THE PYGMY PRESS

PRESENTS

J.J. BONE'S

GOING NATIVE

*A young man's quest for his identity
leads him to an African forest and it's people. . .*

P.O. BOX 359 NEW HOPE, PA 18938

Author photo copyright © 1989 by G.A. Watson

Acknowledgement is made to Bantam Books, Inc. for the
use of quotations from *The Time Machine* (1885) by H.G. Wells

Front cover: (and author's table) Photo by Philip Isaiah Katz,
First Capital Press, Inc.
Faux ivory by Illia Barger, Fine Art Interiors
Illustration purchased by the author from
a street artist in Kisangani, Zaire.
Montage by Chris Heinz,
Kodak Electronic Printing Systems

Maps by Darcy May, after the author (Nduye) and I. DeVore (Ituri Region).

Composition: Get Set, Inc.

ISBN 0-9620069-0-4

Library of Congress Catalog Card Number: 88-62806

Individual copies of GOING NATIVE can be ordered (autographed if requested) for
$14.95 (add PA sales tax of $.90 if applicable) plus $2.00 shipping and handling from:

The Pygmy Press
P.O. Box 359
New Hope, PA 18938

Manufactured in the United States of America

To my parents,
   who took me to France at fourteen

To John,
   with ever-increasing love and admiration

To the memory of Steve,
   for what might have been

To Birdman,
   and what will be

And to the black Africans,
   from whom I learned
   that human kinship
   is everything.

I would like to thank the following for their very special contributions to this book:

John E. Pfeiffer, Colin M. Turnbull, Nancy J. Edwards, Apuobo Aluoka Chamononge, Diawaku Dia Nysela, the Catholic mission at Nduye, the Protestant mission at Kisangani, the Protestant mission at Nyankunde, Merrick Posnansky, Paul Sorelle, Johannes Fabian, George & Louise Spindler, Marc Mancall, Fred Hargadon, Nancy Shavick, Day Boddorff, Rupert Smith, Illia Barger, Christopher Heinz, Darcy May, Philip Katz, Carol Ford, Claire Stra, Susan Simonye, Alma Herman, Clint Czupka, Nancy Wolfe, Greg Watson, Nancy Adam, Bernard Straile, Jacquelyn & Sally Leasure, Beverly Walton, Lynn, and Martine.

GOING NATIVE

MODERN. ORIGIN UNKNOWN.
Width: 31″ Height: 26″
(*from the author's collection*)

Prologue

Winter 1978 / Age 22
Solebury, Pennsylvania
Six months after return from
two years in Africa

O N a spring afternoon in 1968 my friend John took me and a friend of ours scouting for arrowheads in a field bordering the Delaware River. We walked patiently back and forth, occasionally picking up pieces that had been plowed to the surface and exposed by the freshly fallen rain. I began to wonder so intensely about what the life of the people who'd chipped these beautiful stone objects had been like, that I felt happy and melancholic at the same time. I was elated that I'd discovered something that so wholly captivated me, yet sad that these people were no longer here where I now stood, before my eyes, living daily life, so I could see clearly what it was really like. It could never be brought back. "How well they must have known nature," I thought to myself. The world I lived in appeared so insignificant next to the image I had of theirs. I felt ours had lost something essential twelve thousand years ago when all of mankind gave up hunting and gathering and began planting instead. "But what was it exactly?" I asked myself. I dreamt then of the day I would live with people who are still living in remote areas of the world by hunting and gathering.

January 15, 1975 / Age 18
New Hope, Pennsylvania
Eighteen months prior to Africa

Yesterday I had an exciting meeting with Colin M. Turnbull [Born 1924. British cultural anthropologist best known for his books, *The Forest People* and *The Mountain People*, describing life among two African hunter-gatherer societies] at Virginia Commonwealth University in Richmond. While waiting outside his office for quite some time and listening to his cheerful English accent as he spoke to people, I tried to imagine what he must look like. I'd seen a picture of him but the photo had been taken fifteen years prior to this moment. I thought he would look distinctive in a weird way. My prejudices had been formed several ways. First of all, he had lived among hunter-gatherers in the forest and in the desert of East Africa, and, he had been tatooed in the middle of his forehead by two pygmy hunter-gatherers in the Ituri Forest. [Northeastern Zaire, Belgian Congo prior to 1960.] A slit was made with a rusty metal arrow blade and a paste of black ashes made from burnt leaves was pressed into the slit. This organic part of the forest had been made a part of his body so he would always be called back to it.

Furthermore, I had taken a course in experimental, or "living", archeology at Virginia Commonwealth University two years earlier and, in short, my teacher's appearance was a cross between Neanderthal man and an Australian aborigine. He had long frizzly hair and a protruding forehead, enough so, that a cowhide headband didn't squeeze around it but rested on it. And then one of the students from the course had said she couldn't describe Turnbull exactly. I doubt she'd seen him more than once.

When the last person had finished seeing Turnbull, I knocked, was acknowledged, and entered his office to find a tall, slim, lively man who greeted me in a British accent. He was dressed well enough in a coat and tie and desert boots. He looked casual and healthy. He offered me a seat while he finished up on the phone. He put down the phone, took a seat, and asked me how my visa for Zaire was coming.

Now he was close enough so that I could look at his forehead. There it was, a quarter-inch-long, bluish-green line just above the center of the space between his eyebrows. Everything else about him seemed quite normal.

I told him I had an application but the longest visa I could apply for was a tourist visa, and that was valid for only one month and I would check into whatever longer ones they offered when I returned home [New Hope]. Now that I think of it, I may have asked specifically for a tourist visa application in the first place and that's why I've got one now. He seemed to think I could take care of the visa business myself so we moved on to what Zaire is like. I thought this was a bit odd because I expected to be asked first of all why I wanted to go and then some other related questions. I suppose he had a good idea of what I wanted from the first letter I sent him. He assumed I was going and just didn't stop talking from then on practically. I had a hard time asking what I thought were important questions. I was usually cut off.

He talked about this vast dirt/mud road that runs smack through the Ituri Forest, it's width — having been cleared for crops — varying from two to five kilometers, and running seven hundred miles long. He said he remembered it in some places where the trees used to meet over top of the road and form a tunnel. That was about twenty years ago when it was perhaps one hundred feet wide.

He went on to say that the road is extremely muddy when it rains, which must be quite often being in a rain forest. "They are just beginning to become aware of conservation methods." The ruts or holes in the mud sound like solid earth or mud waves. The hills of mud are sometimes five feet high. Traffic is impossible through such a thing until the road crew or the truck drivers take care of it. One can break an axle very easily. He saw people get into mud banks "because they thought their Land Rover was God." The road crew isn't treated very well. The work is hard and the food is fair. One usually doesn't make very good time on the road, but then it doesn't matter because, "Everyone takes things slowly." Their concept of time differs from ours. A truck driver may decide to spend several days with a woman in a village and then move on. Deliveries seem to be flexible.

Some of the trucks deliver beer to the city that's at the end of the road or to villages along the way. The truckers illegally sell some cases to villagers. This sounds commonplace. They tell the company that some of the cases got broken or stolen. The companies know what really happens to it though.

There is much food all around. Villages and crops become part of the edge of the road. In some places of the forest, pineapples and grapefruits can be found and plenty of avocados and nuts also. Game,

IV

especially antelope, is found in the Ituri in abundance. The pygmies roast all their meat over open fires. When asked how the food is, Colin answered, "It is some of the best in the world." He also added that one morning I will wake up and notice that I smell like a pygmy. Much of my smell will be from eating things that have been cooked by fires and my sitting around campfires so often. I will have a smokey scent.

There are loads of mushrooms. Toxic and non-toxic, all different shapes and colors, anywhere from bright pink to white with black stripes, and puffball types.

The villagers are generally friendly and they will ask me who and what I am upon my arrival. They will, in time, really know who I am.

A lot of drinking goes on. "You will drink lots of beer and palm wine with the villagers [versus the nomadic pygmies]." Beer is cheapest in the city and about fifteen times more expensive outside the city. A quart is about thirty cents outside the city.

Palm wine is collected in gourds. Simply, it is the sap from a palm tree. Four special cuts are made and the sap is collected. If the sap is taken in the morning it will have fermented to the point of being mild in alcoholic content, midday is good and much after that Colin found the wine's taste unbearable. The sap ferments during the day. Depending on when the sap is collected and drunk determines the quantity of alcohol found in the wine. Colin likes it. He said I will do lots of drinking and socializing. "People will buy you drinks and you will buy them drinks." He told me he really got plastered once because someone played a prank on him. The prankster had collected the sap from the base of the tree where it is strongest in alcoholic content once fermented, yet tastes mild. "You can drink thinking you are drinking the regular stuff and then suddenly it hits you."

Kenge [Main character and key-informant in *The Forest People*] and Colin were drinking and Kenge decided to climb a nearby tree. Colin started to feel strange and everything began to whirl around violently. He asked Kenge if he felt alright when Kenge had descended from the tree. Kenge replied, "Yes." Then they both passed out. They awoke later in the forest in the cold night to find Kenge's new shoes missing, along with Colin's wallet that contained one hundred dollars, which Colin explained "is a lot of money over there." They returned to the village and got their things back, which had been kept so they wouldn't be robbed while they were passed out in the jungle. Colin said that the people are honest and one is in good hands with them.

Kenge's shoes were new and fancy and he was very proud of them. They were his status symbol, which he usually carried around in his hands rather than wear them on his feet. Maybe he did this because his shoes were more obvious to the observer that way or because they would last longer that way. Colin emphasized what a good place Camp Putnam is [Turnbull's research base. Named after American anthropologist Patrick Putnam, 1900-1960. As an anthropologist (versus missionaries) Putnam knew the Ituri people and languages best] and all the fun I would have drinking with everyone and how good the beer tastes and that when you get a bottle in your hand you don't bother sharing it, you drink it right down just like everyone else. He said he enjoys drinking but not getting drunk enough where things start whirling around. He prefers hangovers to stomach sickness any day. He doesn't like a vomity, sick stomach.

We talked about disease and medicine. I asked him what health problems I'd encounter. He said (matter-of-factly) that I'd get dysentery, which is severe diarrhea with the passage of muscus and blood, and probably malaria. He suggested Lomotil for dysentery which he said would check it immediately. "Dysentery will usually last for three days. You might get malaria. Your temperature will get up to about one hundred and four and you just follow doctor's directions and read the label on the malaria pill bottle. [I'd be able to take care of myself and it would be] unnecessary and cost money to go to a hospital to get it treated." I could do what a hospital would do for me. He recommended lying in bed with plenty of blankets and when I sweated, pour the blankets on to really sweat it out, "and don't make the mistake of taking them off when you sweat or you'll catch a cold on top of everything!" This sounded like a very bad mistake to make. He said he rather enjoyed the recurrent attacks he received about twice each year since then. "You get hot and cold, hot and cold and slip into an enjoyable state of mind, rather like a mild high." When my bout with malaria is over (approximately ten days to two weeks) I'll feel "energetic as hell." All the sweating that comes with malaria cleanses your blood and pores.

He said it is very important that I take the preventative pill for malaria extremely regularly, as close to the hour as possible. He took the pill every week on Sunday morning; when he got up and did the weekly brushing of his teeth. He insisted on how important this was because he had no other methods of prevention. His attitude was this: "I don't like to be worried, bothered or thinking about getting sick.

When I get sick I treat it and that's that." To help avoid dysentery he recommended eating and drinking "what the villagers do." The city milk is great but stay away from milk in the country. I'll get loose bowel movements but this won't always be the sign of dysentery approaching. He doesn't take the pills to prevent dysentery, but waits for it to happen and then checks it dead with the Lomotil. (He must be referring to bascillary dysentery and not the more serious amoebic dysentery.) The village water is bound to give me dysentery. The villagers have built up an immunity to a certain extent, along with the pygmies. The forest water is pure and clean though and insects aren't a problem there.

There is a type of fly in the village that likes to land on your ankles and bite them. He put some kind of cream on his legs to keep them away. Soldier ants are dangerous and if you are bitten don't swat them off, which is the tendency. Run out of their path first. If you spend time swatting them off, more ants will climb up your legs. Their sting is comparable to a bee's and the head stays in your skin.

There are two highly poisonous snakes in the forest, one of which is the Gabon viper. Their venom affects the nervous system. However, snakes bites are very rare because the pygmies know how to avoid them. "Always travel with a pygmy and you'll be safe," he said. They beat the bushes and chatter and make lots of noise to scare everything away. Eventually I'll be able to travel alone. But even pygmies rarely travel alone.

Pertaining to the snakes and the knowledge of the pygmies, he gave this example: These snakes can hardly see, but feel heat with their sensitive tongue. The snakes are born as snakes with pouches of venom. They don't hatch from eggs. A pygmy girl fell into a viper's nest filled with eight babies. Her face was terribly bitten by the young and the mother. "You couldn't see her face by the time she got to the doctor." It looked like a balloon of inflated skin. The doctor wouldn't treat her because he wasn't quite sure how to and if he tried and she died he would lose all his business because no one would be able to trust him anymore. This suggests that Western medicine is mysterious to the villagers and pygmies. The pygmies gathered some leaf medicines from the forest and rubbed them into some small slits they made on her face. The ground up leaf medicine helped her to recover in three days, and she had fully recovered and was back to normal in ten. Colin gave me the impression that the pygmies really know how to take care of practically anything. "They'll really take good care of you," he said.

There is a worm that eats into your toes just below the toenail or in between your toes. About the time you feel this they are ready to come out. "They'll take a thorn or a pin or a nail and dig their egg sacs out," which Colin didn't mind at all. He said it's rather like a "manicure." Then take some iodine and put it on the rotted flesh that the worm created.

None of this stuff such as hangovers, worms, flies on the ankles, dysentery, or its aftereffects, or even some of the current effects of malaria bothered him that much. And upon being asked what his general state of condition was, he answered, "It was all rather enjoyable," with a smile on his face. What he did dislike was being sick in the stomach and feeling nauseous. All these problems could be handled quite well by myself in the village without going and getting professional help.

I asked him about cleanliness. He said he bathed quite regularly, like the pygmies do, who are a clean people. The pygmies cover their genitalia when they wash in the water holes and streams and apparently have always done this even before contact with any other cultures. I asked him what would happen if I dressed like them in a loincloth. He said, "Don't let a villager or an official see you that way. It's improper and unheard of for an American with money to do such a thing and lower himself like that. You may do that sort of thing way back in the forest, which would even seem strange to the pygmies."

He said that while he was in the Himalayas he hardly ever bathed and built up a coating of dirt and oil, or would rub additional oil on himself, because no one else bathed very much, and besides, it would help cut the cold a lot.

There is a law in Zaire that contradicts itself. You are not permitted to photograph pygmies and yet the government says they do not exist. "If you take pictures be careful of the law." He suggested traveling very lightly. Also, if I wanted to go into the forest, always enter with the pygmies to be safe and enter between villages. "Don't let the villagers know that you are associating with the pygmies." Officials don't want people to visit the pygmies. You tell the village that you are leaving or going to the next village and then go into the forest instead. He thought it would be very beneficial to pay Kenge to be my guide and informant.

He kept referring to Kenge as "a real rascal, what a rascal!" Kenge stole sugar from Colin and when Colin asked him why he had done so Kenge replied, "Because you didn't give me any." This was used as an example of pygmy morality differing from ours. "Whatever one has should be shared if there is enough to be shared." They well understand that we need money though and that it guarantees our way home again. He said all in all that he was comfortable the entire time and had a good time.

Pygmies grow to an average height of four feet six inches because they mature under green light. This is a type of light that filters through and reflects off of the leaves into the forest and inhibits human growth. Pygmies are usually going to live into adulthood if they can reach the age of eight. By then, factors such as disease and malnutrition are practically over. The average life span is sixty years.

I asked him what the longest amount of time had been that he had spent exclusively in the forest versus the village clearings. He answered, "Six months."

He also warned me that I should avoid tourists if I intended to get some work done. Many times tourists would drop by and ask to be shown pygmy huts, where to stay, etc. Be careful of imposing tourists.

We talked about city life in Africa. He talked about a Sudanese tribe that walks through the streets tall, proud and as graceful as anything, stark naked; except for a shoulder cloth which comes down and covers the buttocks. They wear this when in the cities because they think that the white man and other dressed people cover their defecating instrument. This tribe defecates privately, therefore they cover their buttocks, but walk around with their genitalia showing. When he said proud as hell and graceful, he acted it out and I could easily imagine the stride and expression on the face of that people.

June 1974 / Age 17
New Hope, Pennsylvania
Two years prior to Africa

I began my high school senior project on Friday afternoon, May 24th, 1974 at about three o'clock. I loaded up my pack with the following things; books, paper, pencil, gourds, gloves for flintworking, sleeping bag, pants, bow, arrows, jacket, sandals, herbal teas, knife, toothbrush, canvas bag, salt, matches, sprouts, clay bowls, nylon cord, metal pot and a sheet of plastic. Almost all of the tools I took were contemporary. I attempted to tan five deer hides and make clothing from them but I was unsuccessful. I made five clay bowls but only one fired properly.

I didn't have enough time to get my fire-making kit completely organized and other things did not turn out because of my lack of experience and time. I literally changed my mind close to fifty times (several times within a few minutes) about whether to do the project authentically or to make compromises here and there. Just as difficult was determining where to draw the line on what and how many compromises to make. If you take this, you might as well take that too, was a frequent thought. Time was running short because of school work so I decided to take the things I did, with the idea that in my spare time spent in the woods I'd replicate some prehistoric tools.

I then hiked about two miles from my home into Burrell's woods, without permission. On my way across the field into the woods, I heard a car speeding along in the distance. The heavy treaded sound of the tires resembled a police car's but I thought the chance of it being one was slim so I continued walking. I turned around to hear a car backing up. It *was* a police car. I pretended to be looking for arrowheads while thinking that the plans for my project might be altered in a minute. Then, over the car's loud speaker came, "That's private property!" So I walked off the field to the police car and saw officer Larry Grawe who asked me what I was doing. I explained that I was looking for arrowheads on my way home from school. (A good time to look for them is when the fields have just been plowed and it has rained.) He seemed to disregard my pack, luckily, and said, "Okay, but it *is* private property." He then drove off. I went down the road pretending I was walking towards home until he was out of sight and then I dashed across the field into the woods, which had become quite overgrown since I was last in them. I decided I would head for a spring near a stream that I had discovered about two months ago. On the way, I recognized some edible plants. There were several types of dock, some milkweed, wild asparagus, jewelweed, nettles, fiddleheads and watercress, all of which I have eaten. I eventually found the spring and set up camp in a clearing next to it. I ran the nylon cord between two small trees and draped my sheet of plastic over it, securing the bottom edges with debris. I took my knife and cut long, tall grass for my bedding. I drank from the spring. It was cold and refreshing. Upon the third time of getting a drink while setting up camp, I saw tiny organisms on the spring bed. I thought I would boil the water from then on even though it was probably pure and I had had a shot for contaminated water. One end of my shelter contained a hearth and the other was blocked off about two feet high with logs, sticks and leaves to keep animals out.

It was getting dark so I explored the stream and a nearby field with my bow and arrows. Around twilight I headed for my shelter feeling quite alone yet excited. Twilight is an eerie time and I welcomed the security and warmth of my sleeping bag. The next day I would worry about food and explore further.

That Friday night I went sleepless. The air was chilly outside. My head, which stuck out of my sleeping bag, got quite cold. Complimented by my allergy to spring grasses, my nose poured mucus nonstop. I spent the entire ten hour night dealing with the mucus the best I could with nothing to wipe it on except my hand, which I would wipe on some nearby grass. Even if I'd had lots of handkerchiefs and my allergy pills with me it would not have done much good. I would still have had to have spent the night wiping my face because, even now, I'm trying a fifth pill out on my allergy which is just as ineffective as the last four. (It was my last chance in pills too.) Nights were long since I went to bed with the sunset. About ten hours long.

The next morning it grew warmer out. My nose stopped running and I slept until I heard the noon whistle, probably sleeping four or five hours. I got up and decided to go hunting. I thought I would worry about getting some meat and if I could not secure any I could always rely on vegetables. First, I made an herbal tea and while getting wood for my fire I killed a two-foot-long snake, hopefully to eat. I ate its liver, which is about the size of a nightcrawler, but the rest of the snake hadn't any meat. I have eaten rattler before but it was much larger and therefore meatier.

I set out after drinking the rosemary tea and decided while hiking through fields and woods that I would head for the woods of Solebury School [my private high school], where I remembered seeing a groundhog and a pheasant's home (while firing some pottery with my anthropology class) complete with animal. I ended up, however, continuing through the fields for several more hours, deciding I would have a better chance of seeing and securing some game in an open field. I didn't see anything, let alone get a shot at it, in the fields, or at Solebury. On the way I ate three robin's eggs from a nest. I ate them raw since transporting them until I reached camp would have been impractical and cooking them would lose a lot of the egg and vitamins, along with protein; not that they contained very much nutrition to begin with.

I heard a pheasant screech in a nearby field and upon entering the field I saw a groundhog in the distance. I chased it into its hole.

Then I walked away from the hole and whistled to let him know I was leaving. I turned around and darted to the entrance of the hole with my bow cocked, ready to shoot. The curious animal stuck his head out to watch me leave and I let the arrow fly for his head. The arrow stuck right where I aimed but the animal had moved his head back into his hole lightning fast. I tried the same trick several more times, the last time waiting twenty minutes, and then gave up.

Minutes later I came across a rabbit and knowing that you can't get too close to them without them scampering off, I took a shot from about forty feet away and missed by an inch. I came across two more rabbits but had no luck. What did I expect for not practicing with a bow before my project? I really don't know that I would have eaten a wild rabbit at that time of year anyway because of rabbit fever [tularemia].

The sun was setting rapidly now and I was getting cold without a shirt on. I headed for camp so I wouldn't be caught traveling in a dark wood, which almost happened the night before while exploring. It's dangerous.

When I reached camp I was feeling slightly exhausted and depressed. I came to the conclusion that I would probably be spending the days to come combing the woods and fields for small game. Though I am a loner, I was beginning to sense that my biggest problem was my loneliness. I had been isolated close to two days and already I felt lonely. I knew how much I liked people before I'd left and this reinforced that knowledge. Hunger wasn't bothering me especially but the loneliness was lowering my morale tremendously. I thought that if one person were with me I wouldn't feel substantially better, and when I asked myself what a comfortable number would have been, I thought at least five, and probably more for longer projects. I should have done some test runs, but the time of year wasn't right.

I could have gone on for some days but that Saturday night was a nightmare because of my nose again. (I seemed to have forgotten about the night before because I had been so excited about the following day.) I couldn't sleep at all, nor the next morning, probably because my body wasn't geared to sleeping those hours. I got up still feeling energetic but knowing that I could not go through another ten hour night of that. I felt depressed but still I had gained something.

I took time in my last hours to think about the future. I pondered whether I was really interested in primitive living or in finding a Utopia and this was my idea of what it was. I finally said, yes, I am interested, why else would I have made and done all the related things?

Hopefully, I am going to a loosely structured college [Empire State College, State University of New York] this fall and my goal is to live with and study some primitive people somewhere. But will I be able to do it, will I ever be able to depend exclusively on nature for my needs, or is it too late and inevitable that I will live in the "civilized" world because I have already been shaped and formed by it?

The hardest question I had to answer was; what did I expect to find? It certainly was just like it should have been.

July 7, 1974 / Age 17
Carsac, France
Two years prior to Africa

I found Bordes' house [François Bordes, 1919-1982. One of France's pre-eminent prehistoric archeologists. Noted for pioneering stratigraphy, which he documented in his classic, *The Old Stone Age*], met him and settled down for the night. The next morning we would dig.

Monday I saw the caves at Pech-de-l'azé [Dwellings of Neanderthals. Immediate precursors of Cro-magnon man—full-fledged human beings—extending from four or five hundred thousand years ago to thirty or forty thousand years before the present]. These are the caves that he has written about in his book, *A Tale of Two Caves*. The caves are very impressive. We dig for eight and a half hours a day at two of the four parts of the caves. Three of us, which includes me, are at Pech number 1 and everyone else is at Pech number 4. We have just completed six days of excavating and today (Sunday) we get off.

There are about twelve to fourteen students and Bordes and his assistant. Out of the students, three are French and the remaining ten or eleven are Americans, half coming from California. The other half come from various places in the U.S.

Admittedly this entry is a bit brief in places up to here but that's because there is something I am very eager to put down. I have been here a week and I am going insane. I told half the people an hour ago how I felt because I was fed up with it all and I had to let it out. I am in a frustrated and sad state right now. I had an idea of what the dig was going to be like and it is a bit more than I anticipated. The digging bores me to death. Bordes doesn't supervise us three because he is at the major site. I try to work very conscientiously but I usually end up taking long rests or throwing rocks at targets, or the one fifteen-year-old and I have dust fights, or we talk about things and hardly get anything done. But I guess the three of us must get enough done to please Bordes. The other one of the three of us is a Frenchman from Haiti and he's thirty years old. He's more mature and does not fool around, but he takes rests for half an hour at times and reads or writes letters occasionally. I'm of some use I suppose, but not much because my heart is not in it.

The digging is part of the problem but unbelievably what's much worse is the people. I can not communicate with all but five or so; let's say half. One girl is the damndest bitch I ever met and probably ever will. She hasn't given me a straight answer to a question yet, so I'm ignoring her. I really thought I was able to get along with anyone but she's impossible. A couple of the others are on ego trips and think they're so together that they're not. This pertains to the vegetarians especially. There are three of them.

A certain amount of the problems stem from myself. I am quite different in many ways. I try to understand, to see their points of view, consider them. Sometimes I just listen and don't converse.

Monday July 8th
Next day

We are starting a second week. I will see how things go today. Bordes told me Saturday that he would be moving us to the major site. I don't think it will be much more interesting. (P.S. Monday p.m. It's a bit better.)

Lunch and dinner are served to us by a restaurant in Carsac. We eat great dinners in Carsac and the big meal of the day is brought to the road near our site and several of us climb down the hill to bring it up to the huge cave. My tentmate and I built two tables and four benches at the mouth of one of the caves. This big cave has two openings. Each go from one side of the mountain of limestone right through to the other.

I like my tentmate. He's a good guy. He is a Frenchman in his late forties who has been Bordes' technician for fifteen or more years. He was a fifth degree black belt in judo three years ago and a European, or *the* European champion. (Since then I've been told there are only four fifth degrees in the world.) We get along fine.

I am one of the few students that get along with Bordes. He has a *terrible* temper which bothers almost everyone and he can be very narrow-minded. Still, he is a nice guy who knows a hell of a lot. And he tells great stories, of which he must know hundreds. [Bordes wrote science fiction under the name François Carsac.] He is very set in his theories. He smokes a pipe twenty-four hours a day.

One thing that's important. It would be best for me to do things on my own money (situations like this) because of the damned obligations involved otherwise. This is the fourth project or so that I'm not that happy about but I'm obligated. Yet swimming in the Dordogne River (cold) and eating these great meals sometimes make it all worth it, and that's what gets me through until the next day.

Just this minute another boy arrived. American or possibly English. He is a flint-knapper [the manufacture of stone tools] also. There is another student flint-knapper who I'm learning some things from. Bordes is usually doing something else instead of flint-knapping when he said he would. But I'm not complaining. After those eight and a half hours at the site I like to go swimming and relax.

The weather has been strange for the first five days. Rainy-looking and very sunny off and on. Very strange. Luckily yesterday (our day off) was beautiful and today is also, so far.

I will need to make an appointment with an allergist when I get back. I'm low on pills and haven't been taking them for two days now. I've decided to save the rest for terrible days (especially rainy ones) and for the flight home. I've been managing.

I just finished lunch. It was splendid as usual. Potato salad, tomato salad, sausage, steak, fresh French bread, three cheeses, apricots. We dine in the cave on the tables.

Meals, swimming, sleep and some other things are what is going to get me through the days. I think I will stay for two more weeks. I told Bordes I would stay three or four weeks, so he expects me to leave, or thinks I will, in two. Someone asked me when I planned to leave and that's how he overheard my answer. It's fine with him. He has plenty of workers. Some are staying ten days, two weeks, three weeks and some as long as six.

I think after my stay I will go to Les Eyzies and see the caves of that area, then possibly northern Spain to the painted cave at Altamira, and then, who knows?

September 26, 1983 / Age 27
Jork, Germany
Five and a half years after
Africa

I feel FREE - FREE - FREE these days. No rent. No bills. (Almost. I am only paying to keep my things in storage in California.) I live in my tiny tent in an orchard that looks like the grounds of Versailles. Such a beautiful view from on high of the plum tree. I am among the rows of cherry trees—"dormant" now. Plum trees across the farm road. Apples in the distance. And a farm house near the hardtop road. I am working for Gerd Lefers. He owns the second largest farm in "Old Country;" Altes Land. He has given me a place to wash. Yes, a hot shower in Europe! I shave these days. No beard or mustache. (The women in Paris made me get rid of it.) Everyone starts work at six-thirty or so. I begin at about nine or ten. Then Gerd can be seen looking at his watch when I leave the w.c. (water closet).

He's a condescending bore. Young—having inherited his dad's farm—and smirky. But . . . of course he has given me much pleasure in living. WOW! What freedom to be in my tent stoned on German beer and it raining like hell on my tent. And that water can't touch me. In Germany—in all the world—I am under two cherry trees nightdreaming, listening to the rain. In the morning I take my hot coffee made the night before and put in a thermos by neighbors. And such nice German chocolate cake this morning with my coffee. I eat so much German sausage, bread, cheese, wine, beer.

TOO MUCH TO WRITE! I make about fifteen dollars a day. At first there were Africans with me picking plums. But it pays very little and so I appear to be alone in the prune orchard. They've gone elsewhere to pick apples. Even the Turks on the farm won't touch the prunes. I laugh. The American doing the shittiest (Scheisse [shit] is used so much in this farming area) work of all on the farm. My years in Africa have shown me, or indicated, what patience is. I enjoy the moment of picking plums. (I was calling them prunes by mistake. I have called them prunes [same spelling in French in the singular] when speaking French to the guy from Côte d'Ivoire [Ivory Coast].)

The quality of my life is excellent. And also, I have big dreams, never knowing if they are just illusions or they will become real. But nonetheless they help me to enjoy life every day. My dreams are to write good novels. But also with all this traveling and my interest in languages I commonly wonder if something good could come to humankind from my experiences someday. One thing that cultural studies can allow one to realize is that horizons are generally only as far as a society "permits" them to be. Individuals break through them every now and again and then society follows. My observations of societies have allowed me to feel this and so I see the potential for me to do many things. These are mostly qualitative ideas or notions and not ways of making money. I feel I could make lots of money if I wanted to but I also fear the possibility of losing the ability to feel life if I had too much money. I like it just the way I am now.

October 8th
Twelve days later

I have been so broke that I could not afford postage until just two days ago when I made a few fast bucks picking huge apples from tiny trees and was getting about fifty cents a box. Had a hot half chicken, French fries, and booze last night. Soooo gooood!

I thought I would be back in the U.S. next week but now that I am picking apples and the money is better I will write my French friend at college and see if I can live in his house in the boonies of France for free. We have talked about this before. It would be super if I could look over my Africa writings and begin to put them together. I still think it would be very difficult to get this done if I returned home right away. In the meanwhile I can't complain.

I've got to get back to the farm now. (I'm at the post office.) Gerd will be looking for me. He's a nice guy afterall.

Historiography

HE Ituri Forest is majestic. Where the Nilotic (from the Nile) Walese (Pronounced WA[ter]-LE[g]-SE [Exactly like the word say, only cut short. The second syllable receives the emphasis]) cultivators have felled the ever-imposing forest to make room for their crops and huts, massive walls of whitish tree trunks reach one hundred and fifty feet to smother the sun. From a distance their appearance reminds one of Dover's chalk cliffs capped with sod. To an outsider its eerie sounds—the half-human cry of monkeys—and stateliness speak of primeval mysteries. Of time stretching back before man's appearance, making a newcomer acutely aware of his frailty and transience. Perhaps it is different for the rhinoceros beetle, the elusive and rare okapi and the nomadic Mbuti pygmies.

The Mbuti have short and powerful light-brown bodies sown with tightly spiraled clumps of hair. Their legs are short in proportion to their torsos; females being on the average three inches shorter than males, who stand four and a half feet. A Mbuti's nose and mouth are nearly the same width.

Within an area of approximately 100,000 square kilometers (about 40,000 square miles, or equivalent in size to the state of Virginia) Putnam estimated the Mbuti population at 40,000 (out of an estimated 170,000 pygmies inhabiting equatorial Africa [Murdock, 1968]. Of these, the Mbuti are considered the "purest" genetically and culturally). He lived and traveled extensively throughout the Ituri area (for more than two decades), as did Schebesta (Swiss Father Paul Schebesta, 1887-1967. Mbuti ethnographer of the 30's. Also wrote popular accounts; *Among Congo Pygmies, My Pygmy and Negro Hosts, Revisiting My Pygmy*

Hosts), who estimated 35,000 Mbuti within the same area. These estimates lent no reason for Turnbull to question them and no evidence indicates a decreasing population. An estimate of the total number of cultivators inhabiting the Ituri area, of which the Walese are one of three primary cultural/linguistic groups, the remaining two being Bantu (linguistically related black cultures of central and southern Africa), has yet to be submitted. For the Walese alone, Murdock (1959) estimates the population at 20,000.

According to Turnbull, Mbuti tribes or subtribes do not exist. These terms are foreign to the Mbuti. Despite the existence of clan names, at least until the early 70's not enough data had been collected to enable any semblance of a clan system to be traced. The only certain units are the nuclear family and hunting bands a number of these comprise.

Schebesta was the first investigator to make an in-depth study of the Mbuti. [Primarily Efe. Not until 1920 did the Western world accept the existence of pygmies as other than mythical, despite ancient Egyptian records dating from as early as 4,000 B.C. describing both, encounters in the forest, as well as the arrival of one brought to Egypt.] Beginning in the early 30's, Schebesta's study ultimately spanned nearly a decade. He used the term Bambuti (*Ba* being a [Ba]ntu plural indicator) in his work to include all the Ituri pygmies, as this is the sense in which it is used by the Mbuti themselves. He then further subdivided them into three linguistic groups. He described the Aka of the north, central, and west Ituri; the Efe to the east; and the Sua to the southeast. To what degree these divisions are anthropologically helpful remains to be explored. Turnbull suggests in his *ethnography* of the Mbuti that a more anthropologically relevant distinction can be drawn based on the two existing hunting economies; Aka being net hunters, versus the Efe and Sua who are archers.

In addition to at least one of the languages of their neighboring villagers, most all Mbuti speak the trade language of the area; Kingwana. The Mbuti add their own very distinct tone when speaking the local dialect of the agriculturalists. These modified tongues are known locally as Kimbuti and what has become of the Mbuti's original language is not known.

Given the history of the Ituri area and Zaire's current economic status, the relationship between the Mbuti and agriculturalists has remained relatively stable when compared to many newly acculturated societies. Additionally, an extremely pervasive ethnic identity is rooted in the hunting and gathering, and agricultural economies of the area.

Although the mutually beneficial relationship maintained between the two cultures has been well documented by anthropologists and historians alike, it remains a much oversimplified view to refer to the Mbuti as hunter-gatherers. This perspective appears to have resulted from the bulk of past, as well as some relatively recent research having been conducted among net hunters by anthropologists who have gone "looking" for hunter-gatherers. Anthropologists have tended to neglect the much smaller population of archers, suspecting that their heavy dependence on garden products raised by their agricultural neighbors has obscured the once traditional hunter-gatherer way of life. (Nets, versus bow and arrow, are an infinitely superior method for exploiting the forest game.)

In fact, DeVore (1979) has pointed out that a more realistic representation of traditional Mbuti life (particularly in terms of social structure—net hunting requires a large cooperative effort—is more likely to be evidenced among the archers because the bow and arrow is an older hunting technique than net hunting, which was probably introduced by Bantu cultivators (Lang, 1919 and Harako, 1976).

The agriculturalists immigrated to the forest about 400 years ago paying the Mbuti with garden products to act as their scouts and mercenaries during intertribal wars. Warfare was abolished with the arrival of the Belgians about a century ago. As a result, the villagers' need for the Mbuti declined sharply, evolving their relationship to one of mutual convenience. The villagers trade foodstuffs with the Mbuti in exchange for primarily meat, building products and labor. Try as the villagers do to dominate this relationship, they are continually being short-changed. They have not been able, for example, to prevent the Mbuti from robbing their gardens, which are far from their compounds due to the nature of shifting cultivation. (Soil fertility is so rapidly depleted that gardens remain productive three to five years, thus forcing a "shift" to a new site.) Although, where they do try to assert authority over the Mbuti is in the village. However, if the Mbuti become dissatisfied with their village counterpart they can easily leave for another, but the converse is not as easy. (For one thing, the Mbuti population is smaller than that of the agriculturalists. Many villager/Mbuti family ties have endured three or more generations.) This enables them (as the Mbuti say) to "eat" the villagers, consequently leaving them with the upper hand in the relationship.

BIBLIOGRAPHY

DeVore, Irven. 1979. A study of the people of the Ituri Forest, an unpublished research proposal.

Harako, R. 1976. The Mbuti as hunters, a study of ecological anthropology of the Mbuti Pygmies. In *Kyoto University African Studies*, 10:37-99.

Lang, H. 1919. Nomad dwarfs and civilization. In *J. of Am. Mus. of Nat. Hist.*, 19:697-713.

Murdock, G.P. 1959. *Africa: Its Peoples and Their Culture History*. New York: McGraw-Hill.

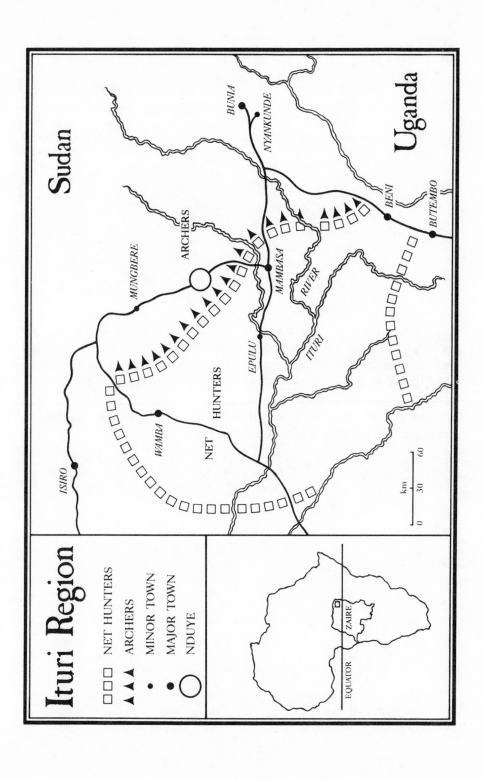

Winter 1978 / Age 22
Solebury, Pennsylvania
Six months after return from
two years in Africa

I had felt for too, too long inhibited by my culture and raped of my identity. White represented sterility and in blackness was the vitality and unrefinedness of black bread. I could not go on with my life until I had breathed, eaten, hunted, danced and slept with the pygmies. And although I was conscious that my desire to do so was far beyond sound reasoning, I was intuitively certain that a dose of this was just what I needed. Then I could continue with my life.

The following chronicle is drawn from letters and a diary the author sent home in installments to his parents and two younger brothers and sisters during his African sojourn of 1976-78.

The degree to which the mission at Nduye influenced the author's interaction with the indigenous population should not be underestimated. For many black Africans, missionaries are the only white people they will ever encounter.

Part One

1

B Y the time I arrived in Nduye Saturday night it was too dark for me to see anything. Some boys and I carried my trunk up the small hill that the mission sits on and we were greeted by the younger Father [a priest] holding a lamp. I explained myself and was given a room, and immediately afterwards, cold beer and a very good meal.

I talked with both of the Fathers while eating and then retired, hardly being able to wait and see what the next morning's light would reveal. I knew there were little mountains in the surrounding area because Father Dave had told me so while in Kisangani.

When I awoke the next morning I saw out of my back window that the hill continued up another hundred feet to its top. Within those hundred freet is a pasture of tall grass with orange trees planted in it. And at the top of the hill are large grey boulders and forest like one would find in temperate regions. It was European-looking and I expected to see cows grazing in the pasture. A couple hours later I did and was feeling quite at home. The orange trees, pasture, cows, temperature, and Italian cuisine, were extremely elevating and soothing.

Then I went over to the window that looked down into the village not far below and opened the curtains. The sight was magnificent and I thought, "What a beautiful place my new home is! I could stay here at least three years and who knows what I'd do after having been here that long."

I met the Fathers and they served me a cup of coffee that was made from the coffee trees that sit below the mission in the plantation.

It's very curious but while I was in Kisangani I dreamt that I would find grey boulders here, a cool climate, and a couple nights ago, of a temperate region's forest. No one told me there were grey boulders here. I also dreamt of finding pine trees here. I haven't seen any here yet, but did see them in Mambasa. The Belgians must have planted them there. No one told me about pines either. While I was in Kisangani last month I recorded that dream:

July 18th
Two weeks earlier

I had some very vivid dreams last night and one was about Turnbull and the Ituri Forest. I'm able to remember certain things about the dream. When I arrived at Nduye [which Turnbull thought would be ideal for my study] it turned out to be a forest, not a jungle. The forest was made up of practically all evergreens. Dark evergreens with pine needles on the ground. And the sun was shining, but not a whole lot of its rays were hitting the forest floor. And behind a shingled shack, like one might find on the coast of Maine, was a stream. It was a North American setting.

I learned from someone that this was Turnbull's shack, office (what have you), and when I inquired if Turnbull was around this man I was talking to said, "Yes." I had a suspicion he was because the front door was open and just a screen door was covering the doorway. It looked as though Turnbull had just stepped out for awhile. When I asked where he was the man told me he was out to lunch and that he'd be back shortly.

The spooky thing about the setting was that all around the house were these long—about three to six feet tall—light grey rocks stuck in the ground like gravestones. Attached to one of the pine trees was a wooden plaque, and carved into it I believe, was something indicating that this was where Turnbull had made his study.

While I was looking at this place, Turnbull came up a path sort of stumbling, and he slapped his hands together, laughing as he came towards me and the entrance to his hut, with whom I assumed were his colleagues. I thought he had been drinking beer. His colleagues seemed quite sober.

Then when we met it was sort of like, "Oh, you've finally arrived. Join the crowd/party." And he said, "If you've got any problems trying to find someone to sponsor you so you can stay in Zaire, I know a missionary near here who can put you up without a doubt." That's about all I remember.

Without analyzing the entire dream, I think the forest symbolized Richmond; the gravestones have something to do with the mission here in Kisangani, the Catholic mission that is at Nduye, monuments to Turnbull's

work, loneliness, coast of Maine; and Turnbull's drinking had to do with
when we drank beer in Richmond at lunch and he told me how good the
beer was in the Ituri, how much I'd drink there with the villagers, and
so forth, and my getting a bit drunk by the time lunch was over and I had
said, 'Good-bye.'

August 5th
Three days later

Here, at my temporary home, I'm feeling a bit sad and uneasy that
I will be leaving it soon to go and live with the villagers. I think within
the next several days I'll be in one of the villages.

After waking up that Sunday morning I took a walk through Nduye
(pronounced *ndu-e*, like the *oo* in sooth and *ee* in bee, two syllables,
the N becoming part of the first syllable) instead of attending the service. I just couldn't wait to pick a site for my hut. While walking out
of the village I started talking to a man and it turned out that right
next to his hut was an unfinished hut that his younger brother had
started building, but for some reason left it unfinished and went to live
somewhere else. He said I could have it to live in, finished, for about
twelve dollars. I thanked him very much but told him I wasn't sure
of anything yet. First I would have to get the chief of Nduye's permission. And besides, I wanted to scout around a bit more.

While I was talking to him a boy about my age came up and
entered the conservation in French. Shortly after that I accompanied
him down a path behind the hut through a bamboo grove to a water
source. I had previously inquired as to the whereabouts of their drinking water. It looked really clean and I tasted it. It tasted fine but I spit
it out just the same.

While at the source we met two pygmies passing by at different
times. I greeted them in Kingwana and shook hands with them. They
were both dressed in cloth loincloths and one was in the process of hunting. He had a large handful of arrows made from bamboo splits. The
tips were sharpened and the fletchings seemed to be made
from leaves.

We moved on down the path until we came to a garden. Here I
had a short look around and asked my companion a lot of questions
about it.

We returned to the huts together and shortly after I parted for the mission.

Yesterday evening I got the impression that I shouldn't stay here at the mission much longer. I think the Fathers feel that a stranger has invaded their territory. It's a little bit peculiar, their acting like this now, because earlier they had invited me to make my quarters here. I told them, "Thank you," but that I preferred, and thought, it would be necessary for me to live with the villagers. They were very skeptical of my idea and are practically dead certain I won't be able to do it. I think they were being polite by inviting me because if I can't live with the villagers it would mean my living at the mission or going home.

It was the younger Father that did the inviting and not the older one who has been here twenty-four years now. The younger Father, Renato or Rene, is here temporarily to build a guesthouse and will be leaving within the next couple of months. He doesn't seem to have been in the position to invite me. He asked Luigi (or Louis) at the lunch table in front of me and Luigi nodded affirmatively.

Now that I've told them I'm going to live in a hut soon, Luigi asked me this morning if my hut was finished. I told him that it hadn't been started yet but that tomorrow or the day after I would be going down to the village to live with a friend until my hut was finished and I would be able to move in. So this is where I sit right now. I've got a lot of not particularly academic things to take care of in the near future.

Soon though, I'll be starting my studies, which will concern agriculture. And then the last twelve months of the eighteen will be more anthropological, hopefully doing something with the hunter-gathering pygmies who are in abundance here. I haven't mentioned my interest in the pygmies to any officials yet because I want to find out more about what their situation with the government is first. They have been a touchy political subject and people wanting to do research with them have been refused since 1972.

I've realized some of the problems I'm going to encounter by just being here. My main one seems to be: Will I have enough researchable material? Anthropological, yes. Agricultural, I'm not so sure. The agriculture practiced here seems awfully simple. I don't believe I'm in a very good position to do a broad survey or make comparisons. For this, I would need a vehicle or need to travel around on trucks, either bringing my food with me or buying it from the villagers, which would prove a bit awkward. Also, I don't have that kind of money and I wouldn't want to do it that way anyway because I want to get to know one community well for my future study; living in one village would permit me to learn the language more rapidly; and my possessions would be safer.

As soon as I find my hut and start living close to the way the Zaireans do, I think I'll be feeling comfortable. That is; more comfortable than I'm already feeling. How long this will last I don't know. I'm pretty sure my home is not here. There's a physical as well as a mental limit as to how far one can go trying to live like the people here do. I want to get a good look at it. The missionaries tell me that even after ten years you don't understand half of what goes on in their minds. It's a different mentality. Although, people are basically the same everywhere, the same needs and so forth, I've been finding.

In general, I believe being settled somewhere will add to a deeper understanding and prove more valuable than a broad superficial one. It will also facilitate contact with one group of pygmies. And of course, personal reasons are involved too.

But I can't help thinking that I shouldn't let too many personal preferences interfere with the work I should be doing. (I can't help feeling a little embarrassed referring to my work as research, having taken only six months of college, and the college being Empire State, where everything I learned was through independent study.)

To summarize, I think I'll run out of researchable agricultural material and end up doing an ethnography, which to me at the moment simply means keeping a diary of daily life with sections of cultural analyses placed throughout. It makes me wonder how academic such a thing is (not that I care terribly), and why it wouldn't be classed as some kind of a writing course.

I hope I can find enough work here to satisfy myself and Empire State College, and enjoy living here as well. This should be a deep learning experience, although of a very different sort, that won't leave me with any better chances of finding a job when I return (not that it matters to me) unless I intend to do some kind of work that involves working with people. I didn't think anthropology or agriculture were my bag before I left, and I still don't think so. My big personal reason might possibly get in the way of things. I'll be talking about my reasons later.

I didn't buy a typewriter in Kisangani (formerly Stanleyville) because it would have cost nearly three hundred dollars and I thought before I make such an investment I should wait to see how things are going to turn out. If I do all my work in handwriting, after eighteen months I'm going to have a lot of typing to do when I return. I don't know that I will care to sit down when I go home and do four to six months of straight typing. If I do my typing here I can go home and start with a clean slate. I'm also concerned about the disruptive sound a tick-tacking typewriter could make, and the alienation from the people that would come with it.

I've not written Turnbull yet to thank him. I suppose he's still wondering whatever happened to me. During his visit to Nduye, he made his quarters here at the mission, possibly in the room I'm occupying now. Nduye mission founder, Father Longo, who ran the mission then, was speared and shot to death by the rebels in 1964. (He pulled the spears from his body and handed them back to his captors!)

August 6th
Next day

I'm enjoying a much different life style. It will surely be much different when I leave the mission and go to live with the agricultural Walese tribe. I can't live with the pygmies yet because I have to discover a way to get permission from the government to do so. The pygmies are a very touchy political subject at the moment and it's a privilege to be in their area, although I will be doing work with the villagers.

August 7th
Next day

I have been here several days now enjoying myself and taking care of things that I should do before I start getting set up. I've got two hours before I go down into the village and look for a temporary place to stay until I can find a hut outside of the main village where I can live and work. At two o'clock I'm supposed to meet with the chief of the collectivity who said he would find me a place to stay.

For the last several days I've done some scouting and question-asking of the area. I climbed to the top of the hill behind the mission, mounted a large boulder and got a good view of the surrounding area.

In the distance—maybe six kilometers away—is a fair-sized mountain that I'm anxious to see. It is sparsely covered with trees and for the most part is solid, grey, bare rock. At the foot of it I'm told, the river Nduye flows. From here it looks like one side of the Delaware Water Gap. I'm especially anxious to see it as it might prove a comfortable place to live.

There is a dirt road that leads out of the actual village of Nduye and comes to a plantation after six kilometers (and the aforementioned mountain) and then continues on another twenty-five kilometers and becomes a path. This path comes to a mine after three hundred and thirty more kilometers. I'm told that beyond where the road becomes a path no inhabitants are to be found, including pygmies. The mine literally must be out in the middle of nowhere.

Shortly I will leave here with a French/Kingwana-speaking guide and we will search along those thirty kilometers for my home-to-be. I'm looking for a hut to buy that is near a drinking water source and the river (fish for protein), has nearby possibilities for a garden, and will facilitate making contact with the pygmies. I'm also looking for a fairly good-size group of people so I will have plenty of people with whom to practice Kingwana (a form of Swahili).

I want to be away from the village of Nduye for several reasons. There are too many people here watching me all the time, and having to answer all their questions constantly I think would prove distracting. I also don't care to be around any town officials or semi-officials. They will only make *my* business *their* business. The chief of the collectivity seems extremely dense. I can understand his wanting to go drinking, never being on time, and forgetting the keys to his office. I have more trouble understanding, and am annoyed by the fact that I have to explain and repeat everything to him at least three times. To add to the confusion of our conversations, he's got a stuttering problem. He's not very considerate. I want to try and avoid people of this type.

I also want to be with people that don't have as many material possessions. I'm interested to see how they make out with their necessities. The villagers of Nduye have an easier time getting what they want because there are a couple small stores here.

Throughout Africa are small stores normally resembling not much more than a vending stand, though they are large enough to have doors. They are usually stocked with laundry and body soap, batteries, cans of concentrated milk for infants, matches, cigarettes, sometimes cloth, and almost always carry cans of sardines from South Africa.

There are also a couple of tailors with sewing machines here and
the people who do have some money are able to keep their clothes repaired.

I also have the feeling that my being a white man out in the bush
alone will cause the villagers to feel some sympathy for me and I hope
they will try and help me live.

Personally, I want to see what it's like to get away from it all and
be nearly totally self-sufficient. This will be one of the greatest lessons
to me; that is, if I can pull it off.

The Fathers don't think I'll be able to do it, nor do the Sisters [nuns]
that live here behind the coffee plantation. Of course they both think
I should give it a good try. Even one of the local inhabitants thinks it
will be very difficult. After this native told me that I did some more
serious wondering.

2

THE day I wrote my last entry I moved from the mission down into the village and ironically I'm now staying with the chief of the collectivity and his family. I've found him to not be so bad afterall.

I intend to be leaving the actual town of Nduye shortly for the bush and may be gone for as long as three months to do some work elsewhere. In four days or so I'll be leaving here with two guides and an interpreter for a village named Kpokporo (roughly, Buck Borough). It is seventy-five kilometers in the bush from the main road that comes through Nduye. Depending on how interesting it turns out to be will determine how long I will stay there. Kpokporo is sixty kilometers from the nearest village in the direction of Nduye, or a two or three day hike through the forest, depending on conditions. I'll try to start from the beginning.

After I had moved in with the chief Saturday afternoon, I prepared to leave that same afternoon to go and look for a hut to buy in a village where I could work. I locked up my belongings in my metal trunk and took with me my snake bite kit, water purification tablets, a coat and my plastic water jug. In a sack I had three kilo's of rock salt and twenty leaves of tobacco for trading or as gifts. The salt was very chunky. The tobacco was some strong stuff from Mambasa. With these things I left down the road that leads to the coffee plantation. I looked for a guide

briefly before my departure, but finding it difficult and being anxious
to see what was down the road, I departed alone. I was so anxious to
find my place, settle down in my own hut, and start my work, that
I left in a slight rain shower.

Along the road to the plantation are scattered huts, and as I passed
them I would greet the people. (I know a very small bit of Kingwana
now.) After three kilometers I came across a villager walking toward
me in the mud with a pygmy that had his hands bound behind his back
and a vine with flowers tangled around him. There was a piece of cord
leading from the pygmy's bound hands into the hand of the villager
who was pulling the pygmy along like a dog on a leash.

The first thing that came to my mind was that the pygmy had stolen
something from the villager's garden. This was confirmed, and I was
told that the vine tangled around the pygmy was not to keep him from
moving, as I had thought previously, but to show people what he had
stolen. It was the vine of a sweet potato.

I arrived at the coffee plantation after another three kilometers
and shortly after passing it the road stopped and a footpath continued
further. The first village I came to after that was where I decided to
clarify where I was headed. The road wasn't doing what I had been
told it would do in Nduye.

I greeted the men who were sitting around under the food preparation shelter (a roofed hut without walls). They thought I had come to
climb Mount Moconza, like other occasional visitors to Nduye, and
fetched me a young boy of fourteen named Tise (Tea-say), who was
being educated at the school in Nduye and spoke French.

I told him that I was a student and so forth, and said that I wanted
to visit the last village. I asked if I was on the right trail; the trail that
came to the gold mine after three hundred and fifty-five more
kilometers. "Yes," was the answer, and he would be happy to guide me
to Andili, the last village on the trail. It was nine kilometers more.

That night I ate peanut butter, sugar cane, sweet potatoes, and
boiled, pounded, manioc leaves mixed with red peppers. The beverage
was my suggestion. We peeled and squeezed the juice out of some sugar
cane and mixed this with lemon juice and water. Then we boiled it
just to make sure I wouldn't get any sickness from the water. The result
was smokey-flavored, hot lemonade. They liked it.

That night I slept in the typical bed that's about a foot too short
for white men and, as usual, I didn't sleep too well. Also, it was cold
and all I had for a cover was my jacket.

The next morning I said my good-byes and thank yous and Tise and I headed off through the deep woods, occasionally coming across small settlements. Here we rested several times, and part of the way we were accompanied by a pygmy carrying his bow and arrows and a letter stuck in his pocket, for delivery I supposed.

Early that afternoon we reached a small village on a hill top by climbing through a large garden situated on the side of the hill. The village consists of roughly five huts and some small pygmy-type leafed domes. These domes are temporary living quarters until huts can be constructed. I was told that the inhabitants had arrived here two weeks before and weren't fully set up yet. Apparently, Andili had been abandoned for a long time to allow regeneration of the forest and soil to take place.

At Andili I learned that there was yet another village past it sixty kilometers further into the forest, really out in the middle of nowhere apparently. The more I hear about Kpokporo the more it sounds like an anthropologist's dream. I've still got a lot of doubts about the place, however.

To get to Kpokporo takes two, or possibly three days from Andili. One camps in the woods at night on the way, in a shelter that's constructed at the end of the day's journey. Food must be taken along, as no one lives between Andili and Kpokporo; as well as guides who will carry spears, a kerosene lamp, and salt, soap, tobacco and palm oil to trade for food at Kpokporo. These last four things are highly prized. We will use them to buy our food, as money can be of no use to us there.

Sometime before we arrive, we'll come down from a small mountain onto savanna. The savanna then stretches a good two hour's hike until one comes to forest again—virgin forest—unlike here. Four kilometers later we will reach Kpokporo.

Everyone I talk to who has been to Kpokporo has told me about the super-abundance of game there. The savanna is full of it. One boy I talked to, while walking the savanna stretch, saw no less than buffalo, leopards, lions and wild boar. Everyone I've questioned has confirmed this fact. In addition, I heard there are giraffes and elephants. Most people have told me that the elephants are in the forest, but some have said they have seen them on the savanna. Just to see some big game should be interesting enough! What could prove extremely interesting is the hunting that is going on there. They say there are many, many pygmies there, many more than agriculturalists. The village of Kpokporo consists of four families of agriculturalists and pygmies. Maybe because of this super-abundance of game there is no need for the pygmies to be nomads. There are huge, wide trees there that make up the virgin forest. The cultivators have their gardens of manioc, sweet potatoes, peanuts and so forth, and especially bananas. They hunt by setting traps. The pygmies there hunt a lot also. They hunt elephants too, unlike here, because the elephant is protected. Whether the pygmies still hunt elephant around here or not, though it's illegal, is something I haven't been able to determine. At Kpokporo there is no one to enforce laws. Everyone says that there is an unbelievable amount of game there. Everyone that has been there has seen and, or, eaten buffalo. One man went as far as telling me that there are so many antelope there that they are occasionally seen wandering through the village. This seems too far-fetched to me.

There are also tons of chickens and eggs. By now, one would probably be thinking that this sounds like the place of every hungry African's dream. No one seems eager to live there however, because of the distance it is from the closest town, and how lonely it is there with only four families of cultivators. I was told they moved there to get away from the Belgians, who had given them some trouble, and also because of the abundance of meat.

Turnbull told me Nduye was the ideal geographical location for my work. Today the English teacher here told me that the pygmies here don't hunt very much compared to the pygmies of Kpokporo. "There, they are real hunters. The pygmies here have been exploited by the agriculturalists," he said.

What could be an important find is if the pygmies are hunting on the savanna and by what means. I'm sure everyone thinks of the pygmies as hunting in the forest. I'm interested to see how much big game hunting exists there.

If it looks like an interesting place, I'll send my guides home and start in on some work. If I do work at Kpokporo it may be more interesting than working here in Nduye, but will probably be slower because no one there speaks French. The cultivators here, and there, are the Kilese-speaking Walese. They also speak Kingwana, a form of Swahili.

Earlier in this entry I mentioned wanting to get away from it all to see what self-sufficiency is about. I would say that it's practically impossible to get away from the modern world and its penetrating influence. When I took that short trip down the path and arrived at Tise's home, there was a man there with a battery-fed radio. This is a sight you practically never get away from. I asked him to hand me the radio when the Beatles came on, and shortly afterward, I listened to a popular number by Neil Young. This kind of thing always makes me wonder what made me decide to come here. Why am I not at home where this is a part of my culture? (It's actually part of their culture now too.) The people here *do* crave the things we have. They don't care if it takes work to get them. They would all come to America if they had the chance. Whether they would all feel comfortable and stay or not, I don't know. I'm slowly getting this thing off my chest finally, this romantic idea of lower material cultures in pre-developed countries. There is a lot to admire here also, I will say. But, I'm finding people to be basically the same everywhere.

When I was at Andili I felt that was about the farthest I've been from civilization, and still, I didn't feel all that far from it in other ways. It sure seemed like a lonely place with a monotonous life style, nearly all of it being devoted to getting the next meal. I wonder how many people are able to realize their potentialities through advanced technology. Here, people don't have the chance. They all work the gardens.

Because Kpokporo is supposed to have even less villagers, I may find it too lonely to live there. I may not be able to leave Kpokporo exactly when I would like to because people don't leave there very often, and I would like to travel with someone who knows the way back to Nduye.

August 11th
Next day

I had a very nice dinner with the chief last night, of chicken, plantains, rice, beans and water from the local source. The chicken was very good and I believe the first I had eaten in practically two months.

We talked about Kpokporo a bit. The chief said the pygmies there are *very* isolated. The more I hear about the place the more it interests me.

The path that leads to Kpokporo continues to another village after forty kilometers and then to another after twenty. The last one has trucks and cars and is back on the main road again. The one before it has a small store.

The last time a white man visited Kpokporo was by a Russian in

1969. He had originally gone there to see the game in the savanna and then returned shortly after to do some research with the pygmies there.

A Belgian visited the place once also, I'm told. And in 1972, an Italian named Nodare, started off for Kpokporo with a party of twenty without the chief's permission. They were stopped and made to return by the military police, who went after them through the jungle. I heard the chase took place at night by lanterns!

The area I'm in is hilly and sometimes mountainous. And very comfortable, exciting and beautiful. I can only say this, obviously, when I'm not in one of my regularly occuring depression stages, which come and go frequently, usually not lasting long.

I'm surprised how well my health has held up during the past four months. I haven't had any serious problems, just some pains in the stomach, occasional diarrhea, and I finally wiped out some fungus I had growing on the inside of my thighs for the past six weeks.

I've found the Africans to be very clean. They wash and bathe more often than I do. Where I am now seems particularly free of maladies, possibly because of the cool temperature and fast-flowing water. I drink the local water which comes from sandy, filter-like sources.

August 12th
Next day

Polygamy is common. The chief of the collectivity currently has two wives and has married four times. He's got quite a few kids.

I'm happy the cuisine is good where I am right now. It's delicious and filling, and these Zairean women really know how to cook, devoting nearly the entire day to the preparation of food. They start with everything from the beginning. It comes from the garden or the woods and then needs to be shelled, sifted, pounded, grated or what have you. It would be too easy to think that their life is boring, preparing the same foods every day. It looks like women's lib is about a thousand years away from reaching Africa. A good wife is one who can cook well, work hard, and produce a lot of children. Wives are bought, and I guess you hope you love the one you've been married to. However, my saying this, is probably what a typical white man would say. I don't know how much love as we know it is involved in choosing a spouse. Things are very casual here.

It's mostly because of Colin Turnbull and his book, *The Forest People,* that I am now here and I am grateful to him for it. And also for the other things he did for me. I just hope that now that I'm here I will be able to make something of this privilege and slightly unorthodox situation. Surely something personal will be gained from this experience, as he said previously. Maybe I'll be able to add a little to the information that's already been gathered about what is going on here. I'm surely lacking a lot of tools, but knew this before I decided to come here, and knew what my reasons were. It was simply a very deep interest in the hunter-gatherer pygmies and their life style. And I got myself here in a way I thought possible so I could perhaps see what it's about firsthand. It wasn't anthropological or agricultural.

I also wanted to work with hunter-gatherers in a comfortable atmosphere—in the forest—and not in the desert or the arctic. Interestingly enough, my having been here and seen them has slightly decreased my interest. It no longer seems as terribly important to me as it did at home whether I make it out into the woods with them or not. I have realized that this is not my home and that I don't really belong here.

August 18th
Six days later

My trip through England, France, Spain and Africa was an education. It put the world in better perspective for me, and that is the main reason I have come here. I have come here to get a better idea of how I would like to live. Now that I am here, I wish I had decided to take a trip through Africa *before* I had decided to do research here. I think that alone would have satisfied my curiousity about what the "simple life" in predeveloped countries is like. Because I traveled so fast my trip was superficial and fatiguing. Now I hope to be able to get an in-depth view of life here. It will only be as deep as the amount of time I spend.

Since I left home I've kept reasonably healthy. Now I'm not sure how my health is going to hold up on a tropical diet of manioc, plantains, sweet potatoes, rice, manioc leaves, corn, beans, palm oil and occasionally a piece of meat, such as chicken or fish. At the moment only dried fish is available because the fishing in the river isn't good during the rainy season. Other meat from the forest isn't available now because the game is defended at the moment. Last night I talked to a villager who hadn't eaten any meat in five months and he seemed to be functioning fine. (October 1st. He ate fish, which he didn't consider meat.)

Shortly I will start off again down the path to the gold mine with my guides, who will be armed with spears, and my interpreter. On my back I will wear a hand-woven basket backpack that Tise's father is making for me. I want to enter with a little style and not with my nylon zip-up pack. In my pack will be paper and pens and little else, less the trading items of salt, tobacco, oil and soap.

I'm feeling pretty well at the moment and am hoping that within the following months I'll be able to do something fairly constructive. Research is probably too strong a word for what I'll be doing. I feel, however, that by the time I return home I will have gotten some romantic ideas of life out of my system. It's not really as romantic as it all sounds, although sometimes it's not far from it. There is a lot of reality here. Sometimes I can't help thinking that I'm going to wake up in my bed at home.

August 23rd
Five days later

It looks like I'm not going to make it to Kpokporo afterall, until possibly the dry season (November—April). I've heard the trip would be too dangerous now because of flooding rivers and trees that get knocked over by the strong winds. There is also a shortage of food there at the moment. Even more importantly though, I've decided to buy a hut here in Nduye and see if I can adapt to life here before I go there. For the past five days I've been going through some pretty heavy culture shock and have had my mind on things other than work. I haven't been able to do a thing. I've decided I had better slow down and try to adapt to life here in Nduye, where things are easier, and some people speak French, and this should make my work go more easily.

As usual, many of my thoughts have changed about things during such a short time, or since I recorded my last entry. I'm happier about this decision and hope it will make adaptation for me here easier.

August 26th
Three days later

I'm still suffering from culture shock and am not able to do anything academic at the moment. I think this must be a very normal feeling and I'm trying not to worry about it. I've decided to direct what little energy I have into finishing my hut, which is just about finished. I expect to be more productive there than I am here, with all the distractions of children playing, radios blaring, and so forth. When I feel energetic enough to write again, and know it's time to, I will.

3

AVING been here for a little while now will permit me to draw a clearer picture of what my situation is, unlike the first entry I wrote while intoxicated by the joy of my arrival. I have a lot I want to say because there is no one here I can *really* communicate with. The English professor who has spent most of his life in Uganda is about my best friend.

I often wonder what I'm doing here, so far away from home, among so many absolute strangers. In fact, this whole experience has been very trying on my emotions. I'm a fairly sensitive person and sometimes imagine the feeling that I have been cast out of my home to partake in the journey of initiation into manhood. It's a very easy feeling to have here.

At the end of my last entry I said I was beginning to experience culture shock. I had finished writing a letter and began reading a book on the twelfth of August. After I had finished the book it seemed to hit me like a tidal wave. I had been very busy writing and was so concerned with it that I was oblivious to my surroundings. It was as though I had looked up from my desk for the first time and asked myself, "I'm going to spend eighteen months here?" The thought of it made me miserable and I threw myself onto my bed sobbing, realizing that I had blown it once again. I thought to myself, "I have come here because of a severe identity crisis and now it is finally finished. It has been killed at Nduye, and now I will return home and be able to continue with my life."

The identity crisis I'm referring to is this: I was just another disillusioned youth who had romantic ideas about "living off the land," "self-sufficiency," "back to nature," "going native," and so forth. I thought I'd be original, and chose the pygmies to do my project with because I thought they were relatively untouched. And now I'm a big fool who went off to Africa ignorant as could be. I was really suffering from anxiety.

Being in a situation like this made me have many, many thoughts and I was uncertain about what to do. I didn't know whether I was thinking irrationally in my state of depression or not. I thought maybe I was thinking this way because my environment was new to me and I was not yet used to it. I thought, "I must stay here and at least try to adapt." But how long would that take? There is probably some length of time it would take for someone to adapt to life here. Both the Father and the English professor had very difficult times adjusting. It took John four months and the Father, Louis, eight. John was assigned here and has not been able to get a transfer yet. This is his second year now. Louis has been here twenty-four years and this Sunday we will be celebrating his birthday, his fortieth year of religious devotion, and his twenty-fifth year of service at Nduye.

It's going to be a big occasion I'm sure. There will be people coming from far away places, such as Kisangani and Isiro. The Brother [unordained, non-clergy] Renato (whom I previously called a Father) has sent some pygmies to kill four antelope for the festivities. I intend to go on the hunt with them tomorrow morning and will spend tonight at their camp.

The only way I can manage to see how these missionaries stay here in Africa, especially in the bush, is for me to think that they think they are doing it for God, and that they have been chosen. I'm not completely serious when I say this of course.

John told me that at one point during his adjustment period, he was having cold sweats while trying to sleep at night. Father Louis told me that he is now of a different mentality than Italians and more near that of the villagers.

Since the day I flew off the handle mentally, I started fixing up my hut so I could move into it. This was an appropriate thing for me to have been working on at the time because my mind was so filled with thoughts concerning my situation here. I also thought that once I had my own place to live in and could get set up and stop living out of a trunk, I would feel more comfortable. Even now as I record this entry I must excuse myself for the disorganization of the thoughts I'm putting down. I'll start with the easiest subject; that being what culture shock is doing to me and what I'm doing about it. I'm not recording this bit in depressing frankness for reasons of self-pity. I am here on my own volition. I feel it is necessary and interesting?

I'm in a foreign atmosphere and I've found that I'm not able to relate to half the things I had anticipated. I'm more of a stranger than I could possibly have imagined, and much of the time I'm a curiousity. (And I haven't even made it out with the pygmies yet. I've only visited camps several times.) Anything one can think of is different; skin color, language, food, habits, ways of thinking, and so forth. Because of this, life for a white man in black Africa, especially in the bush, is very, very fatiguing. I imagine it must get less fatiguing as one adjusts in time. I'm especially tired because my brain functions at practically full capacity every day, from the moment I open my eyes in the morning, until I am tired enough to close them at night. And this is because everything my senses perceive cannot be taken for granted, as many would in my native environment. One just can't tell his mind to stop thinking so much.

One night, just before I went to sleep, my mind was so filled with thoughts that I was curled up on my bed cringing, with my head in hands waiting to fall asleep.

I think every day of the life I knew so well in the U.S., and sometimes even think that I shouldn't return to that life yet because of how well I know it and how ignorant I am of the cultures here. Anthropologists stay in the field for as long as they do, I suppose, because their interest in the work they are doing surpasses their physical and mental discomforts.

Life here among the Walese seems about as slow-paced as life can be. Everyone has their garden, which gives each family their existence. Every day is the same. They spend time in their garden or doing other chores around the home. There is always time to sit around and do nothing. The men are able to do this more than the women because tradition has the women doing most of the work. They prepare the meals each day, which takes a lot of time, having to start from nearly scratch (these self-sufficient people), including the oil they cook with. No choice of professions here. There isn't a large variety of things to eat. You eat what the season has to offer.

Even though I'm living in my own hut now, I'm still taking my meals with the chief, which is very convenient. I've given his wives some money and will give them some more, or my hut, depending on when I leave. The only thing bothersome about taking my meals with him is the irregularity and the infrequency of them. I'm so hungry by the time I sit down at the table that it doesn't matter that I'm eating the same thing day after day. *Every* meal is boiled plantains with either sombe (pounded, boiled manioc leaves with oil and salt) or beans. Or sometimes, if we are lucky, both are served with the plantains. Actually, they are not plantains but one of the many types of bananas that are boiled before they are ripe and sweet, and taste like a tasteless potato. The beverage is consistently water. We usually eat twice a day, midday and in the evening. I forgot. We eat sweet potatoes also. Occasionally we eat meat, but this is becoming rarer as time goes on because the chief has not been paid by the government in over five months.

Likambo, the chief's brother, went to Mambasa as a messenger to pick up fifty dollars for the chief, Apuobo. When he arrived he was told that the money the government had sent out (a little bit to keep everyone working) never got past the hands of the officials in Bunia. It had been pocketed by them. The corruption in Zaire is unbelievable. I've got many stories. I was talking about meat.

It's uneconomical for me to buy an animal and give it to the wives to prepare because I end up eating only one or two of the practically twenty pieces. For instance, the last animal I bought was a porcupine for one dollar. It was prepared, as usual, by several members of the extended family. With Apuobo live his two wives, three children, older sister, younger brother (Likambo, eighteen), and his wife and child. And then there are some other girls and boys about whom I don't know enough yet to be able to figure out how they fit into the situation.

Likambo, Apuobo, and I eat together; men always eating separately from the women and children. In the pot are usually four pieces of meat, two for Apuobo and one for each of us. Whenever there is meat, the chief takes the prime piece. When we come to the table we wait for Apuobo to be seated first because we are eating in his home. Apuobo lives in an abandoned Belgian's brick building with his extended family. Likambo and I usually eat when the chief has come home from work in his office, another abandoned brick building. But this is not always regular, as he sometimes eats across the river with his concubine.

For the past two days I've eaten one meal per day. Because of this,

I eat until there is nothing left or until it hurts, whichever comes first, because the next mealtime is uncertain. This is their habit. They can go comfortably for two days without eating. I'm like a baby here. If my stomach is empty my mind is uneasy. I'm trying to adapt to this eating habit so I don't have to spend time cooking.

Apuobo is quite a character. I never have, and probably never will meet someone again as bumptious and boastful as this man of nearly thirty. I was tired of him after the first time I had met him. I would almost like to be ethnocentric for one moment and say how stupid he is. He's told me so many times, and every meal continues to tell me, how hard he works, what magnificent possessions he has—such as shiny leather shoes, good clothes, an expensive watch, radio, and that's about it—that I'm practically immune to it by now. I actually can't believe the man because I'm sure he doesn't believe what he says about himself, always trying to reassure himself of who he is. He probably also feels insecure around me being a white boy younger than him, having more money than him, and being an American. He's number one man in the village and he lets everyone know it. He's told me that he's unhappy with his life, and how nervous he is because he works so hard. He takes Librium to calm his nerves. You could compliment this man all day and he'd still think you were serious by the end of it.

I think the first factor that is making me uncomfortable is that I have no one to relate or communicate with. Also, to a small degree, I miss some possessions, my old way of life and diet. My work doesn't interest me particularly, but I thought I would be able to get through it because of my great interest in the life of the pygmies. It's difficult having to work at something when you're having enough trouble just living. The villagers aren't happy with their lives. I want to describe them a little.

I don't know if the Walese would admit it themselves, but all the other people who live in Nduye who are from other tribes agree that the Walese are extremely lazy and selfish. They surely aren't known as cultivators, as the people near Bunia are. They do just about enough work to survive, and nothing more. However, there are some women who work extremely hard and, generally speaking, the men are lazier. I'm amazed at what long periods these people can sit and do nothing.

Apuobo had a brother who came and visited him. This man would get up each morning, wash his face and hands, comb his hair, rub some kind of jell on his skin, and admire his face with a hand mirror while sitting in a chair listening to the radio. For an hour or two he'd sit and listen to the radio, and then very often would decide to go back to bed and sleep some more. He would get up later, just before lunchtime, and listen to the radio again, while he waited for lunch to be served. Each meal he had a tremendous appetite and was most greedy at the table. After the meal, he would either take a walk and talk with people or continue sitting on his chair listening to the radio.

September 22nd
Two days later

I stopped writing yesterday when it was time for me to leave for the pygmy camp.

September 27th
Five days later

Here I am again. I didn't get very far on the twenty-second because I ended up leaving for the camp again to go hunting antelope for Father Luigi's festivity. I will describe what happened later.

Before I go on, I should say that when I previously talked about Apuobo I was a bit too harsh on him. Even though there are some things I don't like about him, they are easy for me to disregard. Maybe because I see the man every day. We are friends, and I am grateful to him for what he has done for me and is doing for me.

A couple days later I was in the forest with the pygmies for three days and two nights. And then, when I came back, I celebrated Luigi's affair during the whole of yesterday.

I had begun talking about culture shock. And before I continue, I should probably explain how I see myself here, because ever since I wrote earlier that it's been difficult, the big question seems to be, "Will I be staying much longer?"

I am trying to stay long enough so that I may be able to evaluate objectively what is going on here. What are my interests? Why have I really come here? and so forth.

I intend to stay until about the nineteenth of December, and then I have to go to Kisangani to get my visa renewed. While there, I will spend Christmas with the Fathers on the left bank and see what Diawaku, the vice-rector of the National University of Zaire at Kisangani, has to say about my work—which has amounted to almost nothing so far. I feel guilty and apathetic about it.

Also, when I go to Kisangani, I will by that time have an idea of how to go about asking permission to do work with the pygmies. I'm sure it will come down to asking the commissioner of the region through Diawaku. And after that I would no longer be associated with the university because my work would no longer be agricultural (Thank God!).

After this break, I would hope to come back here with the pygmies. Shortly, I had better start working my butt off. Considering things continue, by the time I get to Kisangani, after five months here, it will still be hard for me to know whether I will feel like working with the pygmies because of the work I'm doing. And even though I'm living in their territory, it's hard for me to know their life. For the moment, the world of the villagers and that of the pygmies is about as different as night and day. The pygmies keep their distance. When I was feeling the most miserable I would visit their camps in the woods, trying to find something there that would stimulate me enough so that I would want to finish my agricultural work and then continue with them. Now, because there are only about eleven weeks until I go to Kisangani, I have no time to visit them. I've got to begin my work. I haven't seen too much of them, but what I have seen has given me a mixed feeling. I feel sixty percent sure, sixty percent of the day, that I'd like to see their life in more detail. I know that whatever happens, I am in Zaire now and will spend some amount of time with them. Here I am able to look at things more realistically, and in another sense, I'm not able to because I'm living in the village and not in the forest. I guess it's time to finally touch on the subject of the pgymies.

The pygmies live in the woods, the villagers in the town of Nduye. The pygmies hardly ever spend the night in the village, unless possibly rain keeps them, and even then I'm not so sure that they wouldn't leave during the night after the rain had stopped.

The English professor had a hard time, but he has succeeded twice now in coaxing a pygmy woman to spend the night. They prefer to live in their camps, almost to the same extent that a villager would not be caught dead spending the night at a camp without good reason.

September 28th
Next day

It is interesting to see that there are two different cultures here living side by side, one not interested in living like the other, and neither one being overpowered by the other. Much of this is due to the two environments; that of the forest and that of the village. I think the pygmies have taken more from the villagers than the villagers from them. The pygmies use metal tools, wear cloth loincloths, and some are doing a bit of cultivation. For example, the last camp I visited had a small garden.

The pygmies have more leisure than the villagers. I guess that is what these people here prefer. They would probably rather do nothing than tend their fields. This they do to the minimum. (All peoples look for an easier way to do things and to live.) Even though the villagers don't believe it, I believe the pygmies have an easier life than they do. One indication being the amount of leisure time they have.

Before I go on, I should mention that the Ituri region is very large, and even though the pygmies have a lot of things in common, they also differ from each other from one place to another. I suspect that the pygmies near Nduye differ from those farther into the woods. Probably the most important difference is that the pygmies around town are living even more easily than the ones far into the forest because almost their entire diet consists of what they steal from the villagers' gardens. They are living very easily at the slight cost of being immoral. They don't steal from one another, but they don't mind stealing from the villagers. Living more easily seems to outweigh the cost of being immoral? I haven't asked the pygmies yet why they steal.

There are also many who work in the villagers' fields for food, money, marijuana, cloth or other things. The character of a pygmy is generally of a happy-go-lucky free spirit. They do most of their living for the moment. They're care-free and do things when they feel like it. They are very friendly and happy people. It's so beautiful seeing these old, wise, wrinkled, toothless grannies smiling at me. They've spent their lives in the woods and their mother will reclaim them. Some of these grown men look as cuddly as a teddy bear because of their smallness, big brown eyes, fuzzy hair, and noses which are very often as wide as their mouths.

When I visit their camps of small, leafed domes of usually five to ten, the men are smiling and very receptive. The women usually smile just as much but are more shy and bashful. If they notice me watching them intently they lower their head and grin and say, "Oo!" or mutter something aloud, which I take to be, "He's staring at me."

When I enter a camp, some of the men rise, walk towards me, and greet me. Then they offer me their authentic chair which is like a tripod, but it has four legs. After they have all had a good look at me, they continue what they were doing before I arrived. Normally, I sit around with the men, who see it as an occasion to smoke, often because I bring them some leaves of tobacco or marijuana; along with salt, oil, or something to eat.

The people here smoke cigarettes with the ash end in their mouth and not the other way around like we do. It's much stronger this way I was told. The pgymies smoke constantly and cough heavily. They can't be too healthy.

Their pipe consists of a hallowed out, long banana leaf stem with a clay bowl inserted at the end which has some pebbles stuck into it to act as a filter. This pipe is very common, although, they have many kinds, ranging from bamboo to gourd water pipes.

They aren't overly generous. I trade things with them. For example, when I was at their camp last, I traded oil and bananas for termites. That's about all I ate during my stay. Termites fried in oil with salt, boiled or grilled bananas, and sombe once. I have eaten termites before in the village, along with leathery-headed grubs and caterpillars on the steamboat in Kisangani. But these were much better cooked in oil, and very rich in protein and fats.

This might be hard to imagine, but I have also been reduced to eating rat, elephant, porcupine, monkey, scaly anteater and countless maggots accidently. It's a little terrifying eating something and later discovering maggots in it. It's possible I've got worms in my stomach. One indication is that if you eat something sweet the worms go wild in your stomach and you can feel them eating ferociously at the sweetness that they love. They don't bother the people here because there's never anything sweet to eat. I was having some very weird feelings in my stomach after the birthday meal at the mission, where sweets were abundant. Suppose I did have them, what would be the point of getting rid of them continuously? I'm eating like the people here, not like the missionaries, and I'd always keep getting them. Nonetheless, I'll check into it.

Here is an inconsistent bunch of things I took note of while at the camp during the antelope hunt: When I arrived, a man was roasting caterpillars. He had them cupped in a broad leaf with hot coals and was shaking and tossing them up and down to evenly brown them. The termites are quite large, and that meal I had of them with grilled bananas was very tasty. We plucked the wings off and cooked the bodies. Actually, there is a bit more to the entire process of preparing termites.

When you walk (in the forest, especially), you find lines of army ants; black, red, and some smaller variation. They've got tremendous biting heads. I've been bitten only once so far by the big ones. Because of this, when I walk on the forest trails, I keep my head down and my eyes on the trail and don't look much at the forest (which is probably one of the most beautiful in the world).

When the villagers are not pounding something in their mortars they lay them on their sides to keep the spirits from using them. The pygmies do the same.

The pygmies are fond of the finger piano. Here is music in a "pre-civilized" culture. They tap their feet or hands to the beat and bob their heads, just as is done universally.

There was singing the night I arrived. Nothing formal. It was as though someone started singing and the others joined in. Each person was in his hut cooking, or lying down, singing. They talk from hut to hut. Everyone always knows what is going on in their big family.

The first night was the second time I had spent the night at a camp. The rain was coming, and because of the wind blowing and circulating in the hut, the smoke from the fire inside was not escaping. It was almost unbearable for me, but not for them. They were indifferent to it. I had my head to the ground and my nose to a crack in between the leaves. It was either that or go outside and get soaked. I was a bit scared that the wind might blow a tree over on the hut, which can happen.

4

ABOUT a month ago a Swiss student was here for two weeks. He came here to go elephant hunting and to partake, as he said, in the "primitive experience." Like Berdj and I, and some others I've known, we have had that age-old idea of the "noble savage." It's easy to wonder about the life of these people when we live in a world so complex with machines and all.

He stayed at the mission and spent time writing and preparing for the hunt. About the second day he was here he started off for Kpokporo with a translator and two provision carriers to hunt elephant.

I was jealous as hell of this guy who had just arrived and was off for the place I'd been refused to be escorted to. I thought, "How do you like this. This guy comes here and is immediately off." I felt foolish having spent eighteen months of spare time at home preparing and still wasn't where I wanted to be.

Well . . . he went off and I remember feeling like he was saying, "See you later sucker." I was thinking of going with him but my hut needed to be worked on, and besides, I decided I'd see what he found. I could always go out there later.

He never got past Andili and returned rather broken-hearted. He went off pretty gung-ho.

Apparently, the chief of Andili had something to do with his not going further. And, he said he heard the elephants were *here*. He started replanning, and over a week later we were off.

There were a lot of complications. Apuobo gave him permission to hunt elephant, even though hunting is illegal at the moment. The chief would just report that the elephant tried to attack a village and was killed. The tusks would be sent to the office of the region or some place.

We went off with an interpreter and five pygmies and spent the night in the forest. The pygmies had previously regarded their custom before an elephant hunt and had done some ceremonial things.

The next morning we were supposed to leave at the crack of dawn. Berdj awoke around eight and wondered what was going on. The pygmies were waiting for something to eat before they started out and we hadn't given them any rice, which was part of the payment for the hunt. It seemed so stupid. They hadn't asked and Berdj forgot.

About nine, we were off. After about a hundred yards we came to the river Biasa, which isn't very big. We had to cross a log to get to the other side. Berdj slowly tumbled into the fast-flowing current as he raised his camera above his head instinctively, and I watched his glasses slip off of his nose into the water. Two seconds later, I wondered why I hadn't grabbed them. It happened so suddenly. It seemed that what had happened in a flash was going to end the hunt. Without his glasses Berdj couldn't see more than a foot in front of him.

I was terribly disappointed, and he more than I. The current was very strong and I thought the chances of recovering the glasses, one in a million.

Minutes later the pygmies and I had stripped and were in the water in what I considered an almost hopeless effort, and I told Berdj so. Ten minutes later a pygmy found them with his feet and miraculously we were off again.

We continued through the forest, the pygmies carrying spears. They had gotten stoned before the hunt, as they do to become fearless they say, and to be drugged into the obsession of one thought: "Kill the elephant!"

After several kilometers we came to a very wet place in the forest with many holes the size of dinner plates in the mud; or elephant tracks. My blood started racing and I thought, "What if we found them?"

We had been warned to run to the right side of an elephant if he charged us. The elephant, for some reason, is very agile and fast when turning to the left.

Shortly afterward, the brush got thicker and we followed the tunnels that had been cleared by the elephants, which were enormous and destructive enough that it might as well have been a bulldozer that had come through ahead of us.

We continued in the large circle we had been making and after about five hours of hunting we reached camp empty-handed and disheartened. Berdj even more so. At least I would have another chance. He was moving on to spend another year with other African peoples.

You would think that this hunt would have been the most amazing and exciting experience. There were some instances of heightened feelings, but I probably could honestly admit that it wasn't all that incredible. In fact, I have found nothing so far very amazing, and that goes for much of my trip. Things have seemed to appear greater than they are from a distance, like when I read Turnbull's book. Upon arriving at the thing, you realize and see that it is very real and you don't see half the magic in it that you did while at home. Life is life everywhere and there's a logical explanation behind everything.

It's like when my family or friends at home read my letters. Things seem more than they are at a distance. Mrs. Evans said, "I envy your fascinating experiences. Life here seems very, very dull."

I would say that life in Nduye is dull at times also, and for me, an outsider, most of the time. I can see why there aren't a lot of whites in Africa. I very often think that I've had enough of this interesting business and should return home and accept the fact that I'm basically just like everyone else. And really, what would be wrong with that?

For some reason there is something inside me that tells me it's too easy to be like everyone else. This conviction is probably something that goes along with being young and idealistic. I've been constantly dwelling on the thought of, "What happens if you always take the easiest choice in life?" Why shouldn't you? It seems the natural thing to do. Why try to be something you're not? I sometimes believe I'd be happy "just" to continue being the woodcutter I was before I left home. How long it would last I don't know. I think I feel some parental pressure to become successful.

What it comes down to is what one thinks of oneself. I've never been in such an awkward position and on top of it, I am in a foreign environment to deal with it. But that is what brought me here. I thought I would be able to look at things more realistically from here, and although confusing at times, I would say it is doing just that. As John, my friend at home said, I will most likely learn more about myself and the U.S. than I will about Africa and Africans.

Earlier, I mentioned that I was going to discuss how I've been dealing with culture shock, which hit me like a ton of bricks physically and mentally. I could feel it in my stomach like there was a hand squeezing my soul as hard as it could, or maybe like someone who's got ulcers. I had zero concentration-power. Each time I would sit myself at my table and try to write, I could not. My mind was elsewhere. I tried reading, which was about as unsuccessful. I'd look up and say, "Jasper, take a walk." And I would, trying to ease my mind, think things out, pass the time that is necessary to adapt to life here.

I *am* making progress. I'm able to do more things now, am hardly crying, and maybe getting involved in my work will help. A little thing, such as the sun being out or not, can affect my mood.

Also, I'm not having so many nightmares and partially sleepless nights as before. A couple of nights ago I dreamt I killed three guys with a broken beer bottle. I've had many, many bizarre dreams since I left. My mind keeps being blown and enriched. This may be a normal feeling for the moment.

Also, I'm trying to push the identity crisis part of my coming here aside and look at the work I might do with the pygmies.

I'm set up in my house now. Four houses down the road from Apuobo, I finished a hut that was practically completed. It needed doors and windows, another layer of mud on the walls and floor, some more leaves put on the roof, and the grounds cleared of weeds to keep snakes away. Also, my neighbors built my outhouse. The price for workers is three cents per hour. I was originally paying them eight, until I finally learned otherwise. Even when I was paying them eight I had to keep coaxing them to work.

The old man several houses down from me was a problem. He built my doors and half of my windows between drinking bouts of raffia wine. He's the proud owner of a raffia tree that sits not more than twenty feet behind my house, and he rakes in the money at ten cents a bottle.

There are a good deal of people who are crazy for the wine as dope addicts are to heroin. They are lined up behind my house many mornings before daylight, waiting to start the day slightly inebriated.

I'm not happy to be awakened by their laughter. When they come for it they are greedy. There are only so many bottles to be had.

There was a child of maybe five years, at the tree recently. He was crying hard with half a bottle of wine in his hand. It was the first time I had seen a child there. After I had asked, I was told that the child was crying because his mother hadn't given him a full bottle. I thought, "The spoiled brat!"

I have one of the nicer huts. Someone had begun constructing it and then left for some reason, so I bought it for twenty-six dollars, finished it off for about twenty-five more, and moved in.

It's quite large for one person. I have a bedroom, entertaining room for people who visit me, a storage room for soap, laundry, and drinking water. And there's my study, which I bet would be fit for any anthropologist.

The nicest feature of my hut is the one large window I have in my study that has glass in it. I bought the glass from the mission; five leftover pieces. My hut is modern-looking with it and sticks out. All my other windows—and those of the villagers—are made of wood, like miniature doors. One wants light, one opens the window. I put the glass one in so I could write while the wind blows, or it rains. Below it sits a long table I got from the girls school.

There are a couple of schools here. Next week I will start French class at the mechanics school, which will help me with my work and add some variation to each day. I'll get to know the students better. Nduye also has a primary and secondary school for the children. There is a soccer field and two teams here. I don't believe I'll be doing much playing, however.

Tise lives with me now. School started on the thirteenth of September and he's been staying here, rather than commute the six kilometers from his home each day. He will, in turn, be helping me with my work and Kilese (the local language, versus Kingwana, the trade language that different tribes living in northeastern Zaire use to communicate with each other). He's not here at the moment and that's why I'm able to write.

I came back from the antelope hunt empty-handed. I wanted to give Luigi some antelopes for his birthday. I ended up giving him a duck.

Sunday's festivities began in the morning with all the Christians going to church at eight o'clock. About six other Fathers helped hold the service. The head of the region was there also. He was black, as almost all the highest ranking religious people in Zaire are now.

The church was nicely decorated, and towards the end of the service tears could be seen rolling down the Father's cheeks. Afterall, he is entering his fortieth year of religious service and his twenty-fifth at Nduye.

After the service, selected people were invited to have something to eat and drink. People such as Apuobo and people of high standing. Or some of the mission's best workmen.

There was plenty of cold beer. And cookies and sweet-coated

peanuts and doughnuts. I had some good conversations with the Fathers and the Sisters who had come from far away.

Eventually it became lunchtime and I realized that only the religious figures were going to be taking lunch. The others had left. My invitation was general and said, "Come and celebrate . . . " unlike the others, saying, "Come for the ten o'clock affair." So I asked Brother Renato to tell me honestly what I had been invited for specifically. Of course he said, "Lunch and dinner." I didn't expect him to say no. He was in good spirits.

We were also celebrating the completion of the large guesthouse. He is here specifically for its construction and that of a garage to follow.

The black bishop (or whoever he was) left very abruptly before the meal, seeing that no other blacks—or Zaireans— were going to be taking part in it.

The meal was thoroughly European. Appetizers of sausages, ham, crackers with butter and pureed sardines and parsely on top. Campari to drink. Three kinds of meat. Sauteed green peppers, browned potatoes, salad, home-baked bread (obviously), beer, *Beaujolais*! grapefruit and papayas for dessert along with plenty of cake.

We also had soup with meat dumplings, and I'm sure I've forgotten some other things. Finished with coffee and whiskey.

I ate to my capacity. There was enough for three meals again. Everyone was in incredibly high spirits, practically all Italians. Singing like mad for a long time after the meal.

One of the Sisters read a very lengthy poem in Italian and Latin honoring Father Luigi. A Father had painted some cute cartoons stereotyping Father Louis' life in Nduye. He has spent the longest time of any of the Fathers in the Ituri region now. Later that night we finished off the leftovers. The Sisters were especially kind and generous to me.

My birthday celebration wasn't quite as big. Tise and I ate cake that the Sisters had brought me as a hut-warming present. We drank water by the light of my kerosene lamp and I sang *Happy Birthday* to myself. The celebration was over in less than ten minutes.

Some random things now to close with: The plastic sandals I bought in Corsica [France] are truly unbelievable. They are perfect for me here, especially when the paths in the forest leading to the camps become streams. Later my feet dry off and are comfortable. If the plastic breaks it can be mended with a hot knife, as my friend Milou in Paris told me they do in Morocco. I could even redesign them to be slightly better. I might write those people a congratulations note.

That's about it. Life should be pretty normal for the next few months, as I hope to get some kind of a report out. Won't be in the forest much, unfortunately. Don't know if I'll have much to write. Have taken this time to keep a brief record of what's happened.

October 1st
Three days later

I stopped writing my last entry because my concentration had become so poor due to the culture shock I was suffering so heavily from. Things seem to be improving gradually, as my being able to write this entry testifies.

While I was writing that last sentence, I felt something like an insect crawling on my foot. I tried to shake it off but it was a bit persistent and heavier feeling than most insects around here. So after the second time I had shaken it off, I decided to look down, thinking it was one of the many toads that occasionally enter my hut. I jumped back off of my stool to stare at a young snake, yelling the name for snake in French to the boy outside who is doing some clean-up for me at the local wage of five cents per hour. He came in with a shovel and I killed it minutes later, finding out from my neighbor that it is the most dangerous snake in the area. That is the first one that has entered my house among the several I have seen people kill. People have died from this snake previously.

I've been here for two months now and I think things are getting better. I'm hoping that it's just a matter of time until I arrive at feeling relatively comfortable. The past four days have been the first ones that I have been able to spend as full workdays. I am working on the agriculture and am in the process of compiling an English-Kilese dictionary with Tyse. (I had misspelled his name with an *i* instead of a *y* previously.)

About the middle of December I'll be going back to Kisangani, from which I am about six hundred kilometers east in the bush. There I will show the people at the university what I have done, and hope to get permission from them to do work with the people I have really come to see; the pygmies, whom I have visited at their camps in the woods only several times. I think from what I've seen so far I'll come back. This forest can get claustrophobic.

5

October 8th
One week later
Meme Kidele

IT'S slightly strange finding myself back in Meme Kidele after having been here two months ago. The last time, I spent the night with Tyse and his family while on the way to Kpokporo.

October 9th
Next day
A cave

I didn't get very far last night because I was very tired and because writing is difficult by lantern. Below this sheet of paper I'm writing on is a sheet of lined paper that shows through this one and serves as a guide for me to write in straight lines. Sunlight is perfect, but lamplight is next to impossible. Yesterday I waited until it was too late to write. Today I also don't have much daylight left, so I'll start with what happened today and go back to tomorrow when I have the time. For now, I will simply say that I have left Nduye to live in a pygmy camp for a couple of weeks if possible because I want to see if they interest me enough to make me return to do work with them after my short break in Kisangani. The village of Nduye was getting on my nerves and the research was difficult for me.

After some complications and a change of plans this morning, I finally left Meme Kidele with two of Tyse's older brothers and a male pygmy in the direction of a hunting camp that was estimated to be about twenty kilometers away. We agreed to travel about ten kilometers in its direction and spend tonight in a cave.

On the way to the cave we encountered several pygmies on the trail who said that the hunting party had left their camp for the village to trade some meat for vegetables, but that they would be returning today as far as the cave to make camp. We went on and arrived here around one this afternoon and I arranged my sleeping quarters and my books and things.

This place they call a cave is actually a huge boulder that slopes outward as it rises and forms a shelter. It's better than a cave because it lets in so much light.

It's starting to get dark now so I'll continue tomorrow from the beginning. A dinner of beans, manioc and bananas is ready now also. I can't wait to see what this place will look like by campfire. Tomorrow, after the early morning hunt, I hope to have plenty of time to go into detail.

October 10th
Next day

I awoke this morning and ate some leftover beans and manioc. Then I went down to the stream to wash my face, brush my teeth, and take my malaria pill, as I do every Sunday morning.

A couple of days before October eighth I decided I had better leave the village of Nduye and go and find a pygmy camp to live in because I wanted to get an idea of what their life is like and if the experience would interest me enough to make me return after my visit to Kisangani in December.

I was also hoping that if the experience was agreeable enough I could return to Nduye and finish a research paper concerning agriculture. I have just about finished all the preparations to begin working with informants in French upon my return. I am finding life in Nduye difficult mentally and physically. My eating schedule will need to be changed in some way upon my return. I can't go on eating at odd hours and sometimes skipping meals completely. I can't do research under such conditions. I'm realizing that this project is not going to be easy. As I sit here now in the cave writing I can see that any future work with the pygmies will most likely be difficult. An example of this is my temporary table which consists of four sticks set up like a tripod.

On top of it sits an aluminum pot cover that serves as my writing surface. It's very awkward and makes writing slow, but with the tools we have I can't think of a better idea.

I had asked Tyse about pygmy camps he knew of. I was looking for one that was hunting far into the forest and not living on villagers' food. He said he knew of one behind the mountain Moconza. I decided to leave for that one on the eighth with him. We would climb Moconza, which is on the other side of the river Nduye, spend the night in the large cave that is there, and the next morning start out for the camp.

October 11th
Next day

Last night the hunters returned with pieces of a young male buffalo they had killed yesterday afternoon. They left here (four of them) about ten minutes ahead of us traveling at a brisk pace, as they usually do, around seven-thirty yesterday morning.

The old pygmy (twenty-five years), two villagers and I, left behind them. If the hunters ahead of us found an animal they would alert us by yelling. They left with each one carrying a spear in his hand, the villagers' hunting dog (Milou), and a small piece of log that was still burning, as they transport fire this way. They took the fire with them in case they had to sleep in the woods. The nights are chilly and the pygmies sleep curled up next to a fire to keep warm. They have no covers like blankets. The pygmies I'm with now don't wear shorts, pants, or shirts like the ones who live closer to Nduye. They wear loincloths made from pounded inner tree bark.

Our party, which was behind, decided not to continue after an hour or so because of a slight misunderstanding. The old pygmy had remained with us behind the four hunters because he said we would not be able to keep up with them, especially if they came across an animal. If they found an animal they would be chasing it at such a speed that we would most likely be left behind. They would be traveling continuously at a fast pace for the entire day, or just until they had found and killed an animal. I told Bololo (His brother is Ubounde) that I wanted to catch up to the others to at least have the chance to see an animal before they set out to chase it. He told the pygmy (Musili) to move faster to catch the others. We moved along at a good pace for a fairly long stretch, sometimes even running, but after awhile Musili told us that it would be too hard to catch them. He knew the pace they move at while hunting and he could also tell from the traces on the trail that they had passed long before us. And they don't march in single file. They streak abreast of each other, each claiming they are the first in line leading the hunt. So there are actually five trails, including the main one.

After they'd found nothing on the main trail, they left it and went bushwhacking, or making their own trails as they went. We could have found them if we really thought it important because Musili knew where they were going to hunt. The pygmies know the forest like the back of their hand for many, many kilometers.

We had gone about three kilometers. We rested for a half hour at a place where we foraged some type of fruit like an olive. Then we returned, picking mushrooms on the way. The rest of the day we spent in the cave talking and preparing food for us and the hunters who would return.

After it had gotten fairly dark, we heard responses in the distance from the returning hunters. We had been yelling from the cave.

October 19th
Eight days later
Ituri Forest

Well . . . I have really, actually, finally made it out with the pygmies. This time I expect to be in the woods with them for about two weeks.

In my last substantial entry I said that I expected to be staying in Nduye doing my agricultural research. Things started looking like I was not going to make it back to Nduye after Kisangani in December, so I decided to take this potentially last trip into the woods with them. I'm somewhere out in the middle of the forest on the fourth day's journey from Meme Kidele and will try to write a little something everyday.

After I return to Nduye, I hope I have the strength to write a research paper for Empire State College. Or I will at least hopefully collect some data so that I can write one in Kisangani.

It looks more certain every day that I won't return here after Kisangani. I like a good challenge, but this is too much. If I stay here much longer I will lose my mind. This change of culture is just too overwhelming for me. I can't go on living here if every day my mind is occupied with anything but wanting to live and work here.

I spend a little bit of each day crying, or if not crying, a large part of the day wanting to. These last few sentences indicate how miserable I have been since about the second week after my arrival. I think I've said enough. I have never been so lonely in my life.

There are some people that can do this sort of thing but I don't seem to be one of them. I was almost convinced at home that I would be a good candidate.

October 20th
Next day

What I wrote yesterday, and have written about in my last entries, are the facts, and I'm disappointed that that is the way this thing has turned out.

October 21st
Next day
Apollo 15 Moon Mission

Yesterday we traveled about fourteen kilometers. Musili was bringing up the rear and we stopped at one point to wait for him to catch up to us.

(December 1st: It was my guide and interpreter Bololo, the villager, who eventually dubbed our mission, "Apollo 15." We had sought the daytime resting place of the moon that the pygmies had told me about. A story I've yet to finish recording.)

November 8th
Seventeen days later
Nduye

In my last entry I thought the month of October was going to be rather boring. Well . . . it seems I couldn't have been more wrong. I think more has happened during this last month (especially with the pygmies and I) than the first two put together. This month has been more difficult for me than the first two.

I'm a little later than usual with this entry and that is because I have been very busy. And it's also because I decided I needed a few more days after my return from Kpokporo with the pgymies to decide whether I wanted to return here after my visit to Kisangani or not.

During the time I thought about it I cleaned my hut and did a large wash in the very small stream near me, that included my backpack, four blankets, and many articles of clothing. There is a noticeable change in my handwriting. This is due to the large amount of laundry soap bars I went through that contain a lot of lye and have burned my hands mildly.

Back from the trip, I was also left with a lot of blackened cooking pots that needed to be scrubbed with sand. I decided to clean everything myself, rather than to pay someone, because this way I knew everything would be very clean. And, because dealing with the Walese usually ends up with some kind of problem. If I had paid someone, I'm sure there would have been at least ten things that could have gone wrong.

Each blanket, while being washed, was so heavy with water that it couldn't be picked up and beaten against the big washing rock as one does with ones other clothes. I was fortunate to be shown by a young girl the way in which blankets are cleaned. First you lather up the blanket, gather it into a small pile on top of the rock, step on top of it and begin stamping and kicking the dirt out of it.

November 9th
Next day

I was talking about making a decision. I've decided that probably in the middle of December I am going to mail Empire State College a withdrawal or intermission form. Actually, maybe at the end of December when I am in Kisangani.

November 11th
Two days later

I have come to the conclusion, or rather, after three months of lying to myself have finally admitted, that living and working here is boring me terribly. I am almost bored out of my mind. I really don't know what to make of it exactly because when I was at home I remember thinking to myself that the Ituri Forest must be one of the most interesting places in the world. And the more I read about the pygmies the more they interested me.

I had an image of the life of hunter-gatherers for at least five years and it was two years ago to this month that I began preparing for this project. What I have actually found upon being here is a lifestyle (of both the villagers and the pgymies) that is very slow and peaceful, and hard in some ways. And for me, rather dull. What I find peculiar is that I still have many of my same old ideas about the beautiful life of a hunter-gatherer even though I have spent time with them and found otherwise. And this must be because that idea was cultivated for five years.

I think many of the pygmies like their lives very much. The villagers generally aren't happy with their lives and often complain about it. The villagers that live here that come from other areas and other tribes find life in Nduye very, very dull and difficult. These foreigners are usually here because they are teachers in one of the schools and jobs are very difficult to find in Zaire. So they continue to live here and suffer rather than give up their jobs.

Anyone who does not have a job supports himself and his family on the products of his garden. In fact, President Mobutu has made it illegal to not have a garden if you are not employed otherwise. If an official of a town such as Apuobo of Nduye learns that someone does not have a garden he will put that person in the small prison here usually for as long as a month. You are locked in a room of darkness, and near dinnertime each evening you are allowed to take a ten or fifteen minute walk. If Apuobo has some kind of work for the prisoners to do he uses them, many times for his personal use.

For instance, he made them construct an outhouse and a bathing enclosure for his family. Or he sends them into the woods to find and cut clusters of palm kernels so his wives can prepare oil.

Many of the officials in Zaire abuse their authority. It was bad enough when the Belgians were abusing the blacks, but now many Zaireans feel worse because the Zaireans in power are crapping on their own people.

For instance, two weeks ago a couple of authorities from Mambasa arrived here and told Apuobo they were going around to all the villages in the Mambasa zone to collect food (especially chickens) because the commissioner of the Ituri region was going to celebrate his third year in office. The commissioner had ordered all the officials in the Ituri region to go around to all the villages and collect food for the festivity. Of course they go around and get it all free.

They come up to a villager and shake hands and chat a minute or two, most likely without introducing themselves because the villager instantly recognizes the men as officials of some kind. Either because he has seen them with the commissioner of the zone of Mambasa when they were here earlier, or because of their good clothes, patent leather shoes and wrist watches.

Then they state why they are here and ask, "Would you like to donate something such as a chicken, or several, in honor of the commissioner's third year in office?"

The villager can't say no, and they take his chickens away. And they make off with bigger booty than that, such as fifty kilogram sacks of rice, peanuts, or coffee.

All the chickens they collected (about twenty-five in Nduye) ended up behind Apuobo's house in two large baskets. *Almost* all of them. We ate chicken to the gills for lunch that day with the officials. We ate it again for dinner after they had left with the two baskets, and continued eating chicken with our meals for the next two days.

And Apuobo served them palm wine, which is an illicit beverage because throughout Zaire Mobutu has declared it illegal to cut down palm trees because of the precious palm kernels that give oil. The only way palm wine can be extracted is by felling the tree. Raffia trees, on the other hand, are tapped, and this *is* legal. Although, after all the wine has been produced the tree dies. This is what I gather because the tree behind my house was cut down after it stopped producing. Palm trees are scarce here but there seem to be enough raffia trees that they can be killed.

I was glad when they cut that tree down. I thought I was going to be able to sleep a bit longer and not be awakened in the early morning, sometimes when the moon was still shining, by the small crowd of people that gathered there talking, laughing, and eventually howling very often.

Well . . . I had no such luck. As soon as they cut the old tree down they began tapping the one next to it. I thought maybe the one they are drinking from now was not going to be good or they would have tapped it before, but it turned out they were just saving it until the other one was finished. And what is worse is that a larger crowd has begun to gather these days. Maybe because the trees producing the wine are becoming more scarce or because this one is producing more and can hold more people.

Every morning at about 5 o'clock I'm rudely awakened by about fifteen cackling people. It's a great social event for them that gets the day off to a good start. It's the first thing they put into their stomach each day and the alcohol and sugar in the beverage gets their body going. Many of them overindulge.

It's curious that these people always have ten makutas [Zairean currency] for a bottle of wine but are always lacking something such as soap, which seems more important to me.

I hardly ever drink. I would rather buy an ear of corn or a papaya with my money. This is more valuable to me. Also, I'm trying to save my money as much as possible. If I leave here at the end of January, I should have enough to get me home if I'm a bit shrewd with it.

Another reason I don't drink is because if I get intoxicated I often sink into a deep state of depression. I remember once getting pretty drunk with this old man on alcohol distilled from manioc. After that I came back to my hut and heavily cried myself to sleep. I've only sipped the stuff occasionally since then.

It's got a very nice rich smoky flavor because it is boiled by fire. Since my arrival, the price has gradually increased from thirty-five makutas per bottle to one hundred—or one zaire—at the moment. I don't know that I'll ever really understand how the people determine at what price to sell their products. Generally, things are relatively expensive here. They usually never sell anything for less than five makutas a piece or per bunch because they say there is nothing in the shops they can buy for less than five makutas.

It's certain that no other experience before has affected my mind as deeply as this one. Never have the grooves in my memory bank been so deeply cut. There have been a couple of instances when I felt I was on the verge of losing my mind. And I am serious when I say this. But I told myself that if it ever began looking serious I would leave before I damaged myself. I sometimes wonder just how mentally stable I am.

I think there are several reasons why this experience is affecting me so intensely. One big one is that I spent two years to this month trying to get here and finally arrived to be horribly disappointed. And so far, all I have really done is try and hold on to something I know I will inevitably lose. It has crushed me but I feel that by the time I arrive home after hitching through the rest of Africa, I will have given myself enough time for my mind to settle down and clear. I feel a bit foolish about what I have done and know that when I return some people will think of me as young and mixed up. All I can say is this experience was either going to turn me on, or not, and so far it hasn't particularly. I sometimes think of it as an experiment, and whether the results are likeable or not, they are the results. I have come here and put every last bit of energy into trying to make this thing work to see the fruits of two years of work. In fact, I can seriously say that I have put three times more energy than I knew I had into this thing and there is nothing more one can do than try to one's limit. It doesn't even really interest me anymore. But I am going to try and produce a report of what I know about the life of the Walese and the pygmies, and their relationship to each other. And I'm going to forget about the agricultural research, mail these papers home, and finish a typed paper for Empire State College (and myself of course) upon my return. If this place truly interested me I guess there would be no amount of culture shock I could not get over.

It seems that recently I've come into a second phase of culture shock: absolute boredome. I was very, very lonely before and uncomfortable in my new surroundings. I feel more comfortable now in some ways and do not find being alone as bad as it was before. Now it just seems like a bore.

I have done some of the more exciting things I could have hoped to do with the pygmies and they have not really turned me on. I have hunted elephant, antelope, hog, and buffalo with them. We have lived in a cave together for three days and spent two of them eating a young male buffalo they killed. I helped transport that buffalo over a long distance. I carried one of the legs wrapped in leaves on a tumpline over my forehead through the forest. I've gone fishing with them, chopped down a tree containing honey and eaten to my capacity while the bees crawled over our bodies. (They were a non-stinging type.) I've also eaten forest fruits with them, heard hunting stories and lived in their domes. I've watched them dance. I've danced with them and the villagers around a campfire in order that the hunters may have better luck in killing an elephant.

Ten percent of the time I enjoy life here but if I'm not enjoying the remaining ninety percent what is the point in my going on? The only time I am really happy is when I find something to eat, or night has come and I take a stroll with my kerosene lamp and go and visit someone in order to listen to *The Voice of America* on their radio. Or I am asleep and have left the reality of this place, though only temporarily, because each morning it is shattered by the laughing crowd of palm wine drinkers or cocks crowing. The sound of the cocks is very shrill and piercing and I swear I would like to kill them all.

Much of this sounds exciting and interesting but I am here and think I know what it is really like. As I've written before, I am still having a hard time accepting the reality of this place and feel that by the time I leave I will probably not have fully accepted it by then either. In fact, I can look back on an experience I had here and see more magic in it after it has happened than while I was actually experiencing it. Many times while experiencing something that I believe should be marvelous I ask myself, "Is this interesting enough to make me stay here?" And the answer is usually, "No."

I have thought so many times that I would rather be doing practically anything else than living here, anything from pumping gas to serving hamburgers. I think that even though it would be a bore and of course I wouldn't do it very long, I would enjoy the comfort of the atmosphere. I would not have to think as much doing that brainless work. I could talk to hundreds of people in my own tongue, eat and drink anything when I wanted to, not be begged, robbed, conived, ripped-off, lied to and abused.

One thing that I have really noticed that a field worker experiences is an absolute lack of affection. Actually, I should only speak for myself and what I am experiencing here. It's the first time I've ever gone so long without someone showing some affection or caring genuinely about me or my welfare. And it wasn't until now that I realized the value of it. When one is out in the field it's no joke. You're on your own. Most of the time it's worse than a lack of affection. It's the contrary. I'm abused.

This experience has been a suppression of emotions and I can't say I've always been able to hide them. If I had to realistically calculate the amount of times I have broken down and cried it would easily reach eighty, and might get up to eighty-five by the end of this week.

I usually don't cry in front of people. My emotional release then is screaming at the top of my lungs. "Yes," I will say that occasionally I am slightly culturally disruptive.

As I have said before, finding and eating food here is a problem for me. These people cultivate just enough to exist on and a little more to sell, in order to buy salt, soap, or cloth, along with a few other necessities. They are so lazy it gets sickening sometimes. They do just a little more work than the pygmies, and I am curious to know if the pygmies' attitude toward life has had some influence on the Walese's outlook. I think hunger pains drive them to work. They simply hate to work and this rubs off on me occasionally. It's not fun working alone. They prize money highly, yet they don't want to work for it.

Here I am in a town of several thousand (I believe I was told, by father Louis) and I have to search really hard to find someone to come and clean the weeds from my place. They love to sit around and talk and joke and eat.

Back to the subject of my being disruptive. The last time I yelled at the top of my lungs was at Apuobo's house. My feelings had been built up in me during the day.

While I was down at the stream washing my clothes, my neighbor Mamada returned from visiting his animal traps in the woods and asked me if he could use my soap, seeing there was a chance to wash himself with soap for a change instead of taking the usual water bath. I thought about it and finally said, "Yes," wanting to keep on my neighbor's good side. But I was so sick of being robbed by the villagers that I told him I was sick of being asked for things by them. He continued to bathe, apparently wanting the bath badly. Which reminds me, the body odor of the people here is a knockout. The pygmies' is especially strong.

Seriously . . . if we are moving along a forest trail and I am ten feet behind a pygmy I can smell him. I could follow a pygmy with my nose smelling and my eyes closed. It's like rancid, fermented, smoke-coated body odor.

When I returned from Kpokporo with my four pygmy guides, we met some other pygmies and villagers on the trail. I bought some hog they had for sale, which I later learned was already two days old. We put it into a burlap sack I had borrowed from the coffee plantation at Mai Tatu and Apanakua (We usually called him by the Italian name, Enzo, the villagers baptized him with) transported the sack on top of his head. I was behind him, so imagine the combination of smells;

pygmy b.o. and rotten hog. And at first I didn't know the hog was in the sack on top of his head and just thought he needed a bath badly.

But believe it or not, the smell was making my mouth water and sometimes I followed behind as closely as possible in order to get a good whiff. I was sick of eating roots, as we did much of the trip, and was ready for some meat.

Incidently, when I returned from that trip it looked like I had been sifted through the forest. I looked like a war veteran. My clothes were shredded, buttons yellowed and shirt blackened, because they had been dried out over a fire. Each foot had no less than four cuts or blisters on it, and my right big toe had gotten infected and began rotting. And that is what brings me to tell that my big toe smelled like the rotten hog.

Later that night, back in Meme Kidele, I ate some of that hog fried in palm oil, but finally gave up because it was too rotten. It was so rotten that you could smush a piece of the meat between your fingers like butter. I gave up because the texture didn't agree with me and the flavor was just too strong. I attempted to eat it because I had been smelling it all day on the trail home. I didn't get sick from it at all, which goes to show just how strong my stomach is by now. The villagers get sick more often than I do, but I'm way off the subject again.

I let Mamadu, my neighbor, use my soap. Later on that day a student came and asked me for envelopes. Then two more asked to borrow English-written books.

Then I went to the chief's house, which is four houses down from me, to see if I could dig up something to eat. He offered me a poached egg, which Likambo proceeded to add salt to—I had thought for me— and gobbled up. Well . . . I hadn't broken down yet.

I bought some unripe bananas the chief's wives had for sale and I told Likambo to tell someone to grill two for me. I gave them to a pygmy girl and Likambo gave her the instructions.

I returned later, hungry as hell as usual, and asked for my bananas, whereupon I found that the girl was missing and so were my bananas. The wives told me she had eaten them because she thought I had given them to her as a gift. This I just found too hard to believe. No one gives gifts to another person in Nduye! I stepped out of the brick cooking house, raised my head to the sky and screamed with all my might. And what do you think the entire extended family did that was sitting in that brick building? They laughed hysterically, of course. And I couldn't

just walk away and say, "To hell with you all!" because then I would
get nothing at all to eat. They replaced the two bananas and served
me some *sombe*.

I spent from October eighteenth to November second in the woods
with the pygmies and two villagers. I went off with them mainly to
see if they would interest me enough to come back from Kisangani and
work with them, and, to give me the will power to get through my work
here.

They said they knew of a place where the moon rests in the woods.
Apparently, there are a lot of shiny rocks sitting in the source of a stream
somewhere. They believe that the moon rests in this place because pieces
of it break off and are left behind when the moon rises in the sky again.
They told me we could reach it in a matter of two or three days. After
the eleventh day, I gave up. We were so far out in the bush that the
pygmies didn't know where they were. We were about sixty to seventy
kilometers from Nduye in the woods.

What I learned from the experience was this: I was not ready for
an adventure like that yet, and, it was the most horrible experience of
my life. It was an unnatural setup. Pgymies can't survive without the
villager's garden products!

We traveled every day looking for the place. The mud was
unbelievable. I thought I was going to leave the forest with a mud
phobia. Twice during the voyage I resorted to yelling, "You little
bastards!" at the top of my lungs, realizing that it was actually all my
fault and I even yelled at myself sometimes.

The height of my misery is when we had to cross through a swamp
where there was practically no footing and sharp, saw-toothed palm
leaves everywhere. You go to grab a tree or a branch to steady yourself
and get thorns in your hand. You step into the mud and sink up to your
crotch in it because an elephant had come through before you and left
a hidden hole.

After I crossed this fifty meter mess, crying and all, mucus pouring from my nose, Musili finds that he's taken the wrong direction.
So fifteen minutes later we were making our way back across the swamp
again.

But this time the pygmies macheteed a clearer path, and cut down
some saplings to step on because they did not like the sound of my crying. It made them afraid, my guide told me. Eventually, they got used to
it. I remember asking my guide, "What do the pygmies think of me?
Do they think I am a child?" All he said was that they feared my crying.

After not having found the moon place, we pushed on for Kpokporo. I hobbled into that village with a very painful toe. I propped up my foot to decrease the pain, and after washing the mud off of my feet, found that the pain was being caused by puss that had built up in my right big toe. After I pierced it, my pain was gone, and the puss oozed out.

That night, I ate an entire chicken with manioc and *sombe*. We were all ready for a day's rest the next day. Even the pygmies, who reputedly don't tire, were more fatigued than I. I danced for elephant that night.

Contrary to what I wrote before, I was told that I *was* the first white man to ever reach Kpokporo, so you can imagine how far out into the bush I was. I sometimes became a bit paranoid when I thought about it. I was the first white man many of the villagers had ever seen.

By the time we left Kpokporo, Nudye looked like New York City, and I was practically running for it. I couldn't wait to get out of that forest.

I swore I'd finish this entry today and as soon as I catch up on my work, I will write again. Tomorrow should be a busy day. I've decided to buy my food and hire a cook. And I've got some recording to do.

I had to quit French class in order to take that trip. It was over my head anyway. I kicked Tyse out of my house. I decided he was more trouble than he was worth. He was also abusing me like many of the other villagers, and ripping me off. His whole family is like that.

I still have that crotch skin disease, and it's getting worse and spreading further. I've had it since the first of July.

I got a nice letter from Turnbull, who is so happy for me. I wish I could get turned on by this place like he was. Kenge, the leading character in Turnbull's book, is still in Epulu I'm told, so I hope to meet him on my way to Kisangani and to give him some beer and cigarettes from Turnbull.

If there were an alternative to living in Nduye (such as moving into a mission somewhere in the Ituri region) that I thought would improve things, I'd do it. Sometimes I wonder if I'm in the wrong town. I feel I'm happier in my hut with the villagers and would only be lonelier if I lived at the mission with the Father and Brother. Also, I learn so much more living here. I feel that if I lived in the mission, it would not be as educational, and I would only isolate myself more from the population.

The life of an anthropologist still fascinates me often.
"Imagine . . . , that man living with such and such a tribe, or the
Eskimos for twelve years!" I just don't think it's me.

6

ONE late afternoon I was sitting at my desk writing when I heard a knock on my door. I asked, "Who is it?" and the person answered, "It's me," as they usually do for some reason, instead of giving their name. I got up and answered the door to find a man that had worked for me before, scraping the weeds out of the dirt around my house with a hoe. All the villagers keep the area around their house free from weeds because snakes like to live in them.

I didn't know it at the time but have since learned this man's name is Kutungoto. He had asked me for work several weeks ago but I told him that I was about to leave Nduye to spend some time with the pygmies and that when I returned the weeds would be high once again. I told him he should return in about two week's time when I get back. He agreed.

Finding him in front of my door, I asked him what he wanted. He answered in a very soft, begging tone of voice, "I would like you to advance me fifty makutas if you could. I will come and work for you on Monday." (He asked me on Saturday. Fifty makutas is about forty-five cents.) My first intention was to say no, because of all the previous times I had been robbed or cheated of my money. And, because the Walese are not very reliable people. I thought about it, however, because he is my neighbor and I felt that he would have a hard time cheating me. If he did, he would have to live with seeing me every day. If he cheated me he would know that I would be his enemy, and we would not be good neighbors.

After asking him, he told me he would come and work for me on Monday at six in the morning. I asked him for how much. Somewhat unbelievably he said, "That is up to you." I told him I would pay him what I have paid my workers previously; five makutas per hour. He agreed, and I impressed the fact upon him that fifty makutas meant ten hours of work, before I handed him the fifty makuta bank note. He said he understood.

Usually when I hand someone some money I do it in front of at least one other villager so I have a witness. This time I was busy and no one was close by so I handed it to him, only the two of us knowing about it. He thanked me and went away.

Monday morning came around and he didn't show up at six. I began my work, and shortly afterward I saw him out of my window walking towards my house on the road. He was apparently returning from the raffia tree, where the villagers love to spend their time.

Shortly after I had finished up what I was doing, and feeling he was in the area, I went to look for him. Seeing he was not at home—the second house to the right of mine—I stepped out onto the road and looked down it in the direction of the raffia tree. There he was with an empty plastic bottle in his hand talking to the people who had gathered to drink. The people were in the middle of the road next to the raffia tree, which sits beside it on a small bank.

A student was approaching me so I stopped and asked him if he knew the name of the man in the red shirt. He said he didn't, but called to him by the name of "red shirt" for me anyway, in Kingwana. The man turned around and upon seeing me I yelled, "Kazi!" meaning work, in Kingwana and Swahili. (Kingwana is a variation of Swahili and many words are the same.) I knew before yelling to him that upon seeing me, he knew what I wanted. He replied in French (of which he knows a fair amount), "I'll arrive at your place shortly." I said, "O.K."

I have learned that to live here I must be very patient with the people. They are in the habit of taking their time and don't always do a job thoroughly. Even more importantly, the experience I am about to relate has shown me that I will have to be more culturally sensitive, think more about what I do and its effect, and if I'm going to live here peacefully, I must learn to always give more than I will receive. It seems that because I am white the people expect me to give more than they will in turn give me. A Father from Kisangani told me that a Zairean told him that he thought the missionaries were here to give things.

The worker, Kutungoto, soon showed up about seven-thirty. He was wearing a red, sleeveless sweater that had become slightly unraveled at the shoulders, and a pair of old shorts. Most of the clothes the people wear here are secondhand and referred to as "Vietnam." I guess this expression has come about because the U.S. gave the Vietnamese a lot of secondhand clothing.

He asked me what work exactly did I have for him to do. I refreshed his memory, telling him of the weeds I wanted cleared from my property. He said, "I will clean your whole place for two zaires." I told him to forget it, and reminded him that he had told me he was going to work for me for five makutas an hour. He responded with, "One zaire to clear all the weeds." I answered, "No."

I asked him if he had a hoe and he replied, "No." I didn't know if that meant not with him or not at all. If he doesn't have a hoe I'm not sure if he's got a garden. I told him to find one and we walked over to my neighbor to borrow one. He gave Kutungoto the hoe and he returned to begin work, of course trying to discuss the price with me again. I told him to begin, and walked the five minute walk into town to find out what time it was from someone who had a watch. I returned and informed Kutungoto that he had started work at seven-thirty.

Going through all I did before I could get him to work is normal. This is how it almost always is. I am sick of it and fairly used to it by now. And while they are working you have to keep asking them to work, as though they were doing you a favor.

About twenty minutes later he told me his food had been prepared and that he was going to eat. I asked him how long it was going to take and he replied, "Two minutes." I told him it wasn't possible and he kept insisting that it was. I walked into my hut and he went and ate two houses down from me. He is staying with his family in my neighbor Nyoka's hut for the time being.

Roughly thirty minutes later, he returned and started working again. I told him I was deducting thirty minutes for his mealtime. He argued he had only been gone ten. I argued thirty. He asked, "How do you know it was thirty? Do you have a watch?" I replied, "No. I am guessing." This went on until I walked back into my hut again.

Thirty minutes later he came to my window and told me he had to leave because the chief had called all the men together to discuss something. Later that day I learned they were trying to find out who had stolen the line to the flagpole. I don't know if it's true or not, but

Apuobo said the penalty for the robber would be death by a firing squad in Bunia if he was ever found. The thief probably wanted the line for his fish traps it was surmised.

When Kutungoto left, he left his wife Sitala with the hoe, and he told me, so that I would not think all was lost upon his leaving. Twenty minutes later Sitala had given up and their daughter of about eleven was giving it a try. She didn't last much longer.

Kutungoto is part villager and part pygmy. It's not easy to tell what the proportion is with these people because they have been inter-marrying over a long period of time. But with him, I would say he is at least half pygmy. This I base on his smallness. It is possible he is the child of a villager and a pygmy and his parents were purely of their race. It is always, I think I may safely say, a Mulese [Walese, singular] man who marries a pygmy woman, and not the contrary. I have never seen, heard, or read to the contrary. The pygmy women come and live in the village with the husband. I have heard they are desirable wives because they are so fertile. The general aim of a married African couple is to produce a large family. A woman who produces many children is greatly admired.

More often, the villagers like to marry their own people, and the pygmies, their own also. Villager-pygmy marriages are not very com-mon. I think one reason is because most of the villagers would be embarrassed to marry a pygmy because of the low opinion most villagers have of them. Many of them believe that the pygmies are similar to animals in many ways because of the way they live. And, because they live in the forest among the other animals.

Kutungoto's wife Sitala — I have been told by my neighbor Nyoka —is a pygmy. Anyone seeing her would have a hard time forgetting her. She has a peculiar gait and her breasts hang down to her waist. But even harder for me to forget is her face, which has one eye half shut. She and her husband have about five children who are all very beautiful and playful.

Later that afternoon the meeting with the chief was over. While stepping out of my back door to use my outhouse, I noticed Kutungoto sitting at my neighbor's place. I asked him what he was waiting for, and he replied it was getting late and he would be back tomorrow.

The next day I saw him next door before noon and after asking him, he told me he was going to start that afternoon. Every time I had seen him he was sitting down and would tell me he was busy at the moment with something or other. At this point I told him he had two days to clear the weeds from my place. It was a three or four hour job only.

Later that afternoon he was still sitting in front of my neighbor Nyoka's place so I walked over to him and said, "You either get to work now or give me my fifty makutas back, or you are coming with me to see the chief." No one likes to see the chief when they are in the wrong. Most of the villagers fear Apuobo, and I felt he did especially because he had already spent time as a prisoner in the small prison of Nduye. It is a mud-walled hut that sits at the northern end of town in the direction of Mungbere.

I was too hasty doing what I did. He panicked and decided his best way out of the situation was to deny that I had given him the money in front of the villagers that were sitting around. He asked, "What fifty makutas? When did you give me it? You didn't give me fifty makutas." He saw that no one else had witnessed that I had given him the money, and knew that I could not prove it, and I suppose figured there was no way he could lose. He feared something however, because he would not come with me to the chief's house.

The man is a *real* actor. Every time he has come and asked me for work he has been very soft-spoken and spoken in a feeble, begging voice, with his sad eyes, occasionally lowering his head to the ground. When I asked him for my fifty makutas back he laughed in my face a bit nervously and denied I'd ever given him the money.

Since the afternoon he took my money he has been himself again. He has not been acting like a feeble soul. And since he has won his case before the chief, he appears to be acting slightly more boldly in front of his family and friends. This incident has strengthened his unity with his relatives, *and* Zaireans, as I will relate.

I left Kutungoto and headed for Apuobo's house in a rage at a brisk pace. It was partly this incident that made me mad, but more so, I was sick of being robbed, asked for things, and in general, abused.

Half way to Apuobo's house I saw him standing on his front porch talking to a small gathering of men. I shrieked at the top of my lungs, partly because I was fed up with it all, because I wanted to show everyone I was serious, and to get their attention, I think. They all looked over at me wondering what had upset me. When I arrived before them I explained myself to the chief and he sent a young man to get Kutungoto. I sat down and Apuobo finished speaking to the men.

Kutungoto arrived with the man and the chief began interrogating him. Kutungoto denied my having given him the money and continued speaking loud and forcefully, as though he were innocent and I had a reason to pick on him by falsely accusing him. He went on in long answers and explanations.

Apuobo, seeing that the matter was not going to be solved shortly or easily, told us to follow him behind his house where chairs were brought out and we sat down. A couple of the men were still hanging around hoping to see some excitement and to see the result of the matter. Besides the men, a large portion of Apuobo's family and relatives were either sitting idly outside of the small food preparation building or preparing some food. The case was going to be solved in front of everyone.

After a couple more questions Apuobo said he was going into his house to get a poison-type drug to give to Kutungoto. I understood it to be a drug from the forest. He said he was going to give him three doses in order to determine if he was guilty or not. If he was guilty he would die within three weeks. If not, he would live.

I have read about trials performed in this manner and don't have much faith in them. The first thing I said to the chief was for him not to give Kutungoto the drug. I said that if he died because of me I would feel miserable for the rest of my life and would never forget it. (And if he didn't die, everyone would think I was a liar and I could never be trusted, I thought to myself.)

We were both interrogated some more, and part way through I became mad enough that I told Kutungoto that if I every found a way to get even with him I would. I gave him an example: I said, "If I ever find your machete, or something else lying around that belongs to you, you will never find it again." I also said I was going to beat him up, but after that, took it back, saying I was not serious. Beating him up would not get me anywhere, except certainly into deeper trouble. Then I called him an imbecile, which turned out to be the worst thing I possibly could have done. I did it because so much anger had built up in me and I wanted to let it out.

Living here has been very, very difficult for me and has meant suppressing a lot of emotions and feelings. I have not always done a good job of it and have yelled at the top of my lungs frequently. I have spent even more time crying. The main reason I get upset as much as I do is because I have come here after two years of preparation and realized that my research and living here is going to be too hard for me to do. It has been very hard for me to accept this reality because nothing in the world meant more to me. When I leave I will never be certain whether I tried hard enough or not, and my main goal will have hardly been reached—that is; living with the pygmies for some time. It has aggravated me, made me feel confused and foolish. Two years of time and money—among other things—practically down the drain. I have come this far and when it actually comes down to doing it, have found it to be a wall I'll never get over. When I leave, it will be like saying good-bye to a way of life, and most likely a career, I might have chosen. The whole thing was a big gamble but I decided it was worth it. I can't help wondering if it might have been different had I gone through college first and arrived here better prepared, older, and more mature. The day I leave will be like jumping off a cliff of no return.

After I called Kutungoto an imbecile the chief told me that was not done and to not do it again. We were here before him in order to settle the matter peacefully. Well . . . it was too late. I didn't realize the seriousness of what I had done. I had publicly shamed him, and worse yet, by doing so, had called all his relatives, *and* the Zaireans, imbeciles without knowing it. This is because their sense of brotherhood is very widespread.

Before I understood what I had done, and had been told that I had hurt him, I replied that he had hurt me and I had not hurt him enough. I could clearly see by that point that everyone was against me. It hardly any longer mattered if Kutungoto had done wrong or not. I had now committed a much larger crime and it was against all. What I had done became the new issue and focus point.

My neighbor Nyoka lied for Kutungoto. He had been called to be questioned concerning the matter. He and I and Kutungoto had been talking in Nyoka's house Sunday night. (Saturday, Kutungoto had asked me for the advance. Tuesday we were both before the chief.) While we were talking Sunday night I got into an interesting but very confusing story with Kutungoto. After forty minutes or more he said he was too tired to go on and wanted to go to sleep. I asked him to please try and finish the story, feeling that it could be finished in about five minutes. I asked him several times for just five more minutes but it was no use. I said I did not appreciate his not wanting to finish the story and that I couldn't understand why he wouldn't just give me five more minutes. I believe it was because he was too confused himself. His French is not

great, and Nyoka, who was doing a good amount of translating from
Kingwana to French, eventually gave up, not being able to understand
Kutungoto's story either. I said, "I did you a favor by advancing you
fifty makutas and now you won't even give me five more minutes of
your time. That doesn't go well with me." I sat there frustrated, thinking how I had sat through practically the whole story and would never
know the ending. I got up and left.

Remembering this incident, I called on Nyoka to be my witness. But
he said I didn't say anything about fifty makutas the night I was in
his home.

Everyone was quite mad at me, especially a young man that was
of some authority in Nduye. I'm not sure of his position exactly, but
I believe he is associated with the national army. He, seeing he had the
right to condemn me for what I had done and that many people were
watching, decided to lecture me in a language other than French. I
believe it was Kingwana, and that he used it deliberately so that all
of the audience would understand his great speech. He was looking at
me and pointing and shaking his finger at me, but he was actually
addressing the small group of people that were scattered around. I could
not understand him, and part way through his speech, I began occasionally saying, "Hapana bwana," which means, "No man (or mister)."
I was trying to tell him he was wrong in the only way I knew how.
Additionally, he was making me mad by mocking me in front of everyone
and getting pleasure out of it. And my retorting was infuriating him,
as I hoped it would. After his fifteen minute lecture he sat down.

At that point I realized that I was never going to get anywhere
and got up, thanked the chief, and walked back to my hut. Half way
to my hut I began crying, thinking to myself that I just wasn't doing
anything right. There was no sympathy shown for a stranger who did
not understand the ways of the Zaireans.

Only several days earlier I had made the serious mistake of not
taking my hat off when I greeted the commissioner of the zone. He told
me, "One takes off his hat when addressing me!" looked down at the
ground, and continued walking past me.

I had goofed badly twice in a matter of only four days. I entered
my hut sobbing, telling myself how sick I was of this place. I felt I was
getting close to having to leave this place because all the villagers would
resent my living here.

I stepped out my back door to get some fresh air and my neighbor

Mamadu (Nyoka's younger brother) told me to come and get my food and pots from his place. His wife would no longer be preparing my meals. I collected my stuff and came back to my hut wondering half-seriously if my hut was going to be burned down. I looked at the large glass window in my study and thought possibly someone might throw something through it.

John, the English professor at the girls school, showed up behind my house at the raffia tree hoping to find something to drink, as he usually does every morning and afternoon. The man in charge of tapping the tree had not shown up yet. I called to John and he came to my back door, whereupon I told him about the big mistake I had made and the consequences.

John is very sympathetic and I tell him all my current doings, thoughts about things, and problems. He, being a stranger to Nduye, having lived a good deal of his life in Uganda, understands what it is like to live here. He finds it difficult living here but has come to accept it, having been here just over a year now. It took him about six months to get settled.

He said he had heard about what I had done and not to worry about it. "There is nothing the villagers will do to you. They fear the chief too much," he said. I agreed he was probably right. He is quite a talker and after we had talked for awhile he left.

I decided the most intelligent thing I could probably do to save my life was to go and apologize to the chief for what I had done. I didn't want to face the next day with everyone angry at me. The man who had lectured me told me he was going to bring me before the chief at his office the next day to see that I was punished. I told him I didn't have time and wasn't going to show up. If he had a problem with me he had better go and see the chief about it. And when I was collecting my things from Mamadu, his wife, Sitala, and all her children were in a big flurry and speaking about me and calling me names. To see the many children chiming in against me, in what I am sure was almost total ignorance, made me even more mad. I mimicked back at them the words they were shouting at me.

When I arrived at the chief's house I found him on his front porch talking with Kutungoto, Nyoka, Mamadu and several other men. I assumed they wanted to see justice done and not let the chief leave me alone just because I was a young, ignorant, white boy who had made a mistake. I had hurt all of them personally by calling Kutungoto an imbecile. To them, calling him that name was calling each of them imbeciles, and all Zaireans.

The first thing I asked the chief was if he would accept my apology for what I had done. I told him I had made a huge mistake and would he please excuse me. I just wanted to get the whole thing over with in whatever manner it could be done. There was no way I could live in Nduye if everyone disliked me. I wanted to repair the damage I had done as fast as possible in a way that would satisfy the villagers.

Apuobo told me to sit down. He told me that what I had done was wrong and against the law. "Against the law?" I thought to myself. He went into his house and came out with a thick pamphlet. He sat down and opened it up on his lap and found the page he was looking for rather quickly. The sun was setting and I was hoping that the matter would be settled by the day's end. His finding the page as fast as he did made me think that he knew the book well and probably knew more about the law than I thought he did. Or maybe my case was a familiar one and he knew well where it was in the pamphlet.

He began to quote an article stating that it is illegal to publicly ridicule or injure someone, and went on to state the fine and penalty for such an offense. The offender could be sentenced eight days to one year in prison and, or, be fined two or three hundred zaires. There were some other minor variations to it regarding the specifics of the offense. He reread it for all to hear and understand three more times.

I was not scared because I felt Apuobo liked me. And being an understanding person, he would not be hard on me. In fact, I felt I would receive a serious talking to and a light penalty. I was a little apprehensive as to what my neighbors had in mind for me though.

Apuobo explained to me what I had done. He said I had spoken like a colonialist, a Belgian, and this was a serious offense. "Mobutu will not tolerate this. Mobutu wants to wipe out colonial attitudes. We blacks are like the whites. We have a brain and a heart. Our insides are the same. We can go to the same schools and receive the same education. The only difference between us is our skin color. Why the good God made us black I don't know, but he decided to. All men are the same regardless of their race," he said. I said, "It's true. We are of the same species. You can give children to any white woman or to a woman of any other race. You can't give children to a monkey however." He agreed, and went on to add he could give children to any woman, whether she be Chinese or pygmy.

"Normally," he said, "if another white had committed the same act he would be deported and made to leave within twenty-four hours." As I was listening to all this I realized that I had been careless and forgotten how serious it is to do something that might seem to contest the government and its revolution, and I told Apuobo this. He told me that to criticize a Zairean is to contest the revolution.

There was a Father in Kisangani who was put on a plane back to Belgium within twenty-four hours because he publicly shamed a Zairean. The authorities told him to pack his bags and never come back. He had to leave his belongings behind.

There is a Father at the Lolwa mission who did the same thing, and according to the chief, this man now goes every day to the commissioner of the zone and pays him a fine of one hundred zaires. I believe only part of this story.

Apuobo said that if he sentenced me to over a month in prison, I would be taken to the one in Bunia. But he was of a good spirit and was not going to do that. If it had been another person I would be leaving the country now. For example, if the commissioner of the zone in Mambasa heard about what I had done, he would send the military here to pick me up and escort me to Bunia. I think Apuobo meant to be put on a plane. I thought that would be a disgraceful way to leave Zaire, and I would not particularly enjoy telling my family and friends that I had been kicked out of Zaire. When I leave I hope it is of my own volition. I not seriously thought for a second that maybe leaving the country because of what I had done might not be so bad afterall. I would no longer have to decide whether I wanted to stay here and try and continue my study or not, and continue suffering from this severe culture shock I am experiencing. I thought it may have been an omen. Or something I did subconsciously in order to make myself leave.

Apuobo let me know several more times of my fortunateness that he was of a good spirit. I told him he was kindhearted and that I wanted to repair what I had done in a way that my neighbors would be happy. I also explained to them all before they made their decision that I had done wrong, and that I had gotten as mad as I had because I was tired to my limit of being robbed and abused by many of the villagers. "There are villagers here who are good to me also," I added. "The villagers do not understand how difficult it is for me to live here," and I stuttered as I said that because I had begun to weep under the cover of darkness. (It also made them feel more sympathic towards me.)

The chief said, "You must buy two chickens and four bottles of raffia wine and eat and drink them together. Then you will be able to start anew. Give the chickens to one of the wives and she will prepare them."

I shook hands with my neighbors as they left and sat back down on my chair glad the matter was resolved. I reflected on what had happened. One thing I remember having thought to myself was, "How do you like that? This guy robs you, then you are disliked by the villagers, and on top of it all, you lose more money by having to buy two chickens and four bottles of wine. And the thief gets a free meal for his good deed!" I had a hard time believing what had happend. I told the chief how grateful I was to him and how lucky I was.

I walked back to my hut and went to sleep, something I really enjoy here. It allows me to leave reality. And very often, I visit my world and people in my dreams. Sleep is never long enough for me here, but even when I was at home I suppose that was true.

The next day wasn't too bad. However, I was sorry to learn by the end of it that several of my neighbors were still having a hard time forgetting the matter and were therefore still angry with me. Thinking back earlier that day, I remembered something I did that might not have gone over too well.

I was sipping wine at the tree behind my house. When we had finished, the gathering of drinkers moved on to the next tree to be tapped a couple houses down from me. While waiting for Mamadu to lower the bottles down from the top of the tree on a line, I sat down. Seeing the ex-chief of Nduye, Primus, I remembered that he said he would repay me my fifty makutas on Wednesday, so I asked him if he remembered his promise to me, hoping I wasn't going to be robbed again. I trusted the man because he was the old chief, and because he usually has some money with him. I felt sure I would get it back because I had lent him a zaire, and he had already paid me back half of it on Monday, as he said he would.

He said he remembered and didn't have my money with him. It was at his house and he said he would send the man sitting next to him with my money. The man was Kutungoto! I advised the old chief that I didn't think that was a good idea. There was a chance he would lose his money if he gave it to Kutungoto, as I had already lost fifty makutas to him I explained. He said he understood and reached into his pocket to pull out a fifty makuta bill. He handed it to me, and I showed everyone publicly that he had paid me and that we were square. (I don't know why he said my money was in his house. I didn't question him about it.)

Maybe my bringing up the issue of Kutungoto having stolen my money stirred up people's feelings again. I didn't know what else to do when the ex-chief said he was going to send my money to me in the hands of Kutungoto. I didn't want him to touch my money. I didn't say he had robbed me, in front of everyone. Instead, I said I had *lost* my money to him.

Later that evening I asked Mamadu a question concerning my research and he replied that he was too tired to answer my question. I asked him, "What is the spelling for *work* in Swahili?" I had an idea it was *k-a-z-i*, but needed to be sure before writing it down in this account. He replied he knew the spelling well but was too tired at the moment to give it to me. "Ask me tomorrow," he said. I asked him once more, saying that it was such a short word, but he refused. I guessed he didn't care to be bothered and could see that he was drunk. He was tapping a raffia tree that had been felled earlier. (After the tree stops producing wine it is felled and they tap a few more bottles out of it.)

Seeing that he didn't want to be bothered, I asked Nyoka the same question, who was sitting outside his hut next to a fire. He gave me the spelling and it turned out that everyone was against him for doing so. They began calling him my collaborator and an American. Nyoka asked me to please go back into my hut because for him to help me would be to go against his family, and that he could not do. It would be hard for him to live with his family. I returned to my hut.

I should also mention, now that I think about it, that I had built up some anger in my neighbors before my dispute with Kutungoto, and I guess they were waiting to let me have it.

I had been sitting around with them in front of their place. I was bored with the slow pace of life here, the laziness of the people, and their abusing me in one way or another. So I decided to indirectly antagonize them by asking them a question I'd had in mind. Part of the reason for asking the question was to see if it was true. And, to see what they, the Walese, would answer.

I said, "I have a question I need answered." They said, "O.K." "There are people who live here who are from other tribes that say the Walese are very lazy cultivators. Is it true what they say?" They didn't like that question at all and thought it was me who was accusing them.

I explained that it wasn't *I*, who was accusing them. They defended themselves, and Nyoka said it was the other tribes who were lazy. (Before I had asked them the question, I knew that the Walese were lazy cultivators. I was interested to see if they would admit it and if their ideals were other than the reality.)

I cited several examples of why there might be some truth to the accusation. "Why is the cost of food here so expensive," I asked. Getting no answer I answered for them, "Because there isn't much." They retorted, "Who sells the food in the market on Sundays? The Walese!" I said that was because practically all the villagers of Nudye are Walese. Adding, "I have a Munande friend who cultivates six hectares of rice each year and he sells almost all of it to the schools."

I asked them how many hours a day a Mulese spent cultivating his garden. The general answer was about four hours, but it depends on the season they said. "I don't believe you spend four hours daily in your gardens," I told them. "Yesterday you weren't in your gardens. Are you going to work in them today?" Nyoka replied, "We only have two hands. I am working on my house at the moment. And the state takes our time away by making us work for it." He cited *Salongo* as an example, and everyone agreed with him. (*Salongo* is the national name for work that the population does for their city or town in order to keep it clean and orderly. It includes various jobs such as digging drainage ditches, to filling in the holes on dirt roads. More commonly, it means slashing the weeds down with a long-bladed tool. The weeds grow so fast in this environment. When I think of *Salongo* I picture a large group of men with their bladed tools called a *coupe-coupe* [*coupe*, in French, means cut] cutting the brush down, and some of the women scraping the weeds from the road with hoes.)

It is true that *Salongo* takes some of their time, but nothing substantial. It is rarely enough to interfere with the tending of their gardens. Usually *Salongo* takes place every Saturday morning until noon or slightly after. Occasionally, when the commissioner of the zone is expected to visit Nduye, five days to a week will be spent in *Salongo* preparing the village for his arrival.

I asked them, "If you don't have the time to work in your gardens, why are you sitting here idly now?" Nyoka replied he was busy with his house and would be starting to work in his garden again after two weeks. The others said they would be going to their gardens later. They were getting tired of me.

I said, "I don't care if it's true or not. If you are happy with your lives that's fine." I returned to my hut next door. "If they are supporting themselves on what they grow, what more do they need?" I thought to myself.

Later that day, while passing by my neighbor's house, I stopped to ask a question: "Nyoka," I said, "If the Walese are productive cultivators, why did the commissioner of the zone, when he was here, tell the population that they were all going to cultivate a huge garden together under the chief's supervision at the beginning of next year?" He sat silently for a moment and then said, "There are some Mulese who are lazy cultivators and it is because of those few."

Seeing that the relationship with my neighbors was still not very good, I wondered why. I thought maybe it was because I had not yet given them the chickens and the wine. I had been looking but had not found any chickens for sale. It's always difficult here.

I went next door to Nyoka and told him I had been looking but had not been able to find two chickens for sale. "If I gave someone the money could they go and search for them?" I asked. He said he thought no one had the time to. Kutungoto, and the others involved, were not around to discuss the matter so I went back into my hut thinking I would take care of it the next day.

The matter was mainly between Mamadu, Nyoka, and I. I found them among the others, waiting for something to drink at the raffia tree down from my house the next afternoon. After asking them, they answered they had no time to go and look for the chickens. I even said I would pay the one that went looking, twenty makutas. I was slightly amazed to be refused. Twenty mukutas is an entire day's wage. I explained to them that if I had the time I would go looking for them. Kutungoto told me he was going fishing the next day but that he might consider the offer when he returned after five days. We all agreed the matter could wait and they said they were in no hurry. After receiving this response, I decided they were just having a little trouble getting over what I had done and were still sore with me. I figured some more time would ease things up.

The next morning I was sitting at my desk writing when I heard a knock on my door. I answered, "Yes," and got up and opened the door to find Kutungoto standing before me. I greeted him and asked him what he wanted. In his soft, sorrowful voice he asked, "Is it possible for you to advance me one zaire fifty? I will come and work for you tomorrow morning." I didn't know what to think. No one else was around at the moment so I thought he must have decided to try and rob me again, thinking I was stupid. Then I thought maybe he had come to me to borrow the money, and this time, he was *really* going to pay me back. And by doing so, thought he would regain my trust in him. I thought maybe he was sorry he had done me wrong and was now offering me a chance for him to make it up to me. One thing I was sure of was that I was not giving him the money, a chance to prove his worth to me, or a chance to make a big fool of me. I kept calm and decided I would listen to what he had to say so that possibly I might be able to understand his way of thinking, and that of the Zaireans.

I told him I could not give him any more money, and that if I did, it would make me a fool. I politely told him he had already taken my fifty makutas, instead of saying, "robbed me of," so that I might not enrage him. He agreed to having taken my money and again asked for the one zaire fifty, explaining that he needed it to pay a fine to the chief because the flagpole cord had been stolen. Each man was to pay one zaire fifty as the penalty because the thief had not been found.

I stood in the doorway silently, wanting to see Kutungoto's intentions. He wanted the money badly and kept asking me for it while I kept refusing. I said, "You admit to having taken my fifty makutas?" He replied, "Yes." The first time he admitted it I was dumbfounded. Upon his reassuring me, I said, "I want you to tell the ex-chief (who was passing by my hut at that moment) this. I called to the old chief, after greeting him, to wait a moment. I told Kutungoto to come with me to the edge of the road where he was waiting, and admit to him that he had taken my fifty makutas.

Wham! I was struck by my enormous folly. Walking past the ex-chief on the road at that second was the *real* Kutungoto! The man I had originally contracted to do the work, the very same one who was standing beside me at that moment, is named *Musaba!*

7

ALL the Walese that I know have a deep fear of toads. At least I have noticed this among the men. But I feel this is because I spend all my time with them. That is why I have not noticed it among the women, and that goes for many things. I know the men far better than I know the women. This is especially true with the pygmies. With them, I have spent practically all of my time among the men.

The role of the sexes is very clearly defined here. Each type of work is either for a male or a female to perform. The exception is people who are not married or live alone. Then they have to do the work that would normally be done by one's husband or wife. Not many people live alone.

They fear toads because they believe they contain poison, especially their skin. They say that if you touch it, your skin will become warty like theirs. I have noticed this at home, only with us it is more of a superstition than a belief. We live so far apart from each other yet we have conceived the same basic idea from looking at the toad.

However, their story is a bit more involved. They say the toad is born with its poison and that the snake draws his poison from them by sinking his fangs into them. "Why else does the snake carry a toad around in his mouth for an hour or two?" they ask. They believe the snake is born without poison and during his lifetime refills his venom sacs with the toad's help. I don't know if the snake kills the toad when he does this.

The Walese's fear of the toad is deep. Toads constantly enter my hut by way of a crack between the bottom of my door and the dirt floor. I think they enter my hut to keep warm at night. The day's heat is trapped in my home and takes several hours to cool off during the night. Several times I have found them the next morning, and as one of my Mulese neighbors would walk by my house I would greet them. After they had turned around to greet me I would toss the toad at them. Seeing it come at them, they would immediately dash out of the way and make a loud exclamation, smiling at me for fooling with them. They were never mad at me. Several times, when the toad did touch them, I think they believed it did not touch them long enough to contaminate them, or just brushed their clothing, which is not serious. They constantly warn me not to pick them up and they back away from me when I do, just in case I decide to toss it in their direction. I found it amusing but don't continue to do it.

One night, the chief called me for dinner. On the way to his house I found a toad and picked it up. When I arrived, I found him lying on a mat on his back porch. I placed the toad near him when he wasn't looking to see what his reaction would be. He is different in many ways from the other Walese. He soon saw the toad and said, "You have put that toad there." Apparently he deduced that the toad had arrived with me and maybe thought it would have been difficult for it to jump up on his porch. I denied it half-heartedly seeing there was no doubt in his mind. I felt rather foolish over the outcome.

I have heard of another belief some Zairean women have, especially the younger ones, if not only them. Even though it doesn't concern the Walese, I think it's worth noting. It is one example—of many—where an African does something in order to get the white man's "magic" to rub off on them. This must take place in large enough places to have barber shops. In Africa, that means at least a small city. And there are white men in them.

The young women who are not yet married, secure the hair of a white man and put a small bunch of it in a lotion that they rub on their bodies. The name of the lotion is Cha Cha Cha. I was told by a Mulese that they do this in order to have good fortune, to become rich, and hopefully marry a white man.

There are many Africans that want to possess something that the white man has even if he has no use for it. It has symbolic power. It's like a good luck charm.

Someone stole the lock off my door, which was rather expensive. What he will do without the keys to it I don't know.

And then there are the students from the school who constantly ask me for books in English or French. I ask them if they know English well enough to read my books and they answer, "I will try. I am studying English now at school." And then I ask, "What is wrong with the books they have for you there? I have seen them and know they are much easier to read than the ones I have. And they are very popular in the United States." Many of them don't know what to answer then. One boy went as far as telling me he had read most all of them. I don't like to lend my things to the people here because they usually don't return them. Maybe they ask me just to start a friendship.

The town of Nduye is not very large. It's not very small either. The Father at the mission told me there are several thousand inhabitants here. A large amount of them don't live in the town itself. They are found living beside the road named Mai Tatu that leaves Nduye and runs six kilometers to a fair-sized coffee plantation. Mai Tatu means, "Three Waters." Apparently the road leads to a place where three sources of water are found. The road becomes a dead end when it reaches the plantation. The name of this small plantation town is Meme Kidele. I don't know it's significance.

After the road, a path continues for another several hundred kilometers and comes to a mining town. Fifty kilometers after the path begins, it forks off. The right part goes to the mine and the left to Kpokporo. Kpokporo is about fifteen kilometers from the fork.

Along the road live the villagers in mud-walled huts with roofs that are shingled with *mongongo* leaves. The huts are scattered along the roadside, and on the average, sit back from the dirt road by at least fifteen feet. This is typical of tropical Africa. They like to be near the roads in order to see the occasional trucks, and more rarely, cars and Land Rovers, go by. It's a form of excitement. It doesn't happen every day.

Sometimes the trucks bring food to sell, such as dried fish or bunches of bananas. And sometimes mail, as there is no steady mail service. More than anything, living next to the road means contact with the outside world. This, all Africans want to have.

Relatives arrive by truck when they come to visit someone. Many times, people on their way to visit someone wave and yell, "Hello," to their friends from the truck as they pass the huts. The passing of vehicles

is exciting. It breaks the monotony of village life. One hears an engine
in the distance, rises from his chair, and walks toward the road to see
the oncoming vehicle.

For me, I am affected even more so by this because trucks are more
a part of my world. It makes me happy to see them because I miss my
world, and unlike many of the villagers, there is a chance they will have
mail for me.

Sometimes I dash out of my hut to catch a glimpse of the vehicle
I heard approaching. I live next to the Mai Tatu road just as it leaves
Nduye. I look down it to where it meets the main dirt road that runs
through town.

Once every couple of days a vehicle will come through Nduye. Only
very rarely does one take the road to the plantation. Usually it's only
the mission's truck that passes by to go and get sand for the garage the
Brother is building. They use it in the cement. There is a small village
half way to Meme Kidele that collects sand from the stream in a large
pile.

When Land Rovers or a car pass, I look to see if there are white
people in them. It is as though I am waiting for someone to come and
visit me. Someone who might speak English and be able to really understand what it is like to live here. Twice I have been visited by whites
and both times it has made me feel very good.

There was an English couple that heard I was here from a missionary in Mambasa, and they came and visited me. I was eating lunch
at the chief's house when I saw the couple walk by on the road through
Nduye. I immediately stood up from the table and walked out the door
to call to them. They were on the way to my hut. I showed them my
hut and we sat down and began talking. I guess it was because I was
so happy to see them that I had a difficult time speaking. I stuttered
and spoke in a confusing manner. By the next day I had calmed down
and they said they noticed quite an improvement in my appearance
and speech. They both thought I wasn't doing myself any good by
staying here.

When the public transportation bus is not broken, it arrives from
Bunia every Saturday, bringing people and often some mail. It has not
been through here in over six weeks. When it does arrive there isn't a
much bigger occasion for the citizens. I can think of only one thing
that tops it and that is when the Father shows a film in the space between the church and the classrooms of the boys school. Almost all the

people of Nduye gather around the bus and look at the travelers. The
travelers get out to stretch their legs and possibly buy something to eat.
They mix with the villagers, talk, and make a larger crowd.

A crowd only attracts more people. Often children are seen among
the people selling peanuts, corn, or other small things. Deep-fried dough
balls are the most popular here. They are made from manioc, wheat,
or banana flour, or in combination.

The shops and homes of the town are built on both sides of the
wide dirt road. In the very center are the shops. There are about five
of them. Only two of them are open most of the day because the other
three have barely anything to sell. They've only got cigarettes, canned
fish, sardines, salt, Bic pens, several shirts and pants, radio batteries,
cloth, and very few other things for sale. They are normally open for
an hour or two each morning before the other two open.

The first store one comes to as he arrives from Mambasa is the
store that has the most things for sale. This one room store is as small
as all the others and relatively packed. This man carries all that the
other stores do and then four times that. I guess this man is able to
make his business work because he always has enough capital to buy
new things.

November 13th
Next day

The officials might resent someone doing a study of their people,
as though they were curiosities. This is definitely the attitude the officials
here in Zaire have concerning people's interest in the pygmies. They
aren't proud of the fact that the pygmies exist in their country. To them,
they represent to the rest of the civilized world, backwardness and
primitiveness. And they don't want to show this to the world. They want
to show they are part of the modern world and equal to us. In fact,
they even try to hide the fact of the pygmies' existence. Photographs are
not allowed to be taken of them. And Mobutu has ordered them all
to cultivate gardens. But his attempts have been unsuccessful so far and
it looks like the pygmies are a long way off from becoming cultivators.

I am really sorry my camera didn't make it here with me. I left
it in Paris because my pack weighed too much. I could have had a lot
of magnificent pictures, such as when we lived in the cave together and

they butchered a baby buffalo. Or the time we spent traveling the
savanna to Kpokporo; black bodies against the tall, light grass, armed
with lances. There still is a chance I'll get some photos one way or
another of this place. It may mean buying a camera and film in Uganda
and returning later with a tourist visa.

This culture shock has affected me tremendously. I've killed a lot
of people in my dreams. I don't know what to make of this one: With
one of the pygmies' lances I stabbed a large white girl three or four
times practically to death, and then went on to make love to her. I was
a midget in the dream.

I have spent a lot of time learning how to live here and have some
amount to still learn. I'm always learning and always paying for it, one
way or another, because of my ignorance. For instance, I have spent
four and one half months keeping a serious skin disease under control,
never being able to wipe it out. Also, this morning will be "wasted"
as I go through my tropical medicine pamphlet. I recall reading about
a disease that sounds like mine. You put Vaseline over the worm holes,
and they stick their head out to breathe so as not to be smothered. That's
when you pluck them out with tweezers. It sounds useless, however.

Part of this day will most likely be spent at the dispensary and walking up to the mission to mail my letters. And tonight I'm going to visit
an old man to buy some food from. How else have I spent this morning?
Well . . . obviously a good part of it writing this entry. And before that,
I cleaned my outhouse, which some very inconsiderate person defecated
in, missing the hole by at least a foot because he couldn't see what he
was doing in the darkness of the night. And because he was in a hurry
so that I might not come out of my hut in the middle of the night to
relieve myself and catch him. And then he would be publicly shamed
and sent to the small town prison. Or maybe my outhouse was dirtied
purposely because he resents a white man living here and living like
the Zaireans. Maybe he sees me as mocking the Zaireans. "Why would
a rich white man leave his good, materially-wealthy world to live in
poverty? Why isn't he at least living with his own tribe at the mission?"
Or maybe it was a careless youngster. I've wondered why so many times
because this is the tenth time now. I think it is done intentionally, because
sometimes they urinate all over the dirt floor.

And why do they come to use my w.c. (water closet), as it is called
here? Because I am the only one who has one. They are too lazy to construct theirs. They would rather go in the woods each time, which is

a lot more impractical. Or they go in the stream. The same stream we all wash our dishes and bathe in. Apparently there isn't enough waste material to contaminate the water. I don't know why. The stream is only four feet wide. I think if the water was warmer we'd be in trouble. It also runs pretty fast.

I thought taking my basket of special leaves they use for toilet paper out of my w.c. would stop them from using it, but I was wrong. Looks like they don't wipe themselves. Hard to imagine on a soft diet of *sombe*, manioc, sweet potatoes, rice, beans and so forth. Now I keep my leaves in my house. Which reminds me, I spent a small amount of this morning picking toilet paper leaves for my basket.

I was happy when a plant decided to grow in my w.c. It brightened up the place and reminded me of a bathroom one often finds at home. Well . . . someone eventually found the leaves large enough to wipe themself with and now my plant is dead. I was sorry for the plant because it had struggled so hard to live, stretching for the sunlight that came through the doorway. It finally looked like it was going to make it, only to be plucked and killed in less than a second.

It reminds me of the Andy Warhol film I heard about. The audience sits painfully through forty-eight hours of watching some grass grow, only to watch a lawn mower come and mow it down in one swipe. I'm sure my reaction could never have equaled theirs.

It's interesting to see that the day I moved in and started digging my w.c., so did my four neighbors begin theirs. It was as though I had set an example. But so far, I believe only one of them has completed his. It's hard work digging down through two meters of soil packed like rock. And that's why I guess they have given up.

Also, I will spend some of today trying to coax one of my neighbors who is a part-time carpenter to construct a door for my w.c. with a lock on it. And of course, we will discuss the price for "such hard work," endlessly.

During this entry, I have been interrupted with attacks of diarrhea because I somehow came across six occasions to eat yesterday, amazingly enough. So I'm a bit sick because I ate so much, and, because I mixed so many different foods, a villager told me. Or it just may be because of the old hog meat I ate.

I spent some time this morning picking burs out of my towel. I mistakenly set it down on the grass, instead of the tree I usually hang it on, when I went to wash this morning. I couldn't hang it in the crotch of the tree because there were too many dishes in front of it due to the women who were washing them.

And the lady next door who prepares tea for me had to be shown three times at what level to fill my cup for the desired strength. And she still didn't get it right. Also, I had to add more tea because she pilfered the first amount I gave her.

These people usually take more than they give. However, yesterday one neighbor brought me a bowl of rice with *sombe.* And upon visiting the old man I will buy food from tonight, I was served a large, delicious platter of rice with the pureed insides of squash seeds. They were mixed with pepper and onions. The rice is being harvested now and I'm happy to eat that familiar food. I can't imagine getting tired of it.

Apuobo is very generous. He has offered to feed me free, and consider me his son and part of his large family. Food is very expensive here and he is supporting at least fifteen people every day from his large garden, which is really saying something. That's at least thirty meals a day.

He has not been paid by the government in over nine months, and by the region, in over five years. He says he's dedicated to his country. He also says that if he does not receive some money from the government by January he will quit his job and become a cultivator. But I don't believe him because I believe he likes his image, authority, and title of "Chief," too much.

My eating with him is an interesting story, which I expect to record today. Part of the reason he is doing it, however, is because he thinks God has sent me to Nduye. He said, "You don't come all the way from the United States to Nduye for no reason. There *is* a reason you are here."

This acculturation process is really something for me. I'm very young for this experience and came here not very well prepared. Imagine! Arriving by hitch-hiking with a pack on my back. Doesn't sound very serious. If I hadn't been so ignorant before I came here I would have never come. It's been very hellish and valuable but if I had known the price earlier I would not have come. Now I am here and will do what I can with it. Eighteen months is a long time if things are hard. I'm constantly being challenged and might just get too tired of it one day and leave. I may leave just to speak my own language among friends, eat a sandwich, or drink some milk. It sounds very immature, but it's a feeling all field workers get I bet. It's hard being alone.

I don't feel close to the people. Of course it would be easier to come home. I'm young, got a lot of time, and will give it a try. I may just find it too hard to say to myself, "I will leave tomorrow." It might be too big a decision and I'll wait for the pre-picked day. Time will tell.

Tonight I drank alcohol distilled from manioc. Several villagers and I were sitting in a garden around the still drinking. They boil a paste of manioc in water in a large can. From the can protrude two large bamboo tubes. One lets off the steam, and of course, the other one, the booze. It's a long tube that lets the alcohol condense and runs a long way to a hole in the ground. In the hole is the bottle which fills up in about twenty minutes. It took only five minutes to finish the bottle sitting around with seven greedy villagers who were just waiting to profit from the white boy who bought the bottle.

Sometimes I push my generosity to the limit in order to see just how far these people will take advantage of me. But that's not to say there aren't any generous villagers here. Yesterday I was served two nice meals, one by my neighbor and the other by a friend of mine. And, as I mentioned recently, the chief of the collectivity has taken me under his wing, called me his son, and offered me all my meals free with him.

There is a choice of about only twenty things to eat here and four to drink; water, palm wine, tea or coffee. I usually eat boiled, unripe bananas, beans, manioc, *sombe* (pounded, boiled, manioc leaves with salt and palm oil), sweet potatoes and rice. Occasionally; corn, fish, and various animals from the bush, such as, pangolin, porcupine, elephant, ground hog, pig, monkey, buffalo, turtle, and others. I even tasted rat, and eat termites in large quantities regularly. My stomach feels capable of handling just about anything now, from putrified hog, to maggots that I've eaten accidentally.

When I spent three days in the cave eating baby buffalo, they butchered it on the ground and boiled most of it up, dirt and all. The rest was grilled. They eat every part of an animal, including the hide, which I found quite tasteless and tough. After all, there isn't much difference between it and a boiled shoe. It made me think of Charlie Chaplin eating his boiled shoe in *The Gold Rush*.

The brain was saved for the old toothless pygmy, Musili, because it was soft and easy for him to eat. He was only twenty-five years old and he won't live more than five more years, which is normal for a pygmy. I once met a women of twenty out in the middle of the woods who looked like she would be ninety in our world.

I've spent at least a third of my time so far with the pygmies and it is so different than the life we live that I find it hard. They love their life very much I'm sure, and find it easygoing. I don't know how I'm going to adapt, having grown up in the civilized world for twenty years. Sometimes I wonder if it's worth the pain. Sometimes pygmy life bores me. They love to sit around in their camps and smoke pot mixed with tobacco for hours on end and recount hunting stories, especially of elephants. Some of these men are incredible mimes, especially after they've smoked and lost some of their inhibitions. These little kids of six or seven have already got the long banana stem pipes in their mouths.

Other than sitting around in their camps feeling bored and lonely, I have hunted elephant, antelope, hog and buffalo with them so far. We've never killed anything. I have seen and eaten animals they have killed while hunting without me. The favorite way to hunt here is with dogs and spears. The dogs pick up the scent of an animal and give chase. A buffalo, for example, will turn around to see the small dogs bothering him and stop to combat them. Eventually the pygmies show up and find the distracted animal and thrust their spears into it before it can flee.

I am living the simple life and I think easier lives can be lived at home. No running water, electricity, flush toilets, refrigerators and so on. I don't know how many months of this weirdness I'm going to be able to handle. I've been here three and a half months to this day and when people ask me when I'm leaving I answer, "When I'm almost dead and have just enough energy to crawl out of Nduye!"

But I *am* still here, and should return after Kisangani if all goes well and the authorities let me continue. I realize I'm supposed to be doing agricultural work, but have found it very difficult, mainly because it bores me. So what I am trying to do now is record life among the villagers. I can't believe that the biggest challenge is yet to come— that's living with the pygmies. Don't know if I'll accept it or be given the chance. Whatever happens, it's all been worth it so far.

8

I'VE never seen such a bunch of lazy, apathetic people as these Walese villagers in my life. They are outright inconsiderate and take me for everything they can get. This goes for most of Zaire's population but for some reason the people here are worse. I don't know if they've always been this way or it has just been since the Belgians left and Mobutu took over. Anyway, the country is an absolute mess and its financial troubles are worse than those of many others who are a part of the current monetary crisis.

These people cultivate just enough food to take the hunger pains away. In fact, the commissioner of the zone was here four days ago, and while addressing the population he told them that because the cultivation is so slack here, everyone at the beginning of 1977 is required to cultivate a section of a huge garden. A large section of the land will be cleared by the entire population of Nduye and the chief of the collectivity will be keeping his eye on everyone to make sure they are doing their work. Most of the day they sit around drinking raffia or palm wine, smoking, talking, joking, and arguing. I really fell in with quite a bunch and I don't think I'm ever going to be able to appreciate their life, be interested in it, or be able to adapt. I feel no more comfortable here now than the first day I arrived.

Other than trying to write, I spend my time eating, walking around the tiny town, talking to the missionaries, or tending to chores. They include washing my clothes in the stream, fetching drinking water, looking for food to buy and discussing its price endlessly, picking toilet paper leaves, cleaning my outhouse that the villagers dirty when my back is turned (I'm putting a door and lock on it), answering the door when people come to sell me an animal, termites or a papaya. Or they come and ask me for money ("Only ten cents?"), or to borrow some books written in English.

I never saw such a lonely town. The three small shops are closed most of the day, making Nduye look like a ghost town. Sometimes I think I write as many letters as I do in order to give me an excuse to walk up to the mission to mail them and speak to the members of my own "tribe," as the missionaries are called by the Walese.

The mission is in its own little world up on top of the hill looking down over the village, and I love to look at it. I hate to admit it but I think the mission is the most beautiful sight in Nduye. Maybe it symbolically reminds me that I will one day return to a place where buildings and life are like that; organized, efficient, and clean. But the mission is a lonely place also and I suppose as long as I'm here I should spend my time in the village.

I guess I'm still trying to stay here so that I'll have something to tell the people when they ask me about the pygmies when I return. "Oh! The pygmies . . . They live in the woods in small leafed domes, hunt animals, eat the forest fruits, dance when it moves them and sit around camp getting high and gazing lazily at the forest." And that's all I might really end up knowing about them after two years of work. But it may be better for me that way in the end. I may be saved more trouble than it's worth.

I still don't have permission from the government to live and work with them, but I've decided that when I get to Kisangani I'm going to ask for it and get it over with. I can't wait any longer. There is a good chance they will say no.

The pygmies are in their own world too. They couldn't care if the rest of the world burned down. They don't have the slightest interest in our world. They have never asked my interpreter when we've been with them where I come from, why am I here or anything concerning my world. I suppose all they know about me is that I come from a land where the white man lives.

All missionaries love their work because God is their employer. So when I ask a missionary if he or she is happy with their life in Nduye they always answer, "Yes." I never take them seriously because of this fact.

There are some people here who deliberately annoy me by speaking Kingwana to me instead of French. And they know French. I just walk away from them now.

I was sitting with my neighbor yesterday afternoon, and because I remembered the date, I decided to tell him what was going on in the U.S. yesterday. I explained to him that a turkey was like a chicken and a duck mixed together, only much larger. When I mentioned that some of the very largest turkeys come close to weighing thirty pounds he was truly astounded. He exclaimed, "That's practically an antelope!"

Later on in the conversation he understood what bird I was talking about and gave me its name in French, which I immediately recalled as the correct one. Then I told him the story of why we celebrate this occasion. (It's amazing how many of those birds are eaten that day.)

My mind has calmed down a bit since the last couple of entries I wrote. It is as though most of the storm has passed. However, I still feel my head isn't completely back together. Although, I don't think it was deranged enough that someone could have noticed it in my appearance. The reason I have calmed down somewhat is because I believe, and hope, that I have made the right decision to leave Nduye near the end of December for Kisangani and come back here only to pick up some mail on my way out of Zaire towards home. I have finally gotten it together to sit down and write that last line. I believe three and a half months has been long enough to make a rational decision. I had been putting this day off for quite awhile.

Often, I think back to the times I told people I was going to live with the pygmies and I try and think about the possibilities of there having been ulterior reasons for my doing so. I've thought it quite possible, if not certain, that by telling people that, I thought that made me someone instantly.

Someone would meet me in the street for example, and ask me what I was up to these days. I would tell them I was selling firewood, and usually add that I was going to Africa to live with the pygmies. I wasn't awfully proud to be selling wood. So I'd tell people about the pygmies so they would know I didn't intend to be selling wood forever, and would think my head was in the right direction by intending to do something interesting with my life. They probably thought, "Oh! This boy is interesting with his stories about pygmies. He's just a temporary woodcutter." I remember telling adults particularly. It was a great cocktail party line. Telling someone what you're going to do is only a very, very small fraction of actually doing it however. Not until you've done it can you really open your mouth about it.

November 27th
Next day

The next couple of weeks I will spend getting ready to go to Kisangani. It will include selling my home and possessions and writing some letters. In five days I am going to the hospital in Nyankunde with a missionary and his wife who live twelve kilometers down the road toward Mambasa. He is called Lubana Bongo by the villagers, which means, "speak to them." It's probably actually one word. I know him by this name only. His wife is Mrs. Lubanabongo.

Nyankunde is just before Bunia. I am going there to finally get my skin disease treated, I hope. I have somehow managed to go five months with it, having noticed it on July 1st for the first time. That was the day I entered Zaire. It seems so foolish having gone five months with it.

I believe I may have picked up the fungus by wearing pants that had not thoroughly dried. While I was hitching, I'd come to someone's house near the end of the day and wash my clothes. My pants were not always dry by the next morning, so I'd put them on and they'd dry on me.

When I got to Kisangani, the doctor told me it was a fungus and prescribed a cream for it. Before I bought the cream I had been washing the area with a soap that contained mercury. I would scratch the area first until it didn't itch anymore and little beads of blood would form. Then I would apply the soap and let it sit for twenty minutes, instead of the recommended five. Twenty minutes was all I could bear. The soap would burn my skin, stop the itching, and retard the malady. I wasn't having much luck with the cream so I continued using the soap with it. The doctor had told me it was serious and that it might take four to six weeks to go away so I wasn't very bothered about it when I didn't find it disappearing right away.

Before I left Kisangani I bought a lot more cream, powder, and lotion of the same product so I would hopefully have plenty to wipe it out once I arrived in Nduye.

The first two months or so here, I burned my crotch daily and kept washing and changing my pants frequently. I thought that it might not be going away because I was not being thorough enough. I didn't know exactly what to make of it. It would eventually disappear after much persistence, only to show up again several days later. I thought that possibly after it disappeared I was not continuing the medication long enough to make sure it wouldn't come back.

By the time I moved into my hut I was out of lotion and powder, and finding the cream useless, I went back to using the soap. Every morning I would go down to the little stream and scrub the soap into my skin with an indigenous hand brush until blood showed. Then I would sit there for thirty to forty-five minutes.

Eventually my skin became so tough that the soap would no longer burn me. I mean to say, I couldn't feel it burn me. I went through layers of skin that kept being burned and flaking off fairly rapidly. About an hour of this each morning began to tire me and after about five weeks I gave up. I wasn't able to start the day until after I had given myself the daily treatment.

After I stopped using the soap I used my fingernails. Whenever it would itch I would scratch it until it didn't anymore. I was pretty sure by then that my malady was not a fungus. I had had it for so long by then that I became used to it and didn't notice it as much as before.

One day I thought about it and decided to go to the small clinic here to see if the Sister knew what the problem was. (I had previously decided that to go to Nyankunde would take too much time from my work and that I would wait until Kisangani. I guess I didn't have too much faith in the clinic here for some reason.)

I remember now why I went to see the Sister. It was because while I was in the forest with the pygmies looking for the place where the moon rests, I began scratching myself so hard, that upon looking closely at my skin I saw something small, slender, and white sticking out of it. I was finally able to get hold of it with my fingernails and pull it out to find a parasite much like a worm, only it was straight and didn't wriggle. It obviously moves but is too hard to see with the eye. It's similar to a tiny splinter.

The first one I pulled out had a black dot at one end, which I assumed was its eye. I squished half of it but I still couldn't see any movement. Looking more closely at my skin, I found others and began pulling them out with my tweezers, but without much success. So little sticks out of my skin that they are hard to get hold of. And when I do begin to pull, I believe I usually only end up with half the critter. It's hard to tell how much remains in my skin.

I discovered them by looking at my thighs in profile instead of directly head-on. I suppose that when I burned the outer layers of my skin I was not killing them, but actually driving them deeper into my flesh. And they would eventually reappear. I went to the Sister and she told me I had a skin disease. She didn't recognize it. She advised me to take tetracycline for four days and gave me another brand of cream. The medications had no effect. In fact, the new cream agitated my skin further. I went back to her and told her what the result was. She said she didn't know what it was, no other villagers had it, and that it would probably go away when I returned home. She told me to continue with the same medicines, and come back and see her if there still was no change and she would try another cream. (I can't imagine a cream used externally killing a parasite that is in my skin.)

I told her all the details of my malady. I've still got it and feel confident that it will be gone by the time I return from Nyankunde. It has a good reputation. American doctors are there and the facilities are good. (You can be sure that if that Sister had my malady she would not wait until she returned to Italy for it to go away.)

It's gotten worse since I first got it. It is now on my buttocks, and my rectum has some small, unhealing, bloody sores. My right knee has two patches growing on it now also. It doesn't bother me too much, except sometimes when I wake up at night to scratch.

One thing I do want to find out while in Nyankunde is if the sickness has been affecting my mind. I intend to get a thorough physical while there, and talk to a doctor about my mental state, what he thinks of it, and what has been affecting it. I believe it is due to the long intensity of this experience.

I went and saw the Sister to see if she thought maybe I was lacking something important in my diet, and that this was affecting my mind. I suggested vitamins (I had a large bottle of them, but somehow the moisture got to them and they began rotting, so I had to heave them) and she agreed it wouldn't hurt to take them. So I've been taking them, and eating regularly now that I've decided to get my neighbors to prepare some of my meals for me. I also still eat with the chief.

It's important to have the tools so that one can cope effectively and as fast as possible with the situation. This is where language is invaluable. To know their language makes one much, much less of a stranger. If one doesn't know the language, he should at least have some background in linguistics to know how to go about learning the language as fast as possible. If a trained anthropologist were in my shoes he would know a hundred times more than what I have learned so far. Without the tools I learn slowly, often by mistakes, the hard way. It is mainly for this reason that I am going home.

Much of the time I am nervous. But more often, and more intense, is my feeling paranoid. There is really nothing more scary than intense paranoia and I have really experienced it here. The most memorable time was when I was out in the forest with the pygmies forty kilometers from Nduye on the moon quest. I thought I was about to freak out. I thought, "Oh my God! Do you realize where you are?" I didn't think I was going to see my home again. I wondered how I was going to get out of the forest and make it home over maybe ten thousand miles, much of it by my thumb. Several other times I thought I was going to pack up my things, get on the next truck to Kisangani, and mail my withdrawal contract to Empire State College from there.

I spend almost all my time doing things other than those that require concentration. I take lots of short walks to relieve stress. I've only thought of meditating to relieve stress, not done it. I have not spent much time writing and have produced no work, and this has added to my paranoia. My intermission form will be sent off to Empire State College in a couple of days.

I have also found that my self-discipline is rather poor. At least it has been concerning my work here. When I mentioned my work in my previous entries, I was working on something at that moment, but most likely was speaking more of my ideal. As I just said, I have produced next to nothing.

It's ironic my sitting here in the bush watching these children go to school each day. They are probably learning more than I am. They all want to go to American or European universities someday more than anything in the world. And most of them won't have the opportunity. Usually to get that opportunity it requires him to exert a lot of strength because so many barriers are in his way. Most of them don't have that much stamina to want to be able to put out for those years for something that is never certain. Coupled with the fact that jobs are very, very difficult to find here even after one's been educated, this leads people to

find more security as a cultivator. Often no one can support them while
they study. Simply, the barriers are endless. The students have a hard
time understanding what I am trying to learn in Nduye. That is one
reason they wonder why I'm not in the U.S. (along with other reasons
as well).

About money; a field worker should have more than enough. It
can save him a lot of time and trouble by working for him. This way,
more of his time can be devoted to his research.

What have I spent my time doing for the past four months if it
hasn't been working? The first three I spent suffering from culture shock
and seeing how incompetent I was at dealing with things. Actually,
the shock has been up to this moment. I stopped my crying bouts when
I made the decision to leave and sat down and began writing this entry.
I've really only given a small idea of what the shock did to me. It was
a traumatic experience. I'd urinate as much as fifteen times a day my
nerves were so on edge. I spent most of my time not alone in my hut.
I visited people in their gardens and homes. I did just about anything
other than sit down and write.

I spent time visiting pygmy camps also. I've slept quite a few nights
in them. Time was spent at the mission also. And some was spent in
laziness. (Why else have I not produced anything?)

I wish I had spent more time with the pygmies. All I got was a
glance at their life. They are in the woods or the villagers' fields most
of the time. That is something I regret about leaving now. But before
I leave I'm going to spend at least a few more afternoons and nights
with my favorite family at their camp, where I will eat boiled rice and
sleep next to the fire in a hut curled up on a hunting net. They are the
friendliest family of pygmies I know. Their camp has a beautiful setting at the edge of a villager's field, in the woods, on a hill. There I
saw the most beautiful child ever. His name is Kapitangani. We are
real buddies.

It looks like the pygmies will be around for a fair while still. A
lot depends on the pace of the country's economy and development.

I went and saw Lubanabongo and his wife last Saturday. They
live at Akokora, twelve kilometers in the direction of Mambasa. I'm
not sure what took me so long to go and see the American couple.

Friday night I decided to go and see them, one big reason being
that I wanted to see if I could possibly stay with them. Or at least to
see if they knew of some missionaries in the Ituri that could put me

up for the month of December to see if it helped. The mission here wouldn't take me (like I thought). That's why I put off asking them for so long.

The same night I had been refused here I felt so miserable I told myself, "I'm leaving Nduye tonight for Akokora." It was the first time I had left here since I arrived, excluding going into the forest.

I was well received by Lubanabongo and his wife and I was terribly happy to see some Americans. Likewise, they were happy to have a visitor. They have so few.

They were born in Norway and later moved to the U.S. Their last thirty years have been spent in various places in Zaire. They are not typical missionaries and they had no influence on my decision to come home. It's not like the missionaries got to me. They were very objective and thought I should at least try for a year and begin learning the language. They told me how important it is to speak the native tongue. They are regularly occupied with going on book-selling trips of several months, so I could see I couldn't stay with them.

I had a good time with them, especially him. Lubanabongo has a great interest in anthropology and linguistics and wishes he had only taken those courses when he was in school. He said, "Anthropology is a great field because it deals with God's last and crown creation: Man."

They are Protestant and did not push their religion on me. They are living much like the Africans, and with them. They have a large garden and eat the same food as the villagers, only more meat usually, and sometimes the preparation is different. They are both in their early sixties and he is quite intelligent.

So, before I know it I'll be leaving the Ituri and Zaire and will be home. That's how time flies. It's frightening.

I should mention that I never saw time crawl along as slowly as here, especially when I've been with the pygmies. During the time I spent with them I never came close to getting used to it. It meant much of the time sitting and doing practically nothing. Talking is the favorite pastime, and that goes for the villagers too. Sitting idly in their camps not being able to communicate was when I felt most like an ugly duckling. There were a couple of other times that I felt quite at home with them. Usually at night while sitting around a fire in their domes. It was a fantastic feeling.

I feel good once again. I did have some great times here, and there will be many things I will miss. I wish I had gotten to know the pygmies

better. Who else in the world lives like them? I don't worry too much
about it because I have a long life ahead of me. And what am I going
to do without my daily portions of *sombe*? It's about as much of the
blacks as their skin color. And palm oil, kernels, and wine? I'll forget
it pretty fast by the time I see what's on the table at home. I also really
missed my camera. But if there is a next time it will be done right.

November 29th
Two days later

Every day now, Apuobo is out with the military supervising the
men of Nduye as they begin clearing the 1000 x 1000 meter swidden
that the commissioner of the zone said Nduye would have. The
authorities follow behind them as they clear. It is because some of the
Walese are lazy that the garden is being made. As long as everyone is
able to support themselves, I don't know what the problem is. Probably
with the new garden less stealing of peoples' vegetables from their
gardens will occur.

A lot of stealing goes on and the pygmies have the biggest hand
in it. Some villagers send them to steal from other villagers' gardens.
I have heard there are some people here who don't have gardens and
they exist on nothing but *sombe* without salt or oil. They just pick,
prepare, and eat the free manioc leaves that grow again right after
they've been picked.

Recently there was a palm oil shortage. Nduye was out of oil for
almost two weeks. All the oil was coming from the trees in the woods.
Oil finally arrived at the small shop and has doubled in price.

In general, things don't seem to be getting any better in Zaire. The
most commonly heard answer in this town is, "Haiko," which means,
"There isn't any." I've been given that answer fifteen times per day
sometimes. I think they do it just to aggravate me. These people are
real characters.

One day I asked the women and children at the chief's house if
there was any food to eat. They responded, "No," while stuffing their
faces. The reason they said, "No," was because no food had been
prepared for the chief and it is only with him that I take my meals.

There is no limit to how much these people would take from me
or another white. And they never give anything in return. More often

than not, when I hand a Mulese a cup of wine, I have to ask him to give it back to me before he consumes the whole thing. Yet among themselves they usually give it back to the person who bought it, voluntarily (normally after they have taken large healthy gulps). The only time I get some from them is when I ask for it, and they are always reluctant or try to refuse. So now I don't give anything. It is only very recently that I have begun drinking (since my decision to leave).

Because the government doesn't have enough money to run the schools properly, they have asked the missionaries to come back and take them over sometime in January. Thus, many teachers will be leaving Nduye then and many will probably be jobless. I understand the missionaries will not have anything to do with the universities.

Apuobo has been very nice to me. He has acted as a father to me. I've been taking all me meals free with him and I intend to give him my hut when I leave. He will most likely give it to his younger brother Likambo and his wife and child. I'd rather they had my nice home than one of the teachers who want to buy it. They'll really like my study with the large glass window in it.

During the time I've been writing this entry, at least a half a dozen people and children have come up to my glass window and looked at what I was doing. They also look at everything on my table and examine the inside of my house. They stay as long as ten minutes very often. (I know this would most likely drive my mother more crazy than anyone I know.)

After my second week here, I found it ironic the day I started reading *The Time Machine*, and came to the paragraphs where the time traveler says:

> . . . To sit among all those unknown things before a puzzle like that is hopeless. That way lies monomania. Face this world. Learn its ways, watch it, be careful of too hasty guesses at its meaning. In the end you will find clues to it all . . . . "
>
> . . . Then suddenly the humour of the situation came into my mind: the thought of the years I had spent in study and toil to get into the future age, and now my passion of anxiety to get out of it. I had made myself the most complicated and the most helpless trap that ever a man devised. Although it was at my own expense, I could not help myself. I laughed aloud . . . . [I couldn't laugh.]
>
> . . . I suppose it was the unexpected nature of my loss that maddened me. I felt hopelessly cut off from my own kind—a strange animal in an

unknown world. I must have raved to and fro, screaming and crying upon
God and Fate . . . .
   . . . It behooves me to be calm and patient, to learn the way of the
people, to get a clear idea of the method of my loss, and the means of get-
ting materials and tools; so that in the end, perhaps, I may make another."
   . . . That would be my only hope, perhaps, but better than despair.
And, after all, it was a beautiful and curious world.

I found it worse than ironic. It was too much. I felt it was predict-
ing my fate!

9

I ARRIVED on Sunday the nineteenth from Nduye early in the morning. I left Nduye on the night of Wednesday the fifteenth, walked three kilometers toward Mambasa, and slept in a village along the roadside. I had intended to walk as far as Akokora (12 kms.) but the night was moonless and it was hard to see where I was stepping. I was afraid I would have sprained an ankle with the roads so eroded and my pack weighing twenty-one kilo's (I found out once I weighed it in Kisangani).

The Sisters, Fathers, and several other people in Nduye thought it would be best for me to leave. The Sisters hadn't expected me to last as long as I did. As I said, "Good-bye" to the Sisters I told them I might decide to come back after Kisangani, and mentioned some ideas for another approach. They seemed disappointed to hear that after I had told them previously that I had intended to leave. (During my stay in Nduye the Fathers were rather cold towards me unfortunately. I have several ideas as to why. Maybe because I was living with the villagers [quite the opposite of themselves], and maybe they just didn't want to be bothered by a visitor.)

When I left Nduye all my neighbors and other villagers didn't give me a going away present, they demanded that I leave them with souvenirs. I told them to forget it. It's not the custom I know. They were just trying to get something out of me. Arne Lenhartzen (alias Lubanabongo) told me that's all they see me as—someone to try and get as much as possible out of. And obviously there is no limit to how much they would take and never give in return.

When a student at the mechanics school learned of my birthday, he asked me to go down to the bar (from the dormitory which sits on the side of the hill just below the mission) and buy drinks for everyone in order to celebrate. I told him I'd bring him something instead. I took a piece of cake that the Sisters had made for me, but he wasn't in, so I left it at the head of his bed. He said he never got it. Maybe he was robbed. Maybe he ate it. Anyhow, he asked for a gift to celebrate the occasion. He didn't really give a damn about my birthday. He just wanted something from me. My birthday had by this time already been over for a week. I decided to buy him a beer. (They only come in the size of one liter here.) I gave him a zaire and he said he'd give me the change. I did it because while I was in Mambasa his family had served me a nice meal. (That was before I had arrived in Nduye.)

Well of course I never saw my change. The whole village, and Zaire for that matter, or even Africa, is filled with types like that. I ended up trusting practically no one by the time I left. I kept giving people a chance to show me that I could trust them until just about the day I left and they never failed to disappoint me. They are devious as hell. I've got a hundred stories of things they took from me. The day I left, my pocketknife finally got swiped. You never want to tell someone you are leaving (white man that is) until you're just about to walk out the door, because if they know ahead of time they say to themselves, "This is our last chance for last grabs." They'll break into your house!

December 25th
Two days later

I'm not certain, but I believe that in order for a person to adapt to a very alien culture there are tools that are available to him that he can find through education. The *language*, linguistics, how to deal with people and so on. He needs something more because he comes from such a different place and also intends to live among the people but not always like them. He always has to remember, that besides being different, he is there as a researcher and not a hunter or cultivator. There will also be a role he will be expected to play, an image to uphold. He will be respected for keeping his pants on and not abandoning them for a loincloth. It is expected of him.

Besides the possibility of missionaries returning to take back the schools, the merchants have also been invited back. Buildings are now being fixed up and repainted. Foreign products will come into the country again. The country should become much better because of Mobutu's decision. He said over the radio that he gave the Zaireans a chance to run the businesses and so forth but they blew it. It was a real mess. Many wished the Belgians had never left it got so bad.

When I was last here in July, I wrote in fair detail about the dream I had of how Nduye would look. Those gray boulders and pine trees were in Nduye alright. No one told me they were there, and I believe sitting here in a tropical forest, it would have been rather difficult to even have the idea that such a thing existed there. I often thought about it while looking at the two things, or sitting on the boulder just above the mission.

A loose interpretation of its meaning could be this: The gray boulders were tombstones. That seemed clear as anything to me while there. In fact—and this is true—they appeared like and were placed like tombstones around Turnbull's house in my dream. So there is no doubt in my mind about that. So what does the death mean? Most likely the death of old ideas and the birth of new ones. (I was actually a bit nervous to find those tombstones upon my arrival.)

Now that I'm writing this out, maybe it's a bit more clear to me. The pine trees could have meant Christmas as marking the death of my project. Christ was born then—my idea for another approach?

Just days before I left Nduye, the director of the girls school's wife gave birth to a dead boy. The pine trees were planted along the road to his house. They were the only pines in Nduye. The sisters had probably planted them, because they aren't indigenous. (Also, some Belgians in Mambasa planted some.) Pines not indigenous symbolized a stranger?

To get to his house, one walked down the road bordered by the pines. And beside his house, or directly at the end of the road, the child was buried. I took part in the ceremony and threw several handfuls of dirt on the casket before it was buried using shovels and hoes.

Yes, I had been thinking then about what it all meant, if anything. Was I letting my imagination get away from me?

The last week or so before my departure I regularly visited a young friend of mine who had just given birth to a boy. I gave her a gift for him.

I am now just at this moment realizing all this. It doesn't really

require one to push his imagination very far does it? It doesn't seem
so fantastic that it really couldn't be true. Afterall, I already have
accepted my fate.

January 3, 1977
Nine days later

My mind really did go through a lot of strange thoughts. I would
often quite vividly imagine myself at home, for instance. While I'd be
in bed I'd imagine I was in bed at home in my room. Or I'd be sitting
in the TV room eating granola. And I'd think about how used to life
I was at home, and how vivid my memory is of it, that I'd say to myself,
"Here I am in a world that's always different. So little do I know about
it. I don't need to go home yet, where I know what that world is all
about." But there were these very human feelings that kept getting in
the way. Things one just can't control. In many ways much of the time
was a suppression of the emotions, or how I really felt. And when I
was at home I didn't take into account the human part of myself that
I was going to have to deal with while in the bush. It's really no fun
at all sitting around in a pygmy camp not being able to talk to them.
And much of the time I'd ask myself, "Is anything worth what I'm going through?" My nerves are still somewhat on edge. As I write this
entry my hands are trembling, as they have been doing since I arrived
here. Or maybe in Nduye also. I never once sat down and made a serious
attempt to record life there. But normally it wasn't something I could
control. I think my inner self finally took over and said, "Go home!"

How *did* I spend my days in Nduye? I would spend them doing
just about anything that didn't take concentration. Washing clothes,
hiking around, looking for and eating food and then doing the dishes,
picking toilet paper leaves for my outhouse, sitting in my hut trying
and sometimes doing some reading or writing, talking to people in
French, buying kerosene at the local store, talking to the Fathers, climbing on top of the big boulder up behind the mission and gazing over
the valley, pounding manioc leaves for a crippled pygmy woman, walking in the woods, sipping raffia wine, talking to the students; anything
to pass the days that I thought were eventually going to lead to my adaptation. I couldn't sit still. I had to find out where I was, what was going on around me in my new world.

At night I always felt good. I felt cozy in the darkness. But the days were different with all those things to look at and deal with. And what to do with each day. At night I'd listen to *The Voice of America* on one of my neighbor's radios, eat, and then sleep. It was nice to slip off away from reality for nine hour's worth of sleep or so.

I was in a rather more remote place than where Turnbull was, but still, the pygmies were doing a lot of living on the villagers' garden products. They ate some wild fruits and occasionally some animals, but the bulk of their diet consisted of food cultivated by the villagers. It seemed it was easier to work in the villager's field for food, and more certain than roaming around the woods for it. The garden food is much more varied and the pygmies have acquired a taste for it.

I don't think all that much hunting was going on. This also depended on how close to the village the pygmies lived. The ones farther away may have done more. Also, if a villager, or one family, had a great desire to eat meat, he'd send "his" pygmies out at least once a week to hunt.

The pygmies seem perfectly adapted to the forest environment. Even as close as they are to it, I would sometimes sense that just because they are human, they are in some ways alien to their environment; just because they are man and not animals.

A humorous note concerning where student of anthropology meets with the culture he's studying: I would give all my scrap paper to my next-door neighbors. They used it to roll their cigarettes. One day I went over to see if they had any use for a sheet of used carbon paper. I was only able to find a young pygmy girl there at that moment, and since she wanted it, I gave it to her. I returned to my desk below my large glass window. Several minutes later, out of my window, I saw how my old sheet of carbon paper had ingeniously been put to use. It now served as the back flap of her loincloth. It was so much lighter than the normal bark ones, that as she would walk along the air would lift it up exposing her fanny.

The villagers thought my trying to live with the pygmies was rather humorous. "Only animals would live in the forest," they would say. "What kind of life is that without salt or oil and moving to live in another spot constantly."

Despite how much the villagers may have ridiculed the pygmies, they loved them very much and may even need them to a certain extent as laborers in their gardens. It was interesting to see many times how really close their relationship to each other was.

January 21st
Eighteen days later

Tomorrow I intend to head back to Nduye to give my hut to Apuobo and sell my possessions. I got my visa prolonged for a month yesterday, so I'll be out of Zaire within then I should think.

Part Two

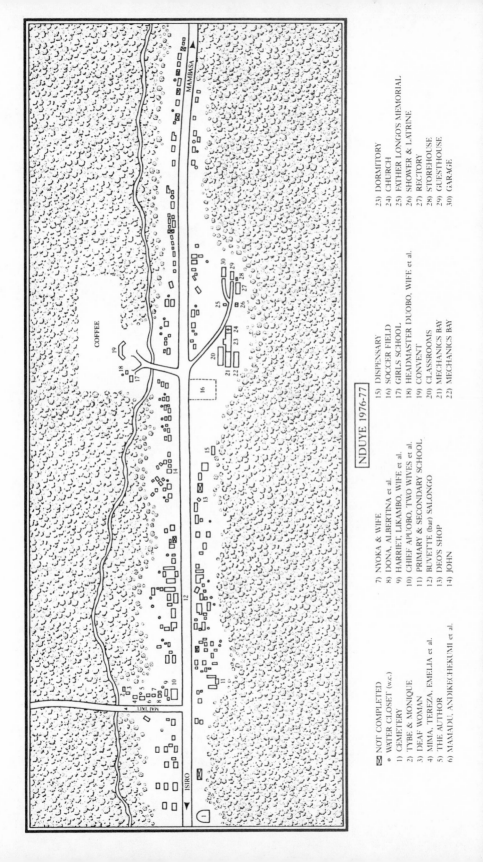

NDUYE 1976-77

ISIRO ▼

MAMBASA ▲

COFFEE

⊠ NOT COMPLETED
∘ WATER CLOSET (w.c.)
1) CEMETERY
2) TYBE & MONIQUE
3) DEAF WOMAN
4) MIMA, TEREZA, EMELIA et al.
5) THE AUTHOR
6) MAMADU, ANDIKECHEKUMI et al.

7) NYOKA & WIFE
8) DONA, ALBERTINA et al.
9) HARRIET, LIKAMBO, WIFE et al.
10) CHIEF APUOBO, TWO WIVES et al.
11) PRIMARY & SECONDARY SCHOOL
12) BUVETTE (bar) SALONGO
13) DEO'S SHOP
14) JOHN

15) DISPENSARY
16) SOCCER FIELD
17) GIRLS SCHOOL
18) HEADMASTER DUOBO, WIFE et al.
19) CONVENT
20) CLASSROOMS
21) MECHANICS BAY
22) MECHANICS BAY

23) DORMITORY
24) CHURCH
25) FATHER LONGO'S MEMORIAL
26) SHOWER & LATRINE
27) RECTORY
28) STOREHOUSE
29) GUESTHOUSE
30) GARAGE

The Mission

The longer we stay
The more we realize
The less we know

VIEW OF FATHERS' QUARTERS OF MISSION (from bottom of its hill). (*from left*) GARAGE, GUEST-HOUSE, DORMITORY, MECHANICS BAY, STOREHOUSE, RECTORY, LATRINE & SHOWER, CHURCH

VIEW OF SISTERS' QUARTERS OF MISSION (from Fathers' side). (from left) GIRLS SCHOOL AND HEADMASTER DUABO'S HOME, CONVENT, MOUNT MOCONZA, WATER TOWER. (foreground) COFFEE PLANTATION, BANANA TREES

The Village

Pima kwanza,
kama weka weza.

Taste first,
for only then shall ye know.

VIEW OF NDUYE (from Fathers' side). (*foreground*) RAIN GUAGE. (*center*)
MARTYR FATHER LONGO'S MEMORIAL. (*left of center*) CLASSROOMS

THE MAIN ROAD NORTH THROUGH NDUYE TOWARD CEMETERY.
CHIEF APUOBO'S OFFICE, PRISON, NDUYE RIVER, MUNGBERE, ISIRO

CHIEF APUOBO ALUOKA CHAMONONGE (in front of his home)

TIBE & MONIQUE'S RESIDENCE (*at left*), DEAF WOMAN'S (*at right*)

MIMA (stepfather of Christina & Angapalaembi; husband of Tereza and Emelia)

CHRISTINA (daughter of Emelia; stepdaughter of Mima) WITH SON TABO, SORTING PALM KERNELS

HARRIET WITH SON LESTER PREPARING MASH FOR MANIOC ALCOHOL (*Katiko*), (older sister of Apuobo & Likambo; girlfriend of John)

TEREZA HUSKING CORN (wife of Mima)

DONA, THE CARPENTER (husband of Albertina a.k.a. "Madame Bons(h)oir")

ALBERTINA (a.k.a "Madame Bons(h)oir," wife of Dona)

JOHN, THE ENGLISH PROFESSOR, DISTILLING MANIOC ALCOHOL (boyfriend of Harriet)

RAFFIA TREE BEING TAPPED FOR WINE (*mabondo*)

TYSE IN FRONT OF COOKING SHELTER (*baraza*)

BROTHERS NYOKA SELINGOBO & MAMADU

PYGMY/VILLAGER UNION

LIKAMBO (younger brother of Apuobo & Harriet)

The Forest

FOREST TRAIL ON THE WAY TO ANDILI

CAMP BIASA

CAMP LIFE (Biasa). (*at left*) SITALA (Gomeza's sister; Kutungoto's wife).
(*at right*) SAKINA (wife of Gomeza) WITH DAUGHTER ASUMINI AND SON KABWANA

GOMEZA WITH POISON-TIPPED ARROWS (father
of Kabibi, Kabwana & Asunini; husband of Sakina, *at
right*)

BARK CLOTH WITH ELEPHANT TUSK BEATER

SAKINA PAINTING BARK CLOTH (*mulumba*),
(mother of Kabibi, Kabwana & Asunini; wife of Gomeza)

CATERPILLARS ROASTING ON ALUMINUM SHEET

ZATU (in front of author's village hut)

ASUMINI SITTING
ON ALUMINUM POT

DAY, THE PHOTOGRAPHER

THE AUTHOR DURING A
LIGHTER MOMENT. (*background*) Kabibi

10

MY handwriting throughout this entry is going to be less than it has been in the past because I have blisters all over my hands. Particularly on my right thumb and forefinger where I grasp this pen. The blisters are due to the work I did around my house since I returned here on Monday. Today is Saturday. I got the blisters from using a *coupe-coupe* to cut down the tall grass that had grown up around my house while I was away.

It turns out *today* is Saturday and yesterday was Friday. I saw one of the ladies in the village yesterday making a beer from rice called *mandarakba* (not sure of spelling), and because she usually prepares it on Saturday and serves it on Sunday, this is what confused me. I intend to go to the Sisters today and get a calendar.

I left Kisangani in the early afternoon of January the twenty-second. I left with about twenty-five zaires in my pocket and decided to try and make it with that much to Nduye. I did end up hitch-hiking successfully from Kisangani to here without paying. I didn't want to bring too much money with me because once I arrived here I would sell my possessions, and I calculated they would give me an additional sixty zaires. I didn't want to have a lot of extra zaires when it came time to leave the country. They aren't worth a thing outside Zaire.

I have begun rereading Turnbull's ethnographic survey, which I received from home upon my return. It's quite interesting and much of what is said I have learned, which means that there really is some kind of work that I can do here without the language, at least to begin with, that is observational work. I am seeing much more than I realize and this has been revealed to me through reading Turnbull's stuff. A lot of what he notes (even as being important), I have noticed also. I just never thought of the things as important. Probably because I don't know what is important concerning research on hunter-gatherers because I have never learned what is and what to look for.

I am now feeling a little bit hungry so I'm going to take a *mandarakba* break and continue when I return. One thing I enjoy about taking a *mandarakba* break is my being able to look at the woman who serves it. She is very, very nice and probably one of the most attractive in Nduye. She is not a Mulese. She is from another tribe from Bunia.

February 7th
Next day

I'm back again. I was interrupted to take care of some chores such as chopping wood, doing my laundry, finding a piece of wood to make an ax handle from, and a few other things.

I ate some more elephant meat three days ago. It was a gift to me. It was smoked, tough and very strong-tasting, so after the first meal of it I gave the rest away to my neighbors.

Later this afternoon I will spend two hours studying Swahili. And later on, record some observations. Maybe tonight I will lie in bed and read one of the magazines which I'm now receiving from home, which is really making life much better for me here. I've got about one hundred and eighty pages of magazine to read between the two copies.

Well . . . I guess it is apparent by now that I don't intend to leave Nduye right away. I have decided to really make an effort and "pull my sox up," as Mrs. Lenhartzen said I should do if I really decided to do it here. I am a little bit perplexed as to what was different about the place upon my return. I guess it seemed more like home the second time, and after being away for six weeks. The only way I am going to stay is by doing the work, which I believe I fully intend to do and keep myself occupied with. Walking around Nduye idly and worrying about where I am is no good at all. I am becoming less lazy and disciplining myself.

Some of my lethargy may have been due to sickness. While I was in Kisangani I decided to go and get examined at the university's hospital. They tested my stool and blood and told me I had two types of intestinal parasites and malaria! I never guessed I had malaria because I don't remember coming down with an attack of it. But one can still get it without having the typical symptoms. There is no way of telling how long I've had it but it certainly is possible that it contributed to my run-down feeling. The parasites aren't dangerous and the doctor said they couldn't be affecting my mentality or stamina. I bought the curative drugs and supposedly I should be cured by now. I must have gotten the parasites from bad water. I'm not taking any more health risks.

So I'm lucky I didn't come down with anything worse, like some intestinal parasite that might have plagued me for the rest of my life. I was cautious during my whole trip to the Ituri, always adding purification tablets to my water. But when I got to Nduye and got settled down I found it easier and more convenient not to purify the water.

Also, I probably still had the idea that the Ituri and the pygmies were a kind of heaven and nothing could be bad there. The water may have looked clean and harmless but obviously a human can't see microscopic parasites. I drank any water that we came across while I was with the pygmies. I once went swimming and drinking at the same time in a river. It was on my way back from my fifteen day voyage [the moon mission] in the woods and I was hot. And after that experience I was feeling like nothing could stop me. I felt like a superathlete.

I was rather ignorant. I did think it was possible I'd get something from bad water, but thought that if the pygmies could live with it, so could I. You know, one doesn't necessarily get closer to people by behaving like them. I would have been much better off if I had tried to communicate with them and been able to converse with them. Then I would have known more about the pygmy and his world.

So I am now boiling all my water for bathing, washing dishes, and drinking. I am taking hot baths every night in order to keep my skin disease under control. I can't seem to get rid of it. And I'm not able to take two baths a day—as the doctor at Nyankunde prescribed— because it is a bit inconvenient. I sold all my pots before I left, so I'm always borrowing them from my neighbors.

My concentration keeps being interrupted in order to scratch myself. I can't scratch and write at the same time. I should feel better after this evening's hot bath of pre-boiled water. I'll continue tomorrow and read for now while I wait for the water to boil.

I am making myself more comfortable than I was before. For two zaires I am having a bathing enclosure built. And after that, I intend to have a cooking shelter built so if it rains I can still boil my water under the roof. The rainy season will be here soon—around the middle of March I believe. The weather is really nice now. It's too bad the dry season is so short.

A few days ago I was out in the woods at a large pygmy camp that is located in a vacant plantation, or large garden. While I was there I asked the *capita* (pygmy chief, or perhaps, "captain?" if it would be alright if I lived in their camp for awhile. He agreed, as I thought he would. The pygmies are very, very friendly, helpful, and cooperative. So for three zaires they are constructing a king-size leafed igloo with a bed and table in it made of sticks. Adjoining my dome will be my necessary bathing enclosure. I happened to go out to the camp because a child had died.

I started walking the road toward Biasa (to the north) because I had heard that six kilometers from here the pygmies were dancing. They went to teach a new dance they created (to other pygmies I assume). Along the way I saw some pygmies returning. I asked if the dancing was over, which I thought strange because the morning had just begun and a villager had told me they'd be dancing for three days. (I later learned they were to dance for a week.) I couldn't understand their answer so I asked a villager, who informed me that most of the pygmies had already returned to camp because a child had died about an hour earlier that morning.

Wanting to see something possibly interesting, I walked back into the woods to the camp that is about a twenty minute walk from the road that cuts through Nduye. Along the way I was wondering if at a moment like that the pygmies would resent my presence, but dying of curiosity I continued on. I had been to that camp many times before and felt I would be well-accepted. Half way to the camp I could hear the loud wailing I expected to hear wafting through the forest from afar.

I arrived and everyone sort of looked up teary-eyed, while others continued wailing and moaning. It was the women who were responsible for the noise. Although, I believe I did see some men with tears in their eyes. I'm not sure. I think among the young men or boys.

I was greeted and conveyed my sentiments in the best way I could by saying, "Iko mbaya, matata," meaning: "It is bad, terrible."

I asked my first question and they were receptive so I knew I was not imposing. There was a girl sitting on the ground with her legs stretched out in front of her. Her hands were bound together with sticks in between her fingers. Her face was smudged with dirt and her eyes showed tears. I learned she was the fetishist who was responsible for the child's death.

I had some salt in my pocket which I gave to the mother of the deceased. She and her husband were sitting on the bed in what I presume was their hut, looking terribly sad. I shook hands with them. In the mother's arms was the dead child wrapped in a blanket—the front of his head, his face, protruding. I believe it must have been the first time I had seen a dead body.

After about fifteen minutes they had told me all I wanted to know, but I didn't understand enough so I went back into town to get John. I bumped into Likambo first and asked him if he'd help me. In exchange, we would drink *mandarakba* together when we returned. He accepted.

About an hour after I'd left the camp for town to look for a translator, I was back with Likambo translating for me while I took notes. I took about as much as I could. The *capita*, Gomeza, eventually got tired. Afterall, a death had occured only two hours previously. This is what I understood:

The father of the dead boy always had everything, plenty of meat, firewood, rice, oil and so on. He never lacked anything. An evil forest spirit became jealous of this man and therefore took his son. This evil spirit manifested himself in the young girl I saw sitting in camp with her hands bound. How they determined it was she who was responsible I don't know. In fact, I'm surprised they named someone at all because Turnbull says only the villagers do this because *they* believe in spirits and the pygmies don't. The pygmies don't believe spirits inhabit the forest. The forest is a good place. I should take back my calling the spirit a forest spirit. I should say spirit, period.

The dead child was buried beside the hut of his parents. Four sticks were planted in the dirt, one at each corner of the grave. Another stick sits in front of the grave. An old, beat up, small aluminum pot sits over the child's head, I assume. I didn't see the burial. One month of mourning will follow, which has gotten me wondering about exactly what kind of atmosphere I will be making my entrance into.

This is another fairly detailed story I will have to go into another time. There is just so much writing I need to do. I really have a ton of work to keep me occupied. I now have the two Turnbull works to read (the other one being his doctoral thesis, *Wayward Servants*) and make my own comments on, letters to write, the language to begin learning and so on.

In addition, I will need to spend some time doing things that the Africans spend their time doing, such as cutting wood—which I like—and making fires. This is what I will do in between academic work. I know that there are going to be some tough times ahead of me but believe I know how to get through them now. I will go hunting, for example, read, write and so forth. This week has been rather good since I returned. I have kept myself occupied.

When I go to Nyankunde in two weeks I am going to buy a radio if possible, to help me through those hard times and to listen to at night. The camp I will be living in is sedentary. It is probably one of the most acculturated camps of all Nduye. Observations could prove interesting in revealing this acculturation process. A villager-type hut has started to be constructed for a pygmy who is associated in some way with the military, I understand. He is one of the fellows who took me elephant hunting with Berdj, the Swiss who was here.

The reason I am going to Nyankunde in two weeks and not sooner is because I need to go to Bunia then to get my visa prolonged that will expire on the twenty-fourth of this month. I'm also going to Bunia to nearly double some of my money on the black market and buy some supplies such as aluminum pots for boiling water and so forth. I left enough things in my hut so that if in Kisangani I had decided to return here to stay, I would be alright. I guess the final decision should have been made here and not in Kisangani.

I have decided it has been a question of culture shock and not a question of my lack of academic training. Does anyone really need academic training to live somewhere? To do excellent field work, yes. I believe I'm getting over the culture shock—learning to adapt to my environment. I think the key to being able to adapt here will depend on my resourcefullness. This may be a lot of hogwash and only time will tell. It's the culture shock I've got to get over and perhaps I am learning how to deal with it now. I haven't cried once since I returned. I'll say it again. It's going much better. I think the safest and best thing for me to say is that I'm still here and am going to make a conscientious effort of it. I think something good can come from it. When I'm gone I am gone and that will be it.

Since my return the villagers have been friendlier to me. I found that these villagers seem good compared to the inhabitants of Kisangani. The Kisangani people often begged me to death. I think I am beginning to absorb something of which is going on as a part of myself.

What I wrote before seems to be merely a justification in order to go home. My problem is the culture shock and trying to get over the big part of it. An outsider like me will never totally get over it obviously.

I'm looking forward to finally spending a fair amount of time with the pygmies when I get back from Bunia. I don't really want to go to Bunia but have to. My vacation was plenty long enough.

With the pygmies it's like one big happy family. I don't think I have, or ever will, see anything more beautiful than a pygmy camp lit by campfires at night.

I didn't end up getting much more done today than finishing this entry afterall. It's been a good day like I thought it would be. I'm doing this because I want to and feel capable now. Besides, there is a slight possibility I'm mistaken. I'm getting along so well with my neighbors now.

February 8th
Next day

Today was a superb day, as I had a feeling it would be upon starting it. This morning I was awake before six, as I usually am, because I go to bed relatively early. And as usual it was my having to urinate that awakened me. I lay in bed however, cherishing the warmth of it and slightly regretting the moment I would finally decide to rise. When the feeling gets strong enough that's when I finally get out of bed. However, this morning something else got me out of bed.

I heard, "Jasper. Jasper. Are you there man?" I replied, "Yes." "Come and drink some wine my friend," the English professor said. "I'll be there in a minute," I answered and hopped out of bed to throw my clothes on. Minutes later we were on our way down the dirt road that passes my house and joins the main road that comes through town. At the main road we made a right and along the way we were accompanied by one of the military men in civilian clothes that live here. He was apparently on his way to fetch some raffia wine also.

We crossed the Nduye River by the wooden and metal bridge. I remember remarking earlier how beautiful the day was starting off in such a chilly, thick mist. John had a sweater on and I, a coat.

The first tree we came to was dry because the wine had already been taken. The villagers get up very early to get it. There are generally twenty or more people each morning waiting at one tree or another hoping to receive a calabash full. Queuing is unknown to them I believe. I've been in Africa ten months now and haven't once seen the Africans form a line to wait for something.

We continued a way farther down the road to another tree John knew of and there we came upon a crowd of people waiting to be served. The people had laid their money down on a piece of bark that lay on the ground. Each bottle cost fifteen makutas, which surprised me, because they are usually ten. It was the first time I had seen them selling for fifteen. I suppose it was because not many trees are being tapped at the moment so the demand is great.

The top of the tree is cut away in a manner that allows the sap to flow freely into a large clay pot they place in the hollowed out part of the tree. I'll have to take another look sometime to see exactly how it is done before I comment further on this. A tree at its prime will yield from thirteen to fifteen bottles per day. A wine-giving tree lasts from three to five weeks, then it will produce no more wine and dies. It is normally cut down after it stops producing.

There wasn't enough wine for everyone to get some. They gave me a half-gourd-full even though I was next to the last to arrive because I had walked from the farthest away, John told me. I didn't hear this until after I had begun drinking it with John, and upon hearing this I remarked they shouldn't have treated me special.

Many times I am treated special because I am a visitor and white. And even though colonialism has been abolished in this country, there are still many inhabitants—especially the old—who show me respect. For example, the men, as well as the women, very often make a slight curtsy while shaking hands with me.

The wine was very nice and sweet and fruity, and warm because of its fermenting. If the wine sits too long in the pot it loses its body and becomes sour and flat. They say it contains many vitamins, which I believe. It is very filling for me, especially first thing in the morning for some reason. Half of the gourd was all I was able to consume. I thanked the tree-tappers for being so kind to me and came back to my hut.

Today has been a fine productive day and I'm hoping the start of something really good finally. I got off to a slow start but believe it is somewhat understandable. Now I need to work hard in order to get permission again to stay here and continue my research. Or I should say—start it.

February 10th
Two days later

It's looking more certain every day that I am now here to stay. The second time back this place looked more like home to me and I told myself I just wasn't going to return home without doing it here. So I've pulled myself together and am overcoming my laziness. I think I may have arrived here forgetting what it was like to work after taking that three-and-one-half month travel vacation overland to get here. In some ways I did feel the pressure to accomplish something, and in other ways I didn't because no one was looking over my shoulder every day demanding some work from me.

After having walked to the mission to post a letter, I returned to my hut, boiled my bath water and took a bath in Apuobo's enclosure. Later, feeling refreshed, I came back and began opening my fungus sores with an Exacto blade from my snakebite kit, and rubbed the yellow powder from my tetracycline capsules into them, stinging me. I repeated the same operation this morning. My right elbow is in miserable shape. I'm going to get a lot of drugs while at Nyankunde to get rid of this mess. I can't go on like this. It is interferring with my work and taking my time away from it.

Food is always fresher here than at home. You can eat a chicken you saw walking around an hour earlier. "Sweet potatoes are like God: They never go bad," Bololo, the villager who lead the moon mission, told me while we camped at the cave prior to that trip. He also told me that according to pygmy philosophy, the "Pygmies eat by themselves and God bless all."

I am now a Zairean when it comes to taking a one bucket shower and it takes me about as much time, or less, than when I was at home. I'm boiling all my drinking water, and water to do my dishes with in addition. My neighbors are cooking my meals regularly. Two days ago I ate a delicious chicken, which are unfortunately hard to obtain in the bush.

While in Bunia, I am going to buy a fishing net and get one of
the locals to go fishing with it for me in order to keep a steady flow
of protein in my diet. He will keep a share and I will remain the pro-
prietor of the net. I may even be able to sell the surplus if there is any
or use it as payment to my cooks. The river is very low at the moment
(dry season) and therefore it's prime time to go fishing.

February 11th
Next day

Yesterday I spent a good deal of the day writing. Gomeza visited
me to inform me that my dome was under construction. The ground
had been cleared and the saplings had been cut to build the frame of
my leafed igloo-to-be. *Mongongo* leaves are hung on the stick frame
by splitting their stems so that they act similar to clothes pins. My hut
is going to be king-size and have a bathing enclosure built adjacent to
it. It's supposed to be ready for me to move into when I return from
Bunia in about two weeks.

I presented the conditions under which I wanted to live with them.
I made it clear to Gomeza—through my neighbor who interpreted for
me—that I didn't expect to support his camp on my pocket. I said, "I
will contribute things occasionally when I can, such as salt. My skin
may be white but I'm a student who is supporting himself and am not
rich. My government isn't paying me for my work," as many Zaireans
assume.

Of course while I talked to him it was more like I was asking him
if it was alright that way, realizing I will be his guest. I told him I
wouldn't take anything away from their economy. I will have to transport
all my food, oil, pots and so forth out to their camp. Maybe in return
for firewood and salt I can get one of the women to prepare my meals.
(We've already discussed the possibility of a boy helping me out in this
respect.) Or more hopefully, the fishing net (or nets) that I bring back
from Bunia will help matters. (Turnbull contributed to the economy
with a hunting net that had been made for him.)

I've spent about a month's worth of days with the pygmies so far,
scattered over the five months I've been here. I've done several hunts
with them but found they don't hunt much here.

I will pass the time there—which may be the most important thing to know how to do while in the bush—reading Turnbull's works on the pygmies, hunting with them, researching, keeping my diary, taking two baths a day to end my fungus disease, learning the language, sitting back, and chopping firewood.

I'm really looking forward to moving in and finally getting to know and live with these extremely friendly people, who I expect will be good hosts. I am now hoping my dream will finally come true; to know them, if only a little. The more Kingwana I learn, the deeper I will go.

I bought a large Chinese-made ax head in Kisangani when I was there in July and am now working on its handle. I am taking pleasure in working it, and can't wait till I put the finishing touches to it by shaving the handle down smooth with a broken piece of glass, as they do here. They do this step after it's been charred and hardened by the fire.

I've changed my mind about what I wrote in Kisangani. I don't need an education (like I thought before leaving home) to live with the Africans. To do good field work, yes. I'm going to do the best I can with what I have. I think I was feeling homesick during the holidays in Kisangani.

Those Fathers in Kisangani are going to flip when I show up at their door. They thought I was so badly off they wanted to see me get on a plane home before Christmas so I could spend Christmas with my family.

One of my intentions was to set out to find the uninhibited savage, but was somewhat disappointed to see such rather civilized beings. Of course, I was glad to—and am glad to—see a healthy portion now and then of this uninhibitedness. But I must also realize that it is due to cultural and environmental dictates. I find something admirable about this momentary living I am witnessing. But there are drawbacks too I would have to assume. I realize this because I cherish both qualities in myself. I need to keep a healthy balance to be the person I want to be. One extreme is no good.

I'm starting to absorb what is happening around me—especially since my mentality has changed and I've become more open to things and am willing to step out and experiment.

I thought possibly the grass was greener here on the other side. Many Africans believe the same thing about the States, which I was reminded of when a student came to me today and asked for Empire State College's address. From talking to him I could see he was ignorant about some things *chez moi*, as I had been of his home.

Many male pygmies wear Western clothes now. Mostly T-shirts and shorts always in dire need of repair. Their buttocks is often seen through the worn-out seat of their pants. Many shirts have large holes in them. They are often rags by our standards, and washed if soap is ever available. Loose-hanging pieces of material are commonly joined together tied into a knot. Cheap plastic or handwoven fiber belts are common, usually not fed through the belt loops if there are any to begin with. Those that don't wear Western clothing don fricus bark loincloths. On chilly mornings pygmies may be seen walking the forest with a piece of burning log held close to their chest to keep themselves warm. They constantly transport fire, lacking the know-how to start them from scratch. I've been told that the pygmies didn't use fire before the villagers invaded their forest.

Yesterday I spent a good deal of the day writing. In between writing I boiled several pots of water, including one for drinking. I made the mistake for the second time of putting the pot on top of the fire first and then fanning the coals with its lid to get a hot flame going. In doing so, I stirred up the ashes, some of which settled in my drinking water. I believe that is why it has a smokey aftertaste that is slightly unpleasant.

I took a raffia wine break at the second house down from me. I really have been fortunate to have what few trees there are being tapped, always next door to me. Two of them couldn't have been any closer to me than directly behind my house. The only problem it posed was that I was woken up very, very early each morning by the drinking crowd.

What a switch the second time back has been. The days aren't long enough now. Before, I didn't know how to kill them. I still haven't had the time to begin learning Kingwana. Even so, I have picked up a limited vocabulary and feel I am on my way. Kingwana is even easier to learn than Swahili. So I'm settling down to some hard work and some simple living, which is one of the big reasons I came here.

I am sitting in my hut at the moment writing by lamplight. From the distance I hear people singing and dancing. I asked my neighbor if it was pygmies who were making the noise. He replied, "No, it's some drunk women making merry." I thought they might have been celebrating something in particular.

Today was a productive day even though I didn't get a terribly lot of academic work done. One thing that took some time and I'm glad I got out of the way, was making my ax handle. My friend Likambo got a pygmy to fetch me a special ax-handle-type of wood. I chopped it down to size with a machete, filed it down and then toughened it up over a fire by charring it. Then I scraped it down with a knife. The handle was finished in a quarter of the time I had expected to take. I mounted the head to it and went to try it out by chopping some wood. That's when I realized I hadn't made it properly. It sure looked professional, however. But that didn't matter. I cut one small, stubby log with my ax, which took forever, and I nearly hurt myself with it before John showed me how to correct the problem. He told me that the warped handle needed to be turned so it curved towards me while holding it; the opposite of how I had it. I had feared having to make another handle.

Dona, my neighbor three houses down from me towards town, fixed the handle further by shortening it and driving a wedge of wood into the top of it. He can be a very fine craftsman when he puts his mind to it. He hacked out the wedge in two seconds with a razor-sharp machete and proceeded to remount the ax head very professionally. Now I'm all set to go and cut my firewood tomorrow morning. I have to do it while it's cool in the morning because I have learned that sweating in the afternoon aggravates my skin disease.

What happens is that the fungus feeds on my salty sweat. So the thing to do is to starve the little beasts. I've been taking hot baths with sterilized water since I returned, every night before bed. It has been a tremendous discovery. Little things can mean a lot in the bush because at home we take so much for granted.

I am just only now making my living conditions as comfortable as possible. Today, my bathing enclosure that was constructed behind my house was completed of palm fronds and bamboo. I had my first bath in it, which I found so much more convenient than hauling a bucket of water to Apuobo's bathing enclosure up the road.

Next, I will have a cooking shelter constructed so I can still boil my water when the rainy season approaches in about six weeks. It's too bad the dry season is so short; three to four months only. During the rainy season it rains every afternoon, especially during the month of August, without fail. But very often it is exciting sitting warm and dry in my hut, or under someones porch, having the strong cold wind blow against me in its fury, and watching massive sheets of rain fall from the black sky. I have seen bright red and pink lightening. I didn't believe it the first couple times I saw it. It was hard to get a good look at because it comes in flashes, obviously.

Most of my time has been spent in the village with the villagers, which has been a good place to start adapting. I arrived here too gung ho and nearly blew it. What I mean is; starting off too fast might not have led me to objectively evaluate my situation. Example: In October, when I went on that fifteen day voyage seventy kilometers into the woods to Kpokporo, I nearly lost my mind. I wasn't ready for it so soon and it turned out to be the most horrible experience of my life. I kept pushing on till I had nothing more in me because I told myself it was my last time with the pygmies and I was going to go all out.

I am just now starting to read for pleasure. Besides the few books I have, I am now receiving two magazines monthly, thanks to my professor; *Time* and *U.S. News and World Report*. It is good for me to know what is going on in the big world, as my professor thought I should. She said it helped her out while she was in the field in Guatemala. After the day is over I enjoy laying on my bed propped up against my sleeping bag reading by lamplight. My sleeping bag is so old now that I'm going to get it restuffed while in Bunia with cotton, I hope. If not, it may mean grass or banana leaves.

I have felt very disillusioned many times throughout this experience since I left home. It has been a searching-for-something trip, mixed with other genuine interests. Many times I felt I didn't know what I wanted to do with my life and I'm finding I'm the kind of person that without some kind of direction, am rather lost. I need to look to something. That's maybe one reason I have decided to stay on—because I don't know yet what I will do afterwards. I feel it will almost definitely be involved with humans, and what and how and why they do things. I wanted to take a look at our ancestors before anything else. I may want to again in the future. I have decided to go further.

I went to Isiaka, the tailor, to see if he had repaired my shorts. He hadn't. I found him dancing and drinking manioc alcohol with some of his buddies in his house. Upon stepping in the door, I joined in the merry-making and they all started laughing in approval. I didn't want to be a cold fish. My favorite song was on the radio too; *Kamiki*. I told them that I had danced to *Kamiki* several times while in Kisangani last.

For the second night now I took a hot bath in my two-day-old bathing enclosure. It's two steps behind my back door—so practical. It appears to be keeping my fungus under some control. I don't itch too much during the day but nights are deadly, often keeping me awake much of the night; such as last night, scratching myself madly until the sores opened up, which makes it worse. Last night was the worst night yet. The fungus seems to come alive at night. I don't know if the warmth of my sleeping bag aggravates it or what. Only ten more days until I reach Nyankunde.

This morning I chopped a good-size log and carried it from the raffia wine tree area (the garden it sits in). I had a few sips of John's wine and then carried it back here on my head. The walk was nearly a kilometer. It's hard work chopping wood by hand and hauling it over a long distance. If the outer layer is rotten it flakes off and sticks to my sweating body, and I wait until I've cooled off to brush the dirt off of me because there never is always enough sterilized water to wash with.

I had some raffia wine from the new tree that's being tapped two houses down from me in the direction of Mai Tatu. It's always very cool and sweet. It's a nice change from constantly drinking water or a very occasional glass of lemonade sweetened with sugar.

February 13th
Two days later

Yesterday morning I went down to the river and washed my long pants, and a new shirt for the first time, that I bought in Kisangani. The river—where I wash my clothes, near the bridge—is a ten minute walk. I put my clothes in my plastic pail with my square block of laundry soap and walked down to the large washing rock. I soak my clothes and then rub the soap into them. I then take the article of clothing in two hands and begin moving my hands up and down while hitting the clothing against the rock. This produces a big lather and eventually loosens all the dirt. I spend about fifteen to twenty minutes cleaning items such as pants or shirts. Sox take no time. A blanket or my coat seem to take forever. It's harder washing clothes by hand than by machine but I don't really mind it. I'm a person who enjoys cleaning and organizing things. After it's well rinsed I wring it out and toss it in the bucket. I came back here and hung my clothing up to dry on a piece of raffia branch that rests under one end of my roof. Each end is inserted in the roof. This sure is simple living.

After I had finished with my clothes I felt very tired and had difficulty writing so I took a snooze, waking up sometime shortly after midday. I had not slept well the night before. I had been kept awake scratching my thighs because of the fungus that lives there. It was the worst night ever for some reason. The places I had scratched stayed moist throughout the night and didn't dry up. I couldn't move my left leg because it would pain me too much. Yesterday it finally dried up.

The camp I'll be moving into appears sedentary. There is a large garden around it that I believe must have once been cultivated by a villager. Now that he has abandoned it for some time, the pygmies are cultivating it to some extent. This, I will be interested to see.

I think they are doing more hunting than I realized. Gomeza says they go every day, but I don't believe they're bringing something home every day.

Now I feel I am finally ready for the pygmies and I'm going to have to be firm while living with them, in the sense that I will not be able to give them something every time they ask me. I hope they will get used to it and allow me to stay with them. I have aided their habit of asking for things by taking them gifts such as salt and tobacco. Eventually, I hope to do some nomadic living with them because it interests me and was formerly more a part of their life. This will depend somewhat on how long I can get a visa for while in Bunia. I'm hoping to not have any complications. I would like to sit down and work undisturbed.

Before noon yesterday, I found I was almost out of biodegradable toilet paper leaves so I picked some more that grow near my house, to fill up my basket. They work very well and are relatively absorbent.

February 14th
Next day

Saturday night I also slept poorly due to my skin sickness and didn't get up until later than usual. The heavy rain that awakened me didn't give me an urge to get out of bed either. So I lay there waiting for it to respite.

I got out of bed to begin a fire, which took some doing with the logs that had been soaked. I brought a piece of burning log over to my hearth from my neighbors' and with the aluminum pot cover began fanning the coals rapidly. Three minutes later I noticed a messy open blister on each hand between my thumb and index finger. My skin breaks open so easily, I suppose because of my insufficient diet. And they take months to heal, normally. And when they do, they leave a light purple scar. When I scratch myself long enough, the skin slides off like I'm a leper.

I finally got the fire going and boiled a large pot of water while I engaged in my weekly shave, brush-my-teeth, and take-my-malaria-pill routine. Hours later the water had cooled off enough for me to take the bath I had missed the night before while talking late into the night with Deo, the largest shopkeeper. I learned from that morning bath to make a better effort to take my baths before bed instead. It made me feel drowsy, in addition to the partially sleepless night before, causing me to take a three hour siesta. If I have to take a morning bath, cold water will be more appropriate, waking me up in place of hot.

After my doze I got up wanting to write. Minutes after I had begun, the rain poured and interrupted me because when it rains, water comes in through the cracks between the five window panes that constitute my window, making my table wet here and there. I moved to the one side of the window to continue writing but found I couldn't sit there because a hole in the roof (the only one in my house) was letting water in on my back. I promptly put a bucket in place to catch the water and began reading a book on philosophy that I had started. I read by the light of my open door. Two villagers took refuge from the rain in my hut. One of them is becoming quite bothersome by wanting to pass the time talking during the day while I'm working because he has nothing to keep him occupied. I've been telling him flatly that I'm too busy, as I tell the others. They complain that I'm always busy. I can see why Turnbull built his house outside of his village.

Many children, as well as adults, come and gape at my window, examining the inside of my study or asking for something such as makutas as I try to write. If they persist for more than five minutes I usually softly yell, "Toka!" which so far as I can tell means, "Get away!"

Sometimes I have to lift my butt from my stool to make it look like I'm coming after them. It does the trick every time because they don't know white people well enough to know when they are serious or playing. They're never sure what to expect of us, as I from them. We could both do something uncommon and pass it off to the other as though it were habitual.

The children sense my playfulness along with my underlying ernestness. A nice advantage however, is having children come up to my window with eggs, pineapples, or papayas for sale. All in all, I prefer to live where I do. If my window were any lower I'd have more faces peering in at me. Sometimes they lift their short friends up to look in.

On the evening of the twelfth I went to see Deo to see if I could borrow his bicycle to ride to Akokora Sunday morning. I wanted to ask Lubanabongo if he could lend me some money to live on until I changed some money in Bunia. I found out that Deo was leaving Sunday for Bunia before I had a chance to ask him for his bike. He said I could join him if I contributed five zaires to the gas. "Is that half the price," I asked, wondering if he was trying to take me. He informed me that it didn't even come close. "The only place one can buy gas now is on the black market and it costs one hundred fifty makutas a liter," he said dispairingly. He calculated that it would cost him forty-five zaires for the gas that would take him the two hundred or so kilometers to Bunia from Nduye. Whether this came out of his pocket or the mission paid for it, I don't know. (It's the mission's Land Rover.) This lead us to discuss all the other problems with Zaire at the moment. He talked about how good it was back in his hometown, Butembo. "There we cultivate all the vegetables the Europeans do. We can eat just like them," he told me.

He said he would come by late Sunday afternoon to pick me up. (February 15th [next day]: Deo had problems with the Land Rover so we expect to leave Monday afternoon.)

February 16th
Two days later

I took some raffia wine with John early yesterday morning and while doing so decided that I wouldn't in the future as often. My mornings would be more wisely spent chopping firewood or studying.

At one o'clock Deo's brother, Kesereka, arrived at my hut on his bicycle to inform me that his brother was leaving and waiting for me at his store. I collected my things and filled my small Jerry Can with the water I had boiled for drinking.

11

BY the time we left Nduye the Land Rover was packed with eight people and loads of the passengers' baggage—particularly one woman's. She sat in the front seat with her child in her arms who had rarely, if ever, ridden in a car and was so terrified that she cried almost all the way to Mambasa. After she had calmed down she became car sick and vomited several times before we reached Nyankunde.

Another boy had an awfully high fever and water streamed from his face while he moaned, waiting to arrive at the hospital in Bunia. His father, sitting beside him, comforted him as best he could. With eight bodies inside it was sweaty to begin with, and sitting on metal seats didn't improve conditions. Our legs were cramped because of the excess baggage, which would occasionally slide around because of the rain-gutted roads, sometimes slipping onto me or being lifted up momentarily as we tipped to one side, to come back down on my foot. Kesereka, Deo's brother, thought the latter hysterical, which caused me to think for the umpteenth time, "Why is the pain or misfortune amusing to the one who isn't experiencing it?" I realized I had often been guilty of the same thing.

Before we started out I could see that it was going to be one of those typically African, compact, uncomfortable rides but was somewhat relieved that I would only have to endure two hundred kilometers. It took us five hours, which is four times better than when I once traveled the same distance in the Central African Republic—a minor nightmare I should never forget.

In Mambasa I brought my coat out of my pack and pillowed my butt with it from there to Nyankunde. By nightfall we arrived at the fork in the road; the left for Bunia, the right for Nyankunde. I began walking the four kilometers from the fork to Nyankunde. Half way, I was picked up by a tractor.

Now for some random notes: The pygmies, as well as the villagers, are highly emotional people, often talking at double our volume. They can be next to you and appear to be shouting.

These people can argue and talk forever. I think it's quite possible that the children begin to speak at an earlier age than ours do because of such close constant contact. Is speaking often an art among people who have so much leisure time?

Last Saturday I tried some local medicine on my skin fungus that a concerned neighbor brought me which his older sister had secured. They were special leaves. I decided to give it a try on my kneecap first, before my thighs. Nyoka took a piece of sugar cane leaf and with the sharp barbed edge, pulled it across my skin repeatedly. After he had made a crosshatch of superficial cuts and blood showed, he rubbed the leaves between his hands and then the pulp into the cuts forcefully. It made me itch furiously at first but I didn't scratch it. Eventually it dried and had a slight effect for the better I believe I noticed. Another friend had previously recommended a chicken's bile mixed with palm oil to put on it. I didn't have a chicken to kill or much faith in the idea.

The female albino pygmy that lives somewhere near the road to Mai Tatu came past my house with her child yesterday on her way into town. It is one of the more peculiar sights I've ever seen.

March 8th
Three weeks later
Paroisse Ste. Marthe
Kisangani

I was talking to the Brother here who says that because mulattoes are neither black nor white, they are outcasts belonging nowhere, just like everywhere else I guess. The blacks call them *muzungus* (whites) but they're only half white actually. When I tell them I don't want to leave kids here they ask, "Don't you want to leave us a big souvenir of the United States?"

I believe pygmy life is more monotonous than village and may be hard for me, having just gotten over tackling village life.

March 9th
Next day

There was a lot of elephant hunting going on just before I left Nduye for Kisangani in December. But I didn't get a chance to see it because I felt all my time should have been devoted to working on something to show Diawaku. I was very regretful at the time, and as it turned out, I never got around to it—the work—afterall. I heard there was a big camp fifteen kilometers back in the woods and it was driving me crazy to know they were hunting elephants. They had been ordered to by Apuobo because Kinshasa wanted ivory for their museum. I still have a chance because hunting of the great beasts goes on in the area of Andili.

March 17th
Eight days later

Maybe many social relations are needed more at my young age and will be easier to do without as I get older. I realize I'm a sociable person by nature but also somewhat of a loner. I'm working hard on trying to acquire more of the latter characteristic because I feel this quality will help me go far in life and enable me to do more of the things I desire. This has also got something to do with why I'm still here. I want to overcome my fear and depressed feeling of being alone so I can walk away from here someday and not possess a fear that would ever stop me from venturing out into the back country of some land again. What I'm saying is, I haven't come to peace with myself yet over this project.

Father David told me when I came back this time that when I had arrived the time before, I had been mentally washed out. They say insane people don't know they're insane but I can say I'm in much better shape. I'm not saying I ever went insane, I'm just relating a fact. Father Dave (whom I'm beginning to like less) told me yesterday afternoon before I left the mission for the right bank, to get my truck ride home, and that the ex-Father Superior or somebody told him to tell me the same thing. He told me I could get sick or lose my mind, but like one friend at home wrote me, "Those are the risks aren't they? Imagine what a dangerous place New York City would be for a pygmy arriving there right out of the bush. He could easily get run over by a truck or a car." There is a lot of truth to that statement. I've got to use my head, and obviously more so concerning my health. I think part of the reason my first four months were difficult was because I was sick and didn't know it. I'll have to deal with the environment differently than I thought previously. I can't go native because I'm not a native (a pygmy), just like everyone pointed out to me before I left home.

Getting back to Father Dave. He could have wished me good luck at least. Like I really needed his advice just before my departure. He thinks I was hanging around Kisangani for so long because I was afraid to go back into the bush, when really I'd been getting my provisions together.

It would really be fine to talk to an anthropologist here sometime. All that these missionaries want to tell me is to go home where all the comforts of civilization are and where I'll, "be right." One told me to settle down and get married. They seem to think that the only people who belong in the bush other than the natives are missionaries. Many of them see no point to what I'm doing.

Part Three

One tribe is as good as another.

12

A S soon as I got back here I had a lot of things to tend to, as I always do upon my return. I sorted out all my provisions and put them away. My hut needed to be swept out. It took me one day to do that, but unfortunately a mouse started gnawing at the food in one of my baskets and while trying to kill it with my hand broom I pulled everything out of place. Now everything is back in order and I've hung my food baskets from the ceiling so rodents can't get at them.

Later that same night I woke up being bitten my army ants and upon lighting my kerosene lamp I found that my whole house had been invaded and that they were all over the floor. It's the first time they've come into my house. I got several logs from my fireplace and soaked the ends in kerosene and burned them out of my home. There were so many it took about forty-five minutes, leaving charcoal all over the floor which needed to be swept out the next morning.

The area that belongs to me around my house had been overgrown with weeds so I cut them down myself, knowing that I would just be wasting my time going around looking for someone to work for me. Even makutas can't get them to work. Work just doesn't interest them. So imagine what it's like when I finally do find a workman. I have to spell everything out for him ten times and prod him along. There's a boy who's been saying he'll be here at eight o'clock each morning for the past four days. They prefer to be paid by the job rather than by five makutas an hour.

Chopping down the weeds with a borrowed *coupe-coupe* gave me the usual blisters I get when I return. My calluses go away while I'm writing in Kisangani. My hands aren't as tough as the natives' because I don't do all the things they do. I don't have a garden that needs to be worked in constantly. After the scrub had been cut down I went down to the river and did a good-size wash, the lye burning the open blisters.

Just about every morning I get a slight attack of homesickness but by afternoon, especially if I'm drinking a cup of *mabondo* (raffia wine) with my friends, I feel at home and know that the day is coming to an end. I go to bed around eight-thirty and read until I fall asleep. I can't write very well just before bed, as I would like, because I'm too tired.

I'm really lucky that John the English professor is here. We are the best of friends and it's good to speak English. He's in his early thirties and spent nearly fifteen years, I believe, in Uganda and Kenya. Since we are both strangers, we are constantly exchanging ideas about life here and making jokes about the people or gossiping about them. He was at one time a social worker and also spent four months among a tribe somewhere until it got too much for him and he decided to leave. He is black and a Zairean.

He and I are now referring to the Walese as the Ik, after Turnbull's book, *The Mountain People*, which is very well-known. John read a review of the play they made out of it that was sent to me, and decided that we were actually living among the Ik because these people are so incredibly self-centered. Not as bad as the Ik, however. Here's a quick example of what happened two days ago. A young girl came to buy some oil from me. I filled her bottle and told her I didn't want any money—that it was a gift. The next day I went to her father to ask to borrow his shovel and his wife said she was going to charge me fifty makutas. Even if it was a joke—it was—it still wasn't very funny. I exclaimed, "Bule!" which means "bull," "rubbish," or "nonsense," as far as I can tell. Whatever . . . it comes in handy very often around here. I told her to give me my bottle of oil back and the husband replied, "You gave the oil to our daughter, not to us." We all knew damn well that the whole family was eating it. It became community property.

I was informed yesterday that my hut at the pygmy camp will be completed in five days, one of them told me. I doubt it, so I intend to go out there Sunday and get them to hurry up. I expect to move in around the first of April.

I'll probably go to Kenya around the end of August if I do decide to buy a camera and possibly a small typewriter. I will also pick up more money there I hope.

There is a lot of food available in Nduye now for some reason and it's roughly half the price of what it used to be. When I'm living with the pygmies I'll probably walk into town every Sunday, or every other, and buy my food at the tiny market.

I forgot to mention that I continued from Nyankunde on to Kisangani because I couldn't change my traveler's checks on the black market in Bunia and I was almost broke. And I thought I had might as well get my visa extended six months at the same time if possible by going to Kisangani.

March 27th
Three days later

On my way back from Kisangani I entered Mambasa at midday on the back of a truck and saw a white banner with black lettering stretched above the road, raising my curiousity. Crowds of people were lined up on the roadside, I assumed waiting for the appearance of an official. I met a guy I knew from Nduye who told me he had arrived in his father's Land Rover from Mungbere (north of Nduye), and that I was welcome to return to Nduye with him and his companions after the commissioner of the subregion had arrived from Bunia and addressed the citizens. As usual, they had been waiting since morning. It never fails. The big cheese always arrives at least six hours late, the next day, or not at all. And the latter is commonplace, as I shall relate further on.

My friend told me their vehicle was hidden alongside the road to Nduye because if they had driven it into town one of the officials might very likely have asked to make use of it, and one can't refuse their demands.

Shortly, the head of the Ituri made his arrival with an apparently makeshift convoy. It's leader arrived on a motorcycle. Behind him was a Range Rover, or two, flashing their headlights; and then himself, in a black Mercedes which was followed by other cars and trucks with lesser officials and military. His car stopped in front of the military and he got out, looking as serious and dignified as possible. The military saluted him and the chief of the zone greeted him, looking just as serious, and very concerned that his guest would be well-received. He walked the road through the enormous crowd and finally let go of a smile and continued to do so in between straight faces all the way to the roofed platform that had been constructed for the occasion.

Each chief gets his chance to receive officials and be received by them. And always, the best of everything is laid out for the guest. A guest can be sure he is in for a good stay when he walks into the host's house and smells what's left from the insecticide that had just been sprayed upon his arrival and then handed a glass of raffia wine. The insecticide is a status symbol. It is used to show that everything down to the last detail has been seen to and that the host has money. Flies are very rarely found in someone's house.

Then after drinking, and even usually having eaten while the population waits in the sweltering heat, the big man addresses the public. Populations have waited days and even then he didn't arrive. They always walk down the road as though they are Mobutu for the day, with their handmade cane (the president's trademark, among others), the leopard skin cap or the skin's immitation, and the typical dress of a short-sleeved suit with a collarless shirt or bare skin underneath; no neckties relating to the Occident.

There's always chicken and fish as part of the meal and almost as often; goat, beef, eggs, or any of the various forest animals. And then a wide assortment of vegetables, the *sombe* having fish or sardines mixed with it.

The dishes are cooked in palm oil, or if the guest is very special, peanut oil or the "margarine" that comes in cans from the capitol, Kinshasa, that's made from palm oil.

Difficulties occur when the guest arrives late by a day or more, or not at all. If he hasn't arrived by the end of the day he said he would, then he probably won't show up at all. It costs a lot of time and money preparing for him and if he doesn't arrive the first day, all the food and wine have to be consumed or it will go bad.

The second day, they wait until he arrives and then work fast as hell if he does. The second day could never match the first. Days are devoted to the first day he's expected. All the weeds are slashed and terraces scraped of weeds with hoes and shovels.

People put on their best clothes, especially the host's wives. They remain in the background during the affair. It is the women who tote the work load here, whether in the village or in the forest.

Apuobo is at an advantage when it comes to entertaining. Because a mission exists in this village, he is able to secure extra oil if he needs it—which he always does—or refined salt from Holland. The latter must be the clincher. Much of the food is prepared with canned tomato paste—expensive also.

The one problem with the refined salt, as opposed to the rock salt normally employed, is that it doesn't pour when the climate's humid. And then one must resort to banging the bottom of the plastic shaker as gracefully as possible and not unscrew the top so as not to embarrass the host.

Well . . . I could go on and on and would like to but I'll have to pick up tomorrow where I've left off. I forgot to mark today's date when I continued writing this morning. Today is Sunday March 28th [next day].

This morning I spent time trying to catch up to today in my diary. About nine-thirty, I went out to the hunting camp I intend to move into in a week. I intended to go yesterday but was delayed. A young Canadian hitch-hiker arrived at my door Saturday morning needing a place to stay, saying that the mission could no longer put him up because a bishop and a Sister were due to arrive the following day. I was reluctant to take him in. I had just gotten set up and started my work when he arrived. Not two days had passed since Alan, another tourist, had left Nduye. And I heard that while I was in Kisangi, a Dutch guy and French girl spent some time here. Some Italian guy in Beni keeps sending them up to see me and I'm mad at him. Before, when I was suffering from culture shock, I welcomed them. It's uncommon to find tourists off the beaten path in Nduye. All that have ever come have done so because they heard I was here. The Italian Father in Mambasa lets them know too. I'll have to tell him, no more of them please.

I sent Alan back up to the mission (They probably sent him down to me), explaining I had no time, and he came down and chatted two nights. He couldn't have caught me at a worse moment; just back from Kisangani with weeds to slash on my terrace, things to unpack, wood to cut, clothes to wash, a bathing shelter that needed repairing, parts of my house needed to be restuccoed with mud, along with a list of other things.

Anyhow . . . Jim said he wanted to spend a few days with the pygmies, so I thought that would mean I'd be setting him up with

supplies and shipping him off into the woods soon. Well . . . I was
wrong. He became very sick yesterday and has been flat out on the floor
of my utility room sleeping ever since. He thinks he may have malaria.
(Turnbull warned me about tourists. That was the last one.)

I went out to the camp to see how my home was coming. It wasn't,
as my suspicions proved true. The ground had been partially cleared
and that's all, but it presented no hindrance. They've offered me a
villagers'-type of hut that they constructed and I've accepted it. If I
really feel like living in a dome when I'm out there I'll have one constructed. This is the most highly acculturated camp I've ever seen, but
more on that later.

There was something that happened there today that made an impression on me. I saw one of the men take one of the small hunting
dogs to the edge of the camp and the forest. He pulled its head upward
while another man held his legs fast. I asked the *capita* of the camp
if they were going to kill the dog because the dog's neck was exposed
and I heard the word "nyama" (meat) mentioned, but still thought it
very peculiar. Dogs are valuable. The man holding the dog tightly by
his muzzle with his left hand, took a small slender twig not much larger
than a thermometer and began ramming it in and out of the dog's
nostrils until the membranes were torn and bright blood gushed out
onto the man's hand and down the dog's mouth mixed with mucus to
rest on the ground.

During this operation the animal was trying frantically to move
but it was useless. Only able to breathe through his nose—his mouth
being clamped tight—proved difficult and blood continually flew out
of his nose like a sneeze through it.

I watched nearly the entire thing, my skin having goose pimples
and shivers running up my spine. Killing I've seen a lot of and it's over
fast, but something about torturing this domestic animal bothered me
and I made some high-pitched sounds of exclamation. The camp
laughed at my near-squeamishness. I didn't know if the pet was being
punished or being treated for a sickness. I didn't believe a punishment
could have been that severe. And then I figured it out. The animal was
having his nasal passages sensitized for the hunt the following day. My
pantomime confirmed my explanation.

It only took a minute or less, and when it was over some kind of
mush that had been put in some fresh leaves was squeezed like a sponge
and the liquid went running down the dog's nostrils until it seemed
he couldn't breathe. Just at that moment he was let go sneezing so

furiously that I thought that if I had just walked into camp at that moment I would have been sure the dog was rabid the way he was carrying on. He shook his head furiously from side to side, wiping his nose on the ground. The dog was probably used to it and being as faithful as dogs are he eventually sat down, in front of what was probably his master's hut.

Gomeza, the *capita*, told me he was serious about trapping some meat the following day. The hunters will travel far in search of game. He hopes to bring me an antelope for sale.

After the first dog had been prepared, a second was. I didn't watch so intently. It reminded me of Turnbull saying he felt the farthest from the Bambuti while watching them hold a bird by its outstretched wings over a fire to roast it. They told him the meat tasted better when it's cooked alive.

I ate some boiled palm kernels and later some roasted ones, and showed Gomeza where I wanted a window knocked in the wall. The villagers aren't fond of windows because they want to keep spirits out. Maybe that's also why my hut at the camp lacked windows.

Where the lath hadn't been filled with mud yet, I showed Gomeza where to fill in and where to leave open to let light in on my writing table. The door is being relocated and the roof needed a few more leaves here and there. My bathing enclosure will be built beside my hut. He said he'll be ready for me in six days. What I witnessed today told me there are a lot more different things in store for me to see.

March 29th
Next day

I'm perturbed. My morning's fire took a long time to start even with the assistance of kerosene and before I knew it, it was ten o'clock. I don't believe I'm joking or am lying to myself when I say I want to get into my work. I realize I've been saying it for months.

At ten I took Jim to the dispensary to get examined but the Sister felt it was unnecessary after we had described the symptoms to her. It sounded like a typical case of malaria—including a splitting headache—I believed also. Before he followed me there I dug two jigger fleas out of his left small toe. He had let them stay in for a long time and the egg sacs took longer than usual to get out.

April 3rd
Five days later

Well . . . here I am into April already. I feel good and very much
at home. I'd feel better if I was caught up on my work but won't despair
because I will be shortly. I say, I will be shortly!

Jim the tourist got in my way to a certain extent. No more tourists!
If I do have any in the future they'll have to be very special. He meant
sterilizing extra water, doing extra dishes, feeding him when he was
hungry not when I was, picking up cigarette wrappers inside and outside of my house, buying his food for the intended forest trip, and becoming his lawyer when some women accused him of taking their photos.
I think that if he hadn't been sick and was still staying here instead
of going out to the camp, it would have been more work. I'm complaining about the situation, not him personally, because he was as courteous
as a normal guest could be, offering to help. But I insisted on doing
it myself because it would get done faster and better because I know
how to do things in this surrounding. When I have a guest I treat him
like one and do the work a host should do.

He couldn't wait to leave, especially because he had a run-in with
Apuobo. Two women accused Jim of taking photos of them. It turned
out to be a misunderstanding, but the town officials played it up to
the moment of truth, finding some uncommon excitement and a way
to pass some time by asserting their authority. Jim became so sick of
Apuobo wanting to take his camera away from him that he kept mut-
tering how he'd like to bust the chief's teeth. By the time he left, he
was so obsessed with that one thought he hoped to meet the chief someday in a back alley of Montreal.

He spent five days here, and by the time he left we were both at
our limits; he filled with Nduye and the chief, and I with him. But
he understood I had work to do and we parted on good terms.

It's getting late into the afternoon and I still have a letter to write
and Swahili to study so I'm going to put down the day's happenings
and do some catching up tomorrow and eventually bring my diary up
to date and keep it that way. I can see that I could do nothing but live
here and keep a diary. I'm going to have so much writing to do and
will do more of it when I get my typewriter in about five months. By
recording what I do every day, it should keep me on my toes, wanting
to make entries recording productive days.

Today was productive. All my clothes have been washed and yesterday evening I cut the lawn, by hand of course, with a *coupe-coupe.* Things like that get me wondering about the machines back home. I whipped it off in about an hour. It would have taken a lawn mower fifteen minutes. It didn't bother me and brought to mind how I keep fit through chopping wood and carrying water.

My diet is also very adequate now. I'm eating papayas with lemon juice squirted in the hollowed out half nearly every morning for breakfast; pineapples, eggs, meat occasionally, beans, rice, manioc tops, palm wine and its vitamins, peanuts, fish, palm oil, bananas. I guess my diet could only be better if I ate raw greens, but then there would always be the chance that they got contaminated somehow before I bought them. All my food is either boiled, grilled, or peeled.

Today being Sunday I got up, brushed my teeth, shaved, and took my malaria pill and then went to the market. I bought manioc, sweet bananas, scallions, manioc tops, and some roots. I'm not sure if the latter are cultivated or grow wild. I returned home, gave my neighbors some of the manioc tops, and some tobacco. In return, they gave me some freshly boiled palm kernels to chew on that I had my eyes on. Once they're boiled they are put in a mortar as fast as possible to be pounded. The oil is loosened more easily I assume while they are hot, but I feel there is possibly a better reason they are pounded instantly. If not, they get eaten up by the children and other passers-by. All it takes is a kid or two to go walking around with one in his mouth and a few in his hand and the good news is out. I still haven't made up my mind as to which I love best, French fries or them. A palm nut roasted on coals is out of this world. I love rich, filling food.

Which reminds me that the three dead raffia trees behind my house that have been rotting for some time have been chopped into by my neighbors in search of *posi* (grubs). I got about twelve out myself and John grilled them on my hearth in oil and salt, along with some attempted bean cakes, when Jim the tourist was here. They are rich in fat. Next time I'll have them prepared with red pepper.

To the side of the road, near the market, many people had gathered outside one of the few cinder block and cement-walled, tin-roofed houses. It being Sunday I knew instantly that the crowd was sipping a brew made from fermented rice mash. Those that had makutas and bought calabashes with them, shared them with their moneyless friends. Sunday here is a pleasant sit back, talk, take it easy and eat well day.

One tries to eat some meat if it's available, or if not, might kill a chicken on the day that God rested. It seems as though the sun always shines on Sunday here. It's a good thing too. I need to buy my food on this day.

To let the public know that *mandarakba* is being served, a beautiful flower or more are fastened to the top of a pole which is planted in front of the host's house. The usual bright red and yellow flower catches one's eye easily. Liking its taste and knowing its nutritiousness, I went over and had ten makuta's worth. My Azande friend had an additional fifteen *k* [abbreviation for makuta] poured into my cup because there was the usual shortage of them.

April 4th
Next day

The road to Mai Tatu passes by my house. If I am standing on it facing my home, to the left of me are my neighbors who cook for me. Their house is less than ten yards away from mine. Mima and his two wives, Emily and Tereza, live there. Tereza has no children, while Emily has five, four of which are living with them now. One is a small boy who has just learned to walk since I arrived last August. His name is Angapalaembi. He used to be terrified of me. Now he never stops managing to say, "Bonjour" somehow whenever he sees me. Probably the only other word he knows is mama. It's a mystery to me.

The next oldest is a girl of about four, Kabibi. Then comes Pkisisi, about six or seven and attending primary school. The *pk* at the beginning of his name must be Kilese and is pronounced by saying the letters *b* and *p* at the same time to make one sound.

Following them, comes Christina of eighteen years I have been told. She does most of my cooking, then Emily and occasionally Terez or Tereza. I'm not sure if her name is pronounced with an *a* on the end or not.

The names I have put down are the names they are commonly called by. Before Zaire gained independence in 1960, everyone had a Christian name. Now that I'm making note of it, I'm not sure if they were also given an indigenous name at the same time or they were adopted later, sometime after independence. I will find out. I believe for some years during post-independence, Christian names continued to be given until less than five years ago when President Mobutu went on his authenticity campaign and declared—among other things—

that giving Christian names was now prohibited, in fact, illegal. Which means that technically, someone could be arrested for addressing another person by his Christian name, and easily so if he were an official. People born after his declaration have only one first name, their *nom d'authenticité*.

Christina has a boy of roughly eight months who's name is Tabo. The paramour who gave him to her is a teacher at one of the schools here. I'm sure I've seen him but don't know who he is.

Just about everyone at least fourteen years old has at least one lover. Before, I was referring to them as concubines, translating directly from the French being spelled the same way, but in English the meaning is slightly different I believe. That is why I have chosen to use the more appropriate term of paramour.

April 5th
Next day

By the age of fourteen or fifteen most every teen-ager has had at least one or more sexual relationships. Sex is seen with a carefree eye compared to our culture in general. I can see that my notes alone on such things in this area as customs, marriage, abortion, disease, prostitution and so forth, would fill up several pages, so I'm going to leave it until I have more time.

Everywhere I passed through in sub-Saharan Africa held casual attitudes toward sex. It apparently is not looked down upon for young girls to solicite men because part of the little money they receive is expected to be contributed to the household. If there is a way to receive payment for a service by which that member can profit solely, the opportunity will be taken. I'm referring specifically to those members of the family such as children, cousins, aunts and uncles, and not to the parents, who are usually responsible for their support. A girl working for the Lenhartzens always asks to be paid in clothing or objects other than money because the former are easier to keep hold of.

After Mima's house, continuing to the left for fifteen yards, one comes to two houses close together. I'm not sure how many people live in the first house but it's not very important because I rarely refer to them. There is a woman who lost her hearing sometime after she had already learned to speak Kilese. I assume she reads lips to communicate.

Next to her is an old couple living in a small hut. The mud walls

are rain-worn and the inside is black with soot. He spends a good part
of most every day making a shallow round basket for sale to winnow
rice with. Tybe's wife, Monique, always wears a black muscle man's
T-shirt and a short fluffy afro. The latter could be considered un-
customary but not offensive. The Zairean women are renowned for their
fanciful hair styles throughout much of Africa.

They are the last of my immediate neighbors to the left of me facing
Mai Tatu, the coffee plantation six kilometers out at the end of the road.

On my other side, at the same distance away, only set back a house's
width farther from the dirt road, is Mamadu and his family. Andikechekumi and he have three young children. The youngest girl was
born while I was in Kisangani in December and January. Foster follows
her. He's adorable and reminds me every time I see him that I must
get a camera here. There are many very interesting faces here that I
want to get pictures of. I don't know the name of his five-year-old sister.

Smack next to his house is his brother's, Nyoka, and his wife. They
haven't had a Christian marriage so technically she's his concubine. She's
apparently infertile, much to her husband's dismay. I feel for him
because I know how much he'd like to have his own child. He often
holds his brother's and coos to her. He complains his wife isn't normal
because she doesn't even want to have children. It's un-African to say
you don't want children if you're someone's wife. She went to the dispensary and the Sister began treating her but she discontinued the
treatment.

A fifteen second walk from his house brings me to Dona's, the fur-
niture maker; his wife, two daughters (one's name is Emily), and his
son Kwimbi of about ten or eleven.

At the moment, Dona is feeding Kutungoto, a pure villager he's
proud to say, but I believe he's got some Bambuti (Kingwana for pygmy)
blood in him. His wife Sitala is a pygmy who's about to burst with a
child. I think it was John who told me pygmy women normally give
birth from nine to twelve months after conception. I wonder if that's
possible. They have about five children. Romain is the cutest by far of
many of the children around. What a smile he has!

Kutungoto has no garden, I think, even though he said he did when
I questioned him. He was living off Nyoka for many months until Nyoka
somehow managed to guide him over to Dona's. I'll have to ask him
about it. Because Kutungoto is part of the family by some remote
relative, he is taken in by his relatives. Relatives can never refuse to sup-

port members of their family no matter how remote. It was common for me to find a man in Kisangani supporting his older brother for years. And it of course includes his brother's family. The loyalty and extent of an African family never ceases to amaze me. Half the time I meet two people of Nduye I may safely assume that they are related somehow.

One day I asked Nyoka when he was going to complete his outhouse. He replied, "When Kutungoto's family leaves. If I finish it now his family will fill it up."

They use the woods like the others who are too lazy to dig their privies. A favorite place is the small stream nearby. They go down to the wooden bridge that's no more than seven planks wide and hang their buttocks over the edge. The waste floats down to the river.

I was just interrupted because I saw out of my window Emily pouring oil out of my bottle into her pot. I went over and asked if I had any oil left and she replied, "No." I called Francophone Nyoka over to translate for me and them. Even though they wouldn't admit it, it was obvious that they've been using my oil and salt. When I would ask to have manioc tops prepared, for example, they would cook theirs with mine and use my oil and salt. This they would take in addition to my payment of food, salt, tobacco, palm wine, makutas and so forth, and I pay them well. I was infuriated that between us we had consumed eight bottles of oil in only the two weeks I've been back. I told them before that the oil and salt was for me alone unless I specified otherwise. Both demand exorbitant sums. A handful of rock salt is fifteen makutas!

I had made a very wise move by buying these same provisions in gross in Kisangani to bring back with me. Too much have gotten out of my hands already and now I must guard every bit with my life. I gave some to friends when I arrived, and four bottles to Apuobo because he said he needed extra oil because he was expecting the commissioner of the Ituri, who never arrived. I'll eventually catch up to that.

Getting back to the last of my immediate neighbors . . . Kutungoto dines at Dona's but sleeps across the road in the bamboo forest in a pygmy igloo his wife built. The man is a drifter, possessing no villager-type hut or garden. He lives for the instant, making me think he's got more Bambuti blood in him than I imagined previously. He walks around during the day with a smile on his face and carrying plastic bottles back and forth from the raffia trees.

There is a path that goes from behind Dona's homestead to the chief's, which sits on the corner of the main road through Nduye and the Mai Tatu road.

The discussion with my neighbors concerning my property has been resolved, hopefully. Christina will do all my cooking in my cooking shelter as soon as it is completed. All my food will stay on my property and I will cut wood for her to cook with.

If I'm not careful, before I know what's happening she will have jumped from her place to my shelter, and finally into my hut, because I hear she's fond of me (among others.) Something else I'll have to go into sometime. I will simply say I've heard many times that these girls can never refuse a white man. It sounds believable because I think they hardly ever refuse their own race.

I will have to continue tomorrow. I write very slowly often. I started at seven this morning and it's nearly four already, having only completed nearly four pages. I spend much time going through my dictionary and thesaurus, and then there are always the daily distractions of chickens for sale, discussions, water to boil and wood to chop. I will have to get a typewriter. Father Dave in Kisangani told me he writes twice as much with his typewriter compared to if he spent the same amount of time writing by hand.

I'm also having a chicken coop constructed at Mima's for my eight chickens. One day I hope to have twenty and eat eggs every day I'm in the village.

My bathing enclosure is being rebuilt because the first was a piece of trash. I'm also having a door and lock put on my outhouse.

While at the table last night, Likambo began to serve me water but I reminded him that I only drank the sterlized water at my house. The chief, feeling that I had looked down on the water he drank, enlightened me to the fact that boiled water has no taste. I told him I agreed and that it was microbes that gave water its taste. Even though I said it half-jokingly just be be safe, he told me that it wasn't true, as I expected. "There are no microbes in Nduye. They are found in Mambasa," he asserted. "I must have been sick from them before because I drank the water down the road near Mambasa," I explained. "Yes. That's it," he answered.

Likambo mentioned bringing another dish of food to the table. "What is it?" Apuobo questioned. "Eggs." He knew, as he always does, that it is I who has brought such and such a gift. That is why he never asks where they come from if he can't reckon that his wives must have secured them. At least he never asks in my presence, whereby he might feel obliged to thank me and belittle himself, being the chief.

I have given his wives game from the forest and eaten it with him, and never once has he thanked me. It is always I who thank *him*, and profusely, because I know he likes it that way, and besides . . . I'm working up to the day I'm going to get him to let me take photos of whatever I like, hopefully. I'm sure if I had a Polaroid it would do the trick.

For the past couple days I have imaginatively glimpsed the people living like children in a dream world away from the complicated modern world. We live in miniature gingerbread-colored houses with leaves for the roof, making me think of Hansel and Gretel. Many, many children run around naked, as well as the women waist up. We sit in a small crowd laughing and drinking under the *mabondo* tree, two and even three times a day. We work and we rest, and we work and we rest when we want to. There is always food in the gardens. All we need to do is bring it home and peel and boil it. While doing so we sit back and talk or maybe have a smoke from a gourd pipe. We pull roasted palm kernels out of the coals and chew the nutritious oil out of them. When nature calls, those of us go into the woods who don't have tiny mud huts with holes in the center of the floor.

At night, certain men, and women with covered enameled dishes of food preferably with some meat in them, slip out of their houses and visit their paramours. Some get pregnant. Others are able to abort with strong drugs. The children that are born are absorbed by the extensive family, and I'm sure I'm not the only one confused by who's who. These are some images I have at the moment, and having been here only six months, I'm sure they must be out of proportion in relative importance to each other.

13

I CAN'T wait to get out to the forest. As soon as I step into the woods I'm under a spell. Their world is different than the villagers'—about as night is to day—or it seems that way at the moment. All my friends are waiting for me out there. In fact, one of them who was in town a couple days ago told me he's angry with me because he's been waiting so long. Well . . . they still haven't fully completed my living quarters.

I was apparently very sick even though I never felt physically ill, except for my fungus. The latter had more affect on me than I realized, now that I've nearly gotten rid of it . . . just some traces left. I'm waiting for some medicine from home to get rid of it with. I couldn't find any here.

I never knew physical sickness could have such a deep affect on the mind. I often wondered during my last month or so here, before I went to Nyankunde, if my mind was really all together. I think the most vivid instance was one afternoon when I was trying to bring my razor to my face to shave and just couldn't manage to do it. I was instantly terribly paranoid and weak, and it was at that moment that I decided I had better go to Nyankunde as soon as possible. I finally took a long time to finish shaving.

When Jim the tourist was here, it was just shortly after he fell sick that he became lonely. He got so homesick that he felt like getting on a plane out of Zaire as soon as possible for his home, Canada. He felt, however, that this feeling would pass and that it was only because he was ill. He started carrying on about the food he used to eat at home, and then he got me going and I could see then that just the presence of my own compatriot was going to distract me. He felt just like I did when I arrived here, and I found it somewhat humorous because it was like looking at my old self. I told him so, and not to worry about it, and that his feeling would go away as soon as he got back out on the road again.

I feel much, much better now and am sorry I didn't have the sense originally to know the proper way to deal with my surroundings. My going home was about as close as it could have gotten.

Sometimes I feel that my sixth sense knew all along that I just wasn't going to let myself leave. When it came down to that last instant of packing up, that's when I realized what I was doing and didn't want to accept it. I told myself to pull myself together *instantly*. That is not to say I'm forcing myself to stay on. I'm enjoying what I'm doing and am even looking more forward to getting out with my friends in the forest, who've been waiting for me for quite some time now. I'm slightly regretful about leaving the village because I'm just now getting very comfortable here with my new chicken coop for my ten chickens, cooking shelter, and bathing enclosure. It's really looking like a villager's home and not some kind of temporary set-up.

One thing, to start with, that will be better about my new home is that I hopefully won't be distracted as easily. Here, everyone loves to come up to my window and see what I'm up to. In fact, as of three days ago, I began eating in my bedroom because everyone who came to my window while I was eating let me know they were hungry. It is the custom here to serve those who arrive. So I no longer eat at my desk where I would feel put on the spot.

Two slobs had come in previously and devoured my lunch, telling me about what a hunger attack they had, and left five minutes later in a rush to drink raffia wine without saying good-bye to me, let alone thanks. I'll never see *them* inside my house again.

My friend at home, John, responded to one of my letters which discussed the question: "Are we all really primitive deep down or are we all really civilized?" He said, "The differences between primitive

and civilized—at least the old conceptions—don't impress him a bit,"
which sounds like a powerful statement for someone to make, and at
first might make one think that he didn't know what he was talking
about, but it's true. Getting to know the pygmies is like finding out
a celebrity is really human inside.

I believe I remember saying that I thought humans were basically
civilized. In response, John pointed out the existence of: cannibalism,
headhunting, the gas chambers, bombing of Hanoi and so on, that have
accompanied the course of man's development, which makes me agree
with him, if primitive means to us crude and unsophisticated.

Discussing this question I find a bit precarious because we are talking about human nature, which scientists are constantly discovering
new things about. So when we say something is primitive, we can also
mean that something that is done today that is crude, is something like
our ancestors might have done, owing to our common nature. But by
the first definition, which accounts for magnitude, modern day man
is more primitive than our ancestors, as John went on to argue.

I also agree with John when he says we're all doing the best we
can, trying to make life as good as possible wherever we are. And that's
why the differences between predeveloped societies and their people,
and the present modern ones, don't impress him a bit, I gather.

Which reminds me: Before I came here, I was putting the physical
world in front of the mental. I wanted to see and live in a society where
everything consumed or utilized was biodegradable. That was one of
my goals and what I based my idea of a perhaps perfect society on.
It rested on the physical.

I felt that all things begin with the physical and that the mental
stems from it. So if the physical was good and pure to begin with, then
the mental, or society, would be good also. I thought a synthetic environment created corrupt living conditions and problems. Much of this way
of thinking was a reaction to my environment. Which makes me think
that the back-to-nature movement exists because of some people's reaction to the environment.

Sometimes I didn't feel comfortable at home, as though I was experiencing culture shock within my mother culture because of how fast
change takes place. Progress is inevitable, or I should say, change. The
ball began rolling a long time ago and there's no stopping or use criticizing it. To criticize the modern world for what it is, is to do so in
ignorance. We can and do criticize what we do with it, however. It

reminds me of a fuel advertisement that states: There are no alternatives, only intelligent choices. And that's what we all think we're making. Our world is probably just as good, or as bad, as anyone else's, and if half the people, or more likely ninety percent of them, who complain about high taxes, food prices, and pollution were sitting where I am, they'd take it all back instantly. I think when they complain it's only half-heartedly because they really know the United States is leading the world with its standard of living. The ones that complain are the ones who've got it too good.

The one thing that I do think is lost as we stray farther and farther away from the natural world, is spirituality. There is something about the simple, basic, and pure that my spirit craves. I will never see anything more beautiful than something created by Mother Nature. There is nothing in the world that evokes deeper emotions in me than the natural, organic world. I think the purity is a big part of what I love about it. That is not to say I think nature is perfect. I love woods, and snow, and that is why one day I will live in the woods at home for some amount of time. I like the smell of it. I like deep, dark, fir forests.

If I had found some Indians living close to the land in North America I would have lived with them. Sometimes I regret I wasn't born a North American Indian a thousand years ago. I am, however, grateful to a small extent that I've been able to see in what direction the world is headed and know that it wasn't going to remain stagnant like I might have thought if I'd been born an Indian. I felt I needed to live with people while living close to the land, and not alone, so that's why I came here.

I'm continuing to guard my good health. Three days ago I discovered my cook was cooking my meals with the brown water I use for bathing. I was a bit shocked, but I'm not sick because I had preboiled it and it got boiled again during the cooking. She now knows to use drinking water for the preparation.

April 11th
Three days later

All is just fine, and by next week sometime a big change will be made when I move into the woods with my friends for about four months, I should think.

April 16th
Five days later

I'm just starting to study my Swahili books. The population speaks a slightly modified version called Kingwana which lacks most of the grammatical complications of pure Swahili, so I hope to make some headway on it pretty fast. My English is decaying because I don't have a chance to use it nearly as much as normal. I've been getting by on my small vocabulary of Kingwana and speaking French with those that were educated in the village's schools.

April 18th
Two days later

I got slightly distracted. Saturday afternoon I walked up to the Sisters' to get my hair cut and, as usual, the one who cuts it did a nice job. I keep my hair pretty short these days, as do the male villagers and pygmies. The women grow theirs out but braid it close to the scalp. You see blacks at home do this.

Today Christina started washing my clothes too. She's similar to a wife but lives with her mother and father and other relatives nextdoor. Her son, Angapalaembi, is just starting the walking stage, I think. Everyone likes to call her my wife, so in front of them I usually do also. When I talk to *her* I say, "Christina." I've become more civilized because of her. She prepares my meals well, sets me a place to eat, does the dishes, sterilizes the water I drink and bathe with, and so on.

Because she was always close by, I began giving her other things to do and am glad for it. Now I've got more time to devote to my work. I'm no male chauvinist. I did everything for myself, except cooking, including hauling firewood and water, and doing so didn't leave me enough time for my work. If I had to cook also I'd have no time at all to work. I'm paying for wood also now. I still cut the "lawn" and keep my property clean, patch the mud walls that get rain-worn. I'm not a villager or a pygmy with time to spend as they do. I'm a researcher and spend a little of my time doing the things they do. This is also necessary so I may taste their lives firsthand.

I just had a cooking shelter completed for Christina to cook under. We're in the rainy season and it rains nearly every afternoon, but the mornings remain exquisitely beautiful, the skies often a deep, deep blue. It's not hot, humid, or jungly here. It's like an early spring or fall day at home.

I'm going to carry a basket of belongings into the woods as far as the first camp. This one has been abandoned, I understand from the pygmy *capita*. They have moved five kilometers farther into the woods to the Biasa River. Somewhere along the way, or perhaps at the abandoned camp, I hope to find someone from the new camp. I sometimes come across men carrying their bows and arrows; or women, baskets or firewood, while walking to and from camp on the forest trails. Before I start out I'll see if I can find a pygmy hanging around town to guide me to the camp. I hope to spend the next four months with them. Undoubtedly, camp will move several times while I'm with them. They move when game becomes scarce and, or, the garbage pile surrounding the camp becomes too large and smelly, and before the water becomes polluted. They do not dig latrines. When I'm with them I squat on a log.

There is a very large tree growing here. The best way I can describe the base of the trunk is that it's shaped like the fletching of an arrow if you were to point it skyward. It goes in and out, looking like the tree has fins. The fin-like walls make very convenient spaces to squat between while answering nature's call.

Just to look up, and up, and up through the ceiling of a tropical forest and hear the half-human cries of monkeys and the voices of strange birds, is often enough to make me feel out of place. I have realized that because of my upbringing I could never be thoroughly at home here, which often makes me ask myself, "Why have I, and why do others, ever do things like this? We are never one hundred percent comfortable. Why live for any amount of time at all like this?"

I've gotten over the major part of the culture shock but there are always those ups and downs. At least *I'm* still experiencing them. Probably the old missionaries don't as much. Everything is always a bit of a struggle. Sometimes days fly by and I think I'll come back here and write a book one day, and other days I feel so blue (not as often as the other days) I wonder what I'm doing here. It's a tug of war between the two. At home there wasn't one. So because I know the blue days pass, I continue. I just assume it must be normal. After I speak Kingwana to some extent and communicate with many more people, I feel I'll be able to evaluate my situation more objectively.

I think, very often when someone leaves the field it is because he's ready to return home, in the sense that his mind and spirit, and possibly body, need it. The work is never finished, unless possibly the information sought was very narrow. I find that the more I learn, the more I realize how ignorant I am of what is going on here. I'm living in my own little world. Sometimes I don't leave my hut and property for several days. I eat, wash, and write.

I've decided to write to more people during the last part of my stay, feeling that keeping in touch can only make things better. That doesn't mean things aren't going along well, because they are. I get slightly blue when I write letters sometimes. And tell myself that that's not the time to write them. But I've got many I want to send off now that I'm back together.

These people talk at twice our volume and argue at four times it. A camp is a place where many humans are living very close together and arguments are to be expected. It's nearly like being born on a full bus that never stops. Tensions are eased when people go hunting, foraging, woodcutting, or go to work in the villagers' fields for payment in food, or more rarely, when they come into the village to dance. They are doing a lot of work for the villagers. Ninety percent of their diet comes from the villagers' plantations. I'm working on the relationship between the Bambuti and the Walese. Nearly all villagers have "their" Bambuti, and the Bambuti their "owners".

The latest biggest local scandal is that one of the Fathers caught a Mulese girl in Brother Renato's room. She's been kicked out of some church group, but the Brother's still at the mission and the girl's parents are demanding why. Good old white justice for you. On top of that, there's a girl in town who may give birth to his child. She has fooled around with others so no one's sure. The Fathers aren't aware of this but the village is. If I was the Brother I'd be going in my pants. I hear he's not really part of the church but a lay Brother. I, myself, don't ever want to find myself with a child here, so I am forbearing.

14

Wednesday April 20th
Two days later
3 kms. from Nduye
in the forest

MONDAY I decided I was ready to make the move to the camp in the forest.

Friday April 22nd
Two days later
Camp Andilifo

I'm back again. I'm still at this camp. Just after I completed that last sentence I decided to ask Gomeza what the name of this camp is. I was looking through Turnbull's material last night and was reminded that camps usually have names. How else could they be told apart when talking to another person about it? The name of this camp is Andilifo, as I have just marked above. The name is Kimbuti. *Andili* means water, is what I understand from him. *Andili* is also the word for water in Kilese as well, I believe. The *fo* that follows *Andili*, is the name of his clan. Before they arrived here, this part of the forest had no name. Gomeza named this camp. He and the rest of his clan arrived here five days before I did. I arrived on Tuesday the nineteenth. They moved from the camp that sits in the abandoned plantation one half kilometer from Nduye in the woods. I'm sure they will return there, as they always do. We passed through it to get here. I think I noticed the doors were closed to the domes, indicating they'll return. Sometimes possessions, such as heavy pounding mortars, are left behind.

I have asked many times, "What is the difference between Kilese and Kimbuti," and every time I am told, "It's the same language. The Bambuti pronounce Kilese with their own accent, and *that* is Kimbuti." I have always asked villagers, and not Bambuti, because I can't speak Kingwana well enough to communicate with the latter. I asked the French-speaking villagers. Only some of the words are pronounced differently, and because of this, some words would be spelled differently, obviously. For example: "What is it?" The Bambuti say, "Aiie?" *(i-e-a-)*, the Walese, "Ochue?" *(o-chu-a)*.

I am sitting at my desk of young saplings that I constructed yesterday. A young boy is enjoying watching me write. He is fascinated by what I am doing. He has just asked me for an orange and made me realize why he came here in the first place most likely. I gave him a lemon instead. I only have two oranges left, which I intend to eat. Their vitamin C will do me some good.

I moved directly into this hut the day I arrived. It was already built when I got here. I found it nearly empty. There were only some tools lying on the dirt floor and some odds and ends stuck between the leaves and their stems that make up the ceiling and the walls. (Where do the walls end and the ceiling start in a dome?)

I am bothered. I feel I have so much work to do that I don't know where to start. I can't write enough fast enough. I usually write painfully slowly, or so it seems. I think. I go through the dictionary and thesaurus and feel guilty about getting lost in them every time I look up a word.

I really hate talking about there not being enough time where I am. Isn't that something that only happens where I come from? I guess that's what I get for coming here with a civilized idea of what I want to do.

I find it hard to concentrate while I'm writing when there is a lot of noise around, such as there is in this camp much of the time. It's nearly six in the evening. Everyone is home. Those that went to the village, and those that went to work in the villagers' fields, have returned, some since three this afternoon. If I find the noise too much of a distraction I may have a special study hut built away from camp, though the idea doesn't appeal to me.

I got up this morning after everyone else had been up for an hour or so I'd guess. Since I got my sleeping bag relined while I was in Kisangani, it's gotten harder to get out of in the slightly chilly mornings.

I drew water from a stream that's a five minute walk away and two feet wide. We dip a cup or bowl into the section that contains a puddle and pour the containerfull into large aluminum pots. I fill my plastic bucket. I walked back through the six inch mud and washed my feet off when I got back here, losing a cup of the somewhat precious water I lugged back.

I was just interrupted to take a look at a heated discussion concerning hunting going on behind my hut. Loud voices, pantomimes and curious gestures. I've never seen anything like a pygmy recounting a hunt, especially an elephant hunt. They speak Kimbuti among themselves, which appears to be a modification of the Walese villagers' Kilese, but they speak Kingwana to me.

The pygmies are poorer than the villagers. Although, I never think of the word poverty while living with either of them. Poverty makes me think of city slums for some reason. Or maybe I never think of it because there's no upper or middle class living among us. They're all in the same boat. I am too, to an extent. (The limitations affect me also.)

The male villagers and many male pygmies wear Western Man's clothing. Much of it doesn't look like more than rags, but just the same, it is clothing from the Occident. The villager women wear a traditional dress made from Holland or Java prints, and have done so for many years. All those exotic fabrics one may have imagined as being African, are actually printed in Holland or England. Many pygmy women wear scraps of these prints as loincloths, as do the men. The two types of loincloths differ, however. Women's are looser than the men's. Both also wear ones made from the inner bark of a tree pounded soft on a log with an elephant's tusk. Then they are painted.

Some male pygmies possess Western clothes in addition to their loincloths. They wear the loincloth in the forest and change into the Western clothes when they reach the village. They change back when they enter the forest, having stashed their clothes at a villager's hut at the edge of it.

I am learning more about the pygmies from their end now.

There are tribal laws here, but in general, people appear to do pretty much what they like. I am rather amazed to find the people lacking many rigid taboos or restrictions. I never even think about violating such and such a custom because apparently few exist. I do always think about what I'm doing however, but if I do something wrong I am pardoned and corrected.

Palm oil is good to put on open sores or cuts. It keeps the flies off. The flies here are not as well-behaved as the ones at home. Here, and in all of Africa, they eat open cuts and can even eat through dried scabs to the liquid.

My bathing platform was built of sticks, just like all the other things, and I'm still taking my nightly baths.

I'm glad they abandoned their old camp because I prefer this place. It seems a more appropriate place for them to live. The camp looks different to me now and then. Sometimes primitive and lost in time. Other times very humorous when I think about these gnomes living in tiny igloos with nature, lying down to sleep when they want to, going to work and dancing as they like. I think its their idleness and carefree attitude toward life that make me smile so often.

Sunday April 24th
Two days later

The day I moved into this camp I found Gomeza in town and told him I was ready to make the move, so he and his brother Pascal (Christian name) and a villager loaded my things into the villager's dugout on the Nduye River and poled down to the bridge. From there, my food, study materials, and other odds and ends, were carried by pygmy women and men to this camp that sits in the virgin forest three kilometers from town.

Life is generally peaceful here. So peaceful, in fact, that it's strange. The old feeling of culture shock seems to have left me. I have adapted enough that I'm comfortable. Even just sitting at a desk all day at home would have taken some getting used to. I spend a lot of time sitting. If not at my desk made of sticks, then around the campfire eating a meal. Today I ate forest chicken, and antelope, with brown and white beans, manioc, and plantains.

Gomeza's wife is cooking my meals. I live next door to them. They cleared out this hut I'm in now to make room for me. My new hut that I'll move into shortly is taller than I am.

The women were confronted with a new problem when it came time to build that baby. They made extra-large chairs to stand on like scaffolding, in order to leaf the roof from the outside of the hut as they always do. All the furnishings are made from sticks; the desk, bed, and shelves. Now all I'm waiting for is a Venetian-blind-type of door and some leaves to make the matress for my bed, and my organic (100%) home will be finished. I'm going to miss my first dome. It's so compact and cozy. It's like a tiny cave. What a feeling I am filled with at night sitting inside here by lamplight!

My Kingwana is picking up because that is all I can use to communicate here. No one speaks French.

A couple days ago the guys almost killed an elephant but it got away. I'm intent on seeing an elephant hunt (a successful one) before I leave. I just hope I have my camera ready when that time comes. The pygmies are apprehensive about taking me along because of how dangerous it is. I asked them last night if an elephant could knock over a tree a foot wide and they answered, "Directly." These beasts sound five times worse than a bulldozer!

Some pygmies go into the village each day in search of work in a villager's garden for payment in food. They return in the afternoon. Others stay behind and rest, sit around, get high, go hunting, and eat. If the person's in a good mood he'll sing; some play the finger piano. I drift off to sleep early at night to finger piano music and the sounds of the forest, its crickets, and their friends. It makes me feel like I'm lost in eternity.

I just stepped outside to watch a man fire a poisoned arrow at a large monkey sitting at least one hundred feet up in a tree. He missed by about only a foot and then the monkey took off. No matter. I am eating the rest of that forest chicken tonight with oodles of mushrooms sautéed in palm oil. Yum!

April 25th
Next day

At the end of three weeks, I'm told, this camp will be abandoned and they will move back to the abandoned plantation. They're moving back to help the villagers with the groundnut (peanut) harvest, and when that's over the men plan to go hunting far into the woods; about fifty kilometers, to start with. I think this supports the fact that the pygmies' work schedule is seasonal to an extent, and they are well aware of when they are in demand.

My young friend Zatu's name is pronounced with the emphasis

on the second syllable. I'm in love with the Kimbuti and Kilese languages. The sounds they contain are fun to pronounce. When I call Zatu I just don't yell Zatu; I yell, "Z-a-a-a-a-t-u-u-u-u-u!" Or in Kingwana, I would add the sound of a long *a* to the end of his name, signifying I was calling him, not speaking about or to him.

This place is really incredible. Here I sit by lamplight watching what is going on outside of my leafed grotto. This hut, by chance, has been positioned perfectly. I see nothing but a line of four huts staggered at various distances from mine, but if I imagine them all to be on the same plane, they would form one continuous line. It has just rained. Kids are running around playing, hugging each other's naked bodies together, smiles from ear to ear. They love to visit me and watch what I'm doing, but I tell them politely to come back when I'm not occupied. Sometimes I am not able to understand why I am no longer experiencing culture shock in this crazy surrounding. I never travel more than one hundred feet in any direction on any given day. And I am more than just comfortable, I'm elated at least half of each day. I have begun to see the beauty of life here. "All tastes are acquired," as the saying goes. All the kids are beautiful, physically and spiritually. There is this little tot running around now with a finger piano clutched under his left arm, chasing a chicken. (I still don't know why some villagers' chickens are kept here temporarily.) It's really something to see the kid when he gets hold of that chicken. He grabs it by its wing with an iron fist and drags it into his hut.

These domes we live in are something contemplative. Small people (average male, four foot six; female, four foot three) living in small domes makes me think of *The Hobbit.*

Something that was a lot of fun about today was yelling Kimbuti, Kilese, and Kingwana words or names about camp. I'm picking up some words and small phrases in Kimbuti. *Bonde, amatonji, semeki bwana.* These mean some kind of relative. I believe a brother-in-law. There is the expression, "Nabode," meaning; I die. And a whole slew of others connoting surprise, such as, "Apao! Undemaingba! Ibe!" I just got these straight from the mouth of Z-a-a-a-a-t-u-u-u-u-u! As long as he's so helpful, it might be a good time to work on my Kingwana with him. These visiting kids are becoming a problem. Although, I've learned several new phrases by wanting to tell them to leave, politely of course.

Gomeza said I wouldn't be able to live with them for much longer. I was disappointed to hear him say that and questioned why. "Because shortly we will be going elephant hunting," he replied. They fear taking me along. The women and children and old men will stay in camp while the young and able hunters will set out and spend possibly up to five weeks hunting. Or if the hunger pains become too great, they'll return earlier. They say that there isn't much to eat in the forest. "We don't carry full stomachs when we go hunting, as we do when we live close to the village," he stated. But the hunger wasn't what worried him about me, nor did it bother me. It's the elephants.

All these hunters are natural mimes and storytellers. They boast and recount stories they've heard rather than participated in. The chief could recount an elephant hunt for thirty minutes and I bet by the time he was finished I could ask him if he was on that hunt and he'd reply, "No." But what good stories they are anyway. And I don't even understand half of what they say. But I do know what a storyteller's arm dangling from his nose is. It's an elephant trunk.

He said, "When a hunter gets an elephant mad, look out!" The elephant, or elephants, start shaking their trunk up and down like an accusing finger in search of the culprits. Only that accusing finger is a five-hundred-pound fly swatter. They begin pushing over trees like they were match sticks. An elephant will grab you with his trunk and set you down under his foot, and after he's stamped on you, he lies down on you to thoroughly finish you off and calm the rage you built up in him.

And those big ears are excellent sound detectors. But I did hear one good note they sheepishly admitted, and that was that an elephant charging after someone gets tangled up in the vines as the pygmy slips through them. I guess they were trying to discourage me by laying all the bad things on me that can happen.

Gomeza asked me if I knew what to do if four elephants closed in on me from four corners. "No," I said. "You squat down low until all of them pass and don't make a sound. Then when the last one is past, you creep up behind him and thrust your lance into the crease behind the knee. Then the war is on!"

Somehow I have to convince them that I'm capable of tagging along. When they detailed me about what a hunt concerned, I felt like I was picnicking where I am now, with three baskets full of food, salt and palm oil, a comfortable bed, towels and soap, and a woman to cook my meals.

That's what excited me. Hearing about these guys in action. They will stop fooling around with monkeys, birds, and antelopes, and go and get Ahab's whale. I'm prepared to rub myself down with elephant dung and all. I won't go near that elephant until he's dead to finally thrust my picadillo in. It's *really* going to be something and I'm sure the twenty-five of them won't return until they've satisfied their blood-thirst. It's all related to how much of a man one is. I think killing elephants is the highest status symbol attainable. Puts one up on the totem pole.

Gomeza's brother, Pascal, is the only one in this camp who's killed an elephant, and he's killed eleven of the enormous beasts. Others have stabbed them but they've gotten away. Gomeza, Pascal, and Sililo are the three brothers living in this camp. All are married. I hear there's a fourth brother somewhere but I don't think it's here.

I began telling them how I walked from Kpokporo to Andili, a distance of sixty kilometers, in one day through the forest. They pointed out savanna was included.

I'm going to get the two lance heads I possess out of my village hut and have them hafted. The men have prepared theirs already. They keep them razor-sharp by rubbing them against a rock. The file I brought out here is used endlessly.

I think they are going hunting just for the sport of it. I doubt they are going to haul a multi-ton elephant back to Nduye through at least forty kilometers of forest. It's possible though. They might even move camp to the elephant and have a meat-eating orgy, as I've heard they do. They look like black ants crawling over the carcass. They crawl inside the stomach and prop it open with trunks of trees and build a fire inside, maybe in order to smoke and preserve the meat. An elephant goes a long way, but it goes, as I've seen it do in the village.

It's time for me to drift off to sleep in my seemingly eternal sur-roundings. But first, a few sentences to close with; there is a special stick used for short-term light. The resin bursts forth a flame. I was finished using mine as a match stick to light mine with, so I blew it out. I was laughed at. Apparently when they extinguish theirs they do it like one does with a cigarette butt.

Killing elephants is not necessary to survive here. They go for the same reason the hunters at home go hunting. For the sport of it.

A romper of two years named Tatakpu just visited me. My extended hand is the same length as his shoulder to his wrist.

There is a pygmy here that looks like the entertainer Joey Bishop. I can't help sometimes smiling inside when I see him.

The name Musaba is given here. How would you like to be addressed as, "Leftovers"?

Tuesday April 26th
Next day

I wrote for a little while this morning, ate beans and plantains, and nearly having finished the meal, I decided it was time for me to take a walk in the woods as long as somebody was going hunting. I was anxious to get out of camp for a spell.

It was a gorgeous day. I'm surprised it's rained so little since I arrived exactly a week ago. I'm beginning to wonder if it possibly rains only in Nduye, just three kilometers away.

It was nearly noon when the five of us set out. Gomeza, Joey Bishop (I'll get his real name later), Zatu and his younger brother, and I, made up the quintet. We began bushwhacking, following no marked trail. I was slightly disappointed my stroll wasn't going to be as easy as I would have liked. But inside I remembered what hunting meant among these people, so I did know to an extent what to expect. This was my first hunt among this clan. I have been on several others with other pygmies of the Nduye area. Usually we went with dogs and carried lances. Today they carried bows and arrows, all of them, and we were accompanied by three dogs.

The black dog, as opposed to the two tan ones (all relatively small, as is usually the case in the Ituri area), was either underfed or sick. He probably wouldn't be capable of hunting if he was sick. Maybe they starve the animals purposely so they'll be more successful trackers. The hair around the ribs was missing, but rather than due to malnutrition, it may have been caused by lying in the hot ashes of a fire in order to keep warm. When the fire is taken into the hut at night, the dogs often sleep on the leftover ashes and the heated ground.

The brush was unevenly thick. Sometimes I'd think about not wanting to ever bump into an elephant in such a place, and others I'd have no trouble running through. Thinking about it more now, I'm not sure which would be better; tangled undergrowth might more easily tangle up a larger object.

I was following Zatu when he streaked ahead, telling me an elephant was following him. He was just trying to show off how fast he could move through the forest or wanting to test my ability. It didn't take me a second to follow him, feeling it was also a good time to show Gomeza one of my capabilities. I have to show him I'm not a clunk in the woods so I can go on that hunt. Zatu (age thirteen or fourteen) stopped before I could catch him. I made a good show and Gomeza was surprised.

(At this point I was interrupted by malaria and my sleep in the woods alone, which I'll record later on.)

15

W HEN my visa expires on the twenty-fourth of August I am going
directly home unless I can find a way for the chief to let me
take some photos. In which case, I will go to Kenya and buy
a cheap camera and come back here and take some, spending only two
weeks at the most if I do come back.

What could have possibly made the change in my thinking? Yesterday I got a slight attack of culture shock, which is nothing new. I get
them from time to time. For some reason I sat back and reevaluated
my situation. Actually, I'd probably be more honest if I said I've been
getting the attacks a bit more often since I moved into the woods. Here,
I don't walk around as I was able to in the village, which can get a
little monotonous sitting in camp all day, even for the pygmies. They
get around more than I do. I'm living with them but still not much
like them in many ways.

The women go into town nearly every day to work for food to bring
back to their families. The men, especially Gomeza, like to hang out
in town, or they go hunting in the forest. Also, as Turnbull points out,
camp gets boring eventually and they move close to the village for a
change of pace.

Anyhow . . . camp was rather deserted yesterday, which is normal for any given day. A couple old people and I were here with the
children. This is when I get to feeling lonely if I don't occupy myself,
and even the children and the old are happy to see the rest of the camp
members by the end of the day. I have seen someone on occasion call

out to the others telling them to come home, half-seriously, because they know the others are too far away to hear them.

Turnbull went hunting with them every day, but here they aren't net-hunters and they don't go hunting as often. Ninety percent of our diet is villagers' plantation food.

I sat back from my desk where I had been writing and was almost suddenly overwhelmed by this new idea. The idea isn't actually new. It's the same one I had before. It concerns how unprepared I am to do good work and that's why I have decided there is no use spending time and money on something that I know perfectly well can be done way better another way. Part of my realization for the second time came because I have once again been confronted with the work to do, which isn't too very palpable to me. I don't have a lot of confidence in myself that I could do good work, and the reason is obviously because I haven't prepared myself properly. The reason the change has come about is because since I left home and have been here my objectives have changed. I no longer just want to live with these people but would like to know more about them, and there is a way to go about it. First, one must know the language. (This would also help me feel like less of a stranger.) Then there are ways of collecting information.

Secondly, I would like to learn to write better and type also. There are civilized ways to get the most out of what I'm doing and that's what I've decided I want; the most. I see no point in doing something halfway when it can be done properly and a lot more enjoyably, I'm sure. I think I'm really ready for a traditional school now, and am certain at least, of a change.

I have realized that I want to be a part of my culture because I like it and also because I can't escape it. It's not in my blood, mind, or choice to live with or be a pygmy or an Eskimo, for example, for the rest of my life. That's why there are anthropologists I guess, and they act the way they do in their environment.

The one thing I still want to do is spend the next four months living with this band and then I'm sure that will be enough. I was not content to leave Kisangani in December for home without having spent time with the pygmies and gotten to know them somewhat.

I have also seen that part of what I came looking for is enigmatic. There were, and are, no answers. And I agree with those people that have said, "It's the venture that counts, for there are no answers."

I think one of the biggest things I accomplished was getting over the culture shock and to see that there was even a point for me where I finally made the adjustment. Sitting where I am now would have been unbearable and even unthinkable three or four months ago. My conception of time, or what people do with their lives, has changed. Other thoughts and ideas would change the longer I stayed, but no matter where I am this will always be true. I could go on and learn some more valuable things from this area and its people but I am grateful and content with what I've gotten out of it so far.

Whenever I eat palm kernels I have to stop writing because when I chew the oil off the pit it makes enough noise in my head that I can't think.

May 5th
Two days later

I was wondering if this was going to happen; I am ready to go home as soon as possible.

I am sitting in my dome at the moment three kilometers out in the woods with the pygmies who are sitting around. Some went hunting, some went to hang out in town, the children are playing in the woods close by, and many adults are just sitting in camp eating, cooking, talking, smoking, painting bark loincloths, or playing the finger piano.

I have been here nearly three weeks and I can see that I am just not going to have the patience to continue for even several more months. This is the way it really is with the pygmies of this area. I have observed them off and on for nearly ten months now. I know a lot about what daily life is for them. I am satisfied, unlike when I was in Kisangani in December about to start home.

Yesterday I was so happy about my decision that I decided to walk into town and spend the day there. I also wanted to step out of the forest into the clear and think about it in another environment (where I could see for miles).

I bought some manioc flour at the village shop and gave it to Christina to prepare with one of my chickens. Gomeza, Christina, and I, ate the delicious meal along with some drunken, uninvited slob who ate all the chicken, and the flour (cooked paste) too, for that matter.

He came wandering into my house smelling food. He practically washed his hands in the gravy, feeling for the meat that was in it. He absolutely repulsed me. I can't say I won't be happy to get back to a country where I'll be given something instead of being asked for something all the time. Even these "self-sufficient" pygmies can get a bit tiring always demanding something from me. I can not help thinking that a person who asks something from me thinks less of me than a person who asks for nothing from me. I like to be looked at as a person and not something to try and get something out of. I don't think I'll know by the time I leave here to what extent the people had an interest in me. Some do and some don't, to varying degrees.

May 6th
Next day

I finished reading Turnbull's *Wayward Servants* this morning for the first time ever, having started it two days ago. My general conclusion from reading it is that I should go home and learn more. It's just overwhelming to see what and how much he found out using the techniques he did. He spoke French, Kingwana, and Kibila fluently. I never knew so much existed around me until I read what he had to say. He knows Epulu ("his" village of about 100 kms. straight distance from here) practically inside out. He goes into sorcery, witchcraft, magic and many, many other phenomena. Where he was and I am, are really very different.

He says that the Epulu net-hunters could live solely on forest products but eat village food instead because it's mutually convenient. Pygmies are paid for their services to the villagers in plantation foods. I don't know that the pygmies here could ever live solely off the forest. Since I've been here they've killed two small antelopes, a rat, a forest chicken, a turtle, and some crabs. They eat forest nuts occasionally and lots of mushrooms. I have never seen the pygmies eat any berries. I'd say as much as ninety-five percent of their diet comes from the villagers' plantations. Gomeza tells me there is no food in the forest. The buffalo is a repulsive animal to the Epulu pygmies and never hunted. Here, it is hunted with pleasure.

I am thoroughly at peace with myself. Nothing is tormenting me inside. There is nothing more I want to do here now except maybe climb

Mount Moconza before I leave. I don't care that I never saw an elephant—a whole living one. I came back and got over culture shock. I think that was the most important thing to me. I feel I could live anywhere now.

My fungus is just barely visible and not bothering me. I am keeping it under control with what I have left of the Whitfield's Ointment I brought back from the Kisangani mission. I've got about a month's worth more and then I don't know what I'll do. The fungus has been with me nearly a year now! (In English, my fungus seems to be known as "ringworm," partly because it grows in rings, which are reddish.)

Saturday May 7th
Next day
Camp Biasa

"Kuhama! Kuhama!" Today was *kuhama* day. We decamped two kilometeres further into the forest to make a total of five kilometers from town now. We are less than five minutes from the Biasa River.

About nine o'clock we packed up everything in baskets and strolled to this clearing in the woods. Because the grass was low and the ground clear of trees, I could tell they had been here many times before. They didn't fetch water until after their huts had been constructed, which means they knew beforehand where the water was.

Monday May 9th
Two days later

This is a great camp. Tore the forest Godhead must be pleased with us. We have been here two days and we have already caught four antelope. This morning they got a *lendu*, which is an antelope about the size of a goat.

I am having the time of my life. I'm having so much fun and such a great time. I'm eating well, playing with the kids, and observing the natural beauty. I speak enough Kingwana to get along fine, and it's only what I've picked up without studying.

I just this moment came back from another band that is camped less than a ten minute walk away. It's nice to have nearby neighbors.

I hear there is another camp across the river and at that camp are lots of oil-giving palm trees. Gomeza and I are going to pay them a visit within the next few days.

Tuesday May 10th
Next day

Just about two weeks ago I got sick one night. At first I thought it was because I had eaten too much palm oil, but it turned out I had malaria on top of it. I didn't sleep well that night and felt weak the next morning. I felt the normal loneliness that accompanies sickness here, and knew I wasn't going to get a shred of work done that day, so I walked into town through the forest. All the hunters had left by the time I had gotten up. The one boy in camp, Zatu, was asked to accompany me but he refused. Apparently, no one thought it mattered much so they let me go alone. I felt I simply had to get in to town to walk around, talk, and breathe.

I arrived fine and spent the day. I went in to talk to John and to get some vitamins from the dispensary. There weren't any, so I looked for some pineapples instead. I saw Gomeza and told him that I would return the same day.

Rain fell late in the afternoon and delayed my departure until just about sunset. John had asked me to stay but I told him my sleeping bag and all my other stuff were out at this camp. I also wanted to begin taking the malaria treatment that night and the Nivaquine (the drug) was back at camp. I started off really set on arriving. I started to get panicky. I had no firebrand or my flashlight with me. It gets darker sooner in the woods than in cleared areas and I hadn't taken this into account as fully as I should have. I contemplated returning after the first one half kilometer but continued. When I arrived in camp I'd have a meal, a hot bath, medicine, and a warm bed to sleep in. Some of my poor judgement in taking the gamble may have been due to my sickness.

I came to the abandoned camp in the old plantation after about one kilometer. It was still faintly light out. I thought for a second of spending the night in one of the decaying huts but it didn't sound too inviting, so I continued at a brisk pace into the forest thinking I would be able to call to the pygmies at the camp and they would come and get me. I thought I'd make about one more kilometer and call for them to take me the last kilometer to camp, the camp being three kilometers from town. I had remembered hearing village drums while sitting in the camp, and even trucks passing through, so I had no doubt in my mind that they would hear me when I called the only one kilometer left. I soon learned that the sound of drums travels at greater distances than a human's voice. My voice was thoroughly deflected by all the trees and swallowed up by the forest. I began yelling toward the sky, meanwhile rotating my body while calling because I was no longer sure in what direction the camp was situated.

It became too dark and I began feeling for the path with my bare feet. My sandals had come off earlier because of the deep mud. I held them in my hands. Also, I hoped to feel out the trail more easily in bare feet. The whole time I inched forward I was *so* confident because I was thinking that as soon as I could go no further I would simply call out and they would come to my rescue. I shortly lost the trail and began feeling with my hands. There was a touch of moonlight finally to see faintly by, but it had come out after I had lost the trail. So I learned there is a period of darkness between sunset and moonrise. I wished I had sat patiently until the latter had appeared. By that time it was too late. I looked up through the trees and thought I saw a clearing which reminded me of a second old camp I had passed through on the way to the camp I was now living in. I thought I'd sleep there. I kept moving forward in my bare feet and shorts, somehow always avoiding the thorns by such luck. I kept thinking about snakes but remembered how they would normally flee from the noise I was making. At this point I had my sandals full of mud in my jean shoulder bag, along with a small sack of peanuts I had brought from my hut, a few oranges, two books, one hundred envelopes, and a map of Africa!

I continued, the whole time cursing myself. It was quite obviously becoming the most stupid thing I had done since I left home. Twenty minutes later I realized the clearing perpetually ahead of me was an illusion caused by looking up through the forest canopy at a certain angle. By the moonlight I tried to retrace my way back to the trail I had lost, but it was no use. At one point, I walked on top of a long rotten tree trunk that lay on the ground. When I got near the end, it gave way and I fell until my shoulders were level with it. On the way down some jagged edges scratched my side under my left armpit, shredding my shirt and cutting my skin. I didn't know how deep the

cuts were and couldn't see any blood in the darkness. When I felt for
blood all I could feel was wetness due mostly to the rain that had just
begun to sprinkle, I assumed. The cuts weren't deep so I figured if any
blood was being lost it wasn't much. But at this point I realized I had
better not go a step further and settle down for the night. What if I
did cut myself badly? Then I could lose a lot of blood and then I would
really be in trouble. It could easily be fatal.

I climbed the trunk of a medium-size fallen tree that stood at a
forty-five degree angle. This is when I did my longest and loudest yelling while turning my head in circles. I made high, long, shrieking sounds
mostly, but getting tired of that I occasionally yelled, "Gomeza!" and
"Kuja hapa," come here. I also yelled, "Uo! Uo!" which in Kilese states
ones whereabouts and demands another's. After five minutes I was in
trouble. I continued for about ten more, also hoping that the racket
I was making would scare any nearby animals away. Although, I didn't
know if all I was really doing was signaling to nearby leopards and
gorillas that I was something helplessly in distress and easy prey. This
became the thought that preoccupied my mind. I remembered Gomeza
telling me he'd seen gorillas around, and John told me just before I had
left the village that a nearby leopard had been snatching dogs and goats
at night. I was helpless. No fire, no nothing. Just a penknife.

I decided it was better to remain completely still and not traipse
around the forest any longer, which would leave an even larger trail
of scent for some animal to pick up. Although, maybe my odor would
appear clear to them and scare them away. A human's must be very
different than another animal's.

I walked toward the base of the tree I was standing on until I came
to another tree it had fallen over and formed an X, like that of scissors
but not a cross. I snuggled into the crotch that was filled with bent
saplings and vines and tried out my bed-to-be, hopefully. I didn't want
to search any more than I had to for a place to sleep. This one I felt
comfortable in because it was clear above. I could see the sky and it
let in enough light to see for a little distance around me, owing to the
two fallen trees I had decided to sleep between. My head lay against
the upper one.

First I decided to eat in order to get my body working to digest
the food and throw off some heat. I hadn't eaten in a day due to my
sickness. I didn't much look forward to shelling peanuts and eating
oranges as sour as lemons. I wasn't even hungry. But I was getting cold

in the rain. I ate one of the three oranges and maybe five handfuls of peanuts. The rest I dumped on the ground below in order to use the empty sugar sack as a blanket. This I used, along with my jean shoulder bag. I opened up the cover flap and spread it out to make the second blanket. Here I was, getting down to survival techniques and recalling all I knew, which was probably about as much as anyone from home knew. The books and papers, I stuck inside my shirt to try and keep dry. I began thinking about the hobos who, while riding trains in the cold as stowaways, would shove balled up newspaper in their clothes for insulation. I knew I could make it through until the morning even if I shivered all night. It was thinking about animals that bothered me. I would try to run from gorillas I decided, but if a leopard came I was finished. I couldn't even go up a tree to get away from a leopard. If either showed up I would first shriek the loudest shriek I ever in my life did shriek and hope the animal would take off. If not, then the chase would be on. Certainly any animal in the surrounding area knew from my previous yells where I was. I urinated several times off the bough thinking maybe they'd smell my urine and stay away. I bedded down huddled into the tightest ball possible. I had to cut some sticks out of the way that were pressing into my back. Then I just wished to awake the next morning. I said to myself, "I pray for morning to arrive—that I may see it." But I was wishing, not praying, because I'm not religious.

Just as I had settled down something took off out of the bushes just in front of where I lay huddled up. "Probably an antelope," I thought. Then I kept swearing I heard twigs cracking under the weight of something's foot perhaps. I just tried to pass it off as my imagination getting the better of me, but the sound was undeniable. I finally decided it was certain rain drops falling on *mongongo* leaves. I kept imagining a gorilla's arm reaching up from the ground and taking hold of me, but first I'd surely hear him approach I thought, questioned? I became my normal self and said, "If it happens, it happens. Until that time there's no use worrying about it." If I did die it'd probably be fast. I had had a good life up to that point so it wouldn't be so terrible. But what about my family. They'd flip out. My father would surely show up with an interpreter and maybe even John, my friend at home. I could just see it now. Parents get letter of, " . . . son is missing." Maybe just a telegram. (I was surprised to read yesterday in Turnbull's stuff about some villagers never returning from the woods after they've gone in for one reason or another.) "My parents would be regretful they ever let me go," I thought.

Wednesday May 11th
Next day

I pulled my makeshift blankets up over me, covering my head. I pulled my jean cap down tight on my head. I'll never forget my high school geometry teacher telling us on a backpacking trip that sixty or ninety percent of a human's body heat is lost through the head. Maybe he said eighty. I'm not sure.

I closed my eyes knowing it would be an hour, or more likely two, until I might go to sleep. Minutes later the rain fell a lot harder and I finally decided to lower myself to the ground and take shelter under the two trees I had been lying on. I felt safer up on those trees than on the ground and that is why I was hesitant about moving down. I sat huddled up, the ground being too wet to lie on. I was getting about as wet as before, and soon I was thoroughly drenched, so I moved back up on top of the trees to where I could at least lie down. There I spent the night tossing and turning until I finally fell asleep. I thought God has sent the rain to thoroughly punish me for my stupidity. I thought then that it was *undoubtedly* the most stupid thing I had done since I left home.

Turnbull had told me to always travel with a pygmy. Pygmies seldom travel alone, and if they do, they sing or make some other kind of noise. Turnbull tells of a women being killed by a buffalo while foraging alone. When the news reached camp the first thing someone said was, "Wasn't she singing?" The answer was no, she hadn't been singing. Which means someone had been close enough to her that they would have heard her if she was.

The night did not drag on, strangely enough. Which meant I had slept for substantial amounts of time in between waking. I knew I had made it. I thought my chances were very good the night before. The rain had stopped an hour before dawn just when I would have shivered uncontrollably had it continued, and then I might have gotten really sick. Luckily my malaria attack had been on the fever side during the night and not on the chill side.

I lay still for about fifteen minutes. Monkeys were being noisy nearby. I knew the pygmy women wouldn't leave camp until seven or eight o'clock and that it would take awhile for them to pass by me on the trail, so I didn't start yelling until I got up. I was going to leave the peanuts in the tangled brush below but crawled through it and scooped them up, leaves, twigs, mud and all. I was later glad I did. They made good eating. The fallen trees became the base from where I struck out in four different directions hoping to run across the trail which I knew was nearby.

After I had traveled the third direction about to take the fourth, I was getting discouraged. The fourth one was the lucky one. I walked toward the rising sun on the new-found trail because I knew it would lead me to the village or the old camp in the plantation nearby. I had observed the sun's pattern while in the camp.

Within ten minutes I arrived at the old camp. That's when I realized that I hadn't gone as far as I thought I had the previous night. I also realized I had taken the wrong trail from the old to the new camp. I set out for the camp again. Two hundred yards later I found Sililo. He asked me where I had slept and I told him.

I was a miserable sight. My tan, torn, shirt looked like a tea bag. It had been dyed in mud. It was shredded on the one side. I had looked at my scratches. I might have told someone a leopard scratched me lightly because the cuts were in the pattern of a cat's paw. But they weren't that bad because they have nearly healed in the two weeks since then. I think the scars will eventually disappear.

Sililo was astounded, but less than I expected. He was on his way into town. He showed me the trail. He showed me with his arm to bear right as I continued to the camp. I walked and I walked and I walked. Every time I came to a fork I went right and soon I realized I was lost again and becoming very angry. I began yelling a mixture of Kingwana and English and then I stopped finally because I thought I heard something. It was Gomeza yelling, "Joseph! Joseph! Joseph! [Gomeza's name for me]" "Uo! Uo! Uo!" I replied until we finally faced each other. He was with his older brother Pascal. They had heard my story from Sililo. Now *they* were as astonished as I believed they would be.

The first thing I told them was what a bad thing I had done, over and over. We walked until we came to another camp member who was preparing wine from a palm tree illegally. That sure tasted sweet after a long cold night, and made me feel just right for a hot bath and a sleep.

We ate some of my peanuts and then carried on until we came to another trail I knew well. I realized then how disoriented I was. I had just made a four kilometer circle. We reached camp. Everyone was happy to see me. I felt closer to all. There were more than just a few giggles and smiles going around camp then. Before I arrived I was told never to walk the forest alone.

Maybe I had thought that if I had arrived the night before I would have proved I was more capable in general than everyone thought. Now I proved nearly the opposite, except perhaps that I was strong to have gotten through that night. I almost began wishing I had slept in the village.

Just as I sat down near the fire to warm up and was thinking about that hot meal and shower, a villager arrived. Instantly I knew the news was out and that he was sent to get me.

I was very tired at this point. My muscles ached because they had been contracted tightly throughout the night fending off the cold. I knew I couldn't refuse Apuobo's command no matter what the circumstances were. We sat down and had hot powdered milk together. I thought the milk sugar would do me good and give me the energy to make it back into town. Asked if the chief was mad, he said, "No." I guessed the chief was feeling bored and needed something to do. Maybe even a little money in his pocket. What I understood was that he wanted the details. He wanted to know who was responsible for the mishap.

Gomeza, the villager of some authority, and I, returned to town. By the time I arrived I was a celebrity. Two hours after Sililo had known, all of Nduye knew and Gomeza made full use of spreading this humorous story. Everyone had a good laugh when they saw me.

We arrived at the office. Apuobo was away in Mambasa. It was his younger brother, the assistant chief, who had called me. I explained how it was my fault and exactly what had happened. The assistant chief (I forget his name) told me that Gomeza didn't want me in his camp. That *really* woke me up.

Gomeza is the *capita* of all the Bambuti in the collectivity of Nduye. When I am in his camp he's responsible for me at all times. If I died the state would hold him fully responsible.

Now I fully realized the seriousness of what I had done. I told him I had been disrespectful and begged his pardon. He appeared to enjoy the fact that I, a white man, was asking a pygmy for forgiveness. And on this condition he would reconsider what he had said and allow me to live with him.

I had explained to the assistant chief that I'd never walk alone in the forest, always listen and respect Gomeza, and contribute salt, tobacco, and other things to the camp, and he told Gomeza this in Kilese.

Everything was back to normal again. I think another reason Gomeza didn't want me around at first was because of how intent I was on going hunting for elephant. This I no longer wanted to do and made me realize that I had better start listening to the people who know the forest. What would I, a stranger, know about it?

At one point I was asked what I would do if I couldn't live with Gomeza, and I told the assistant chief I'd probably go home. Gomeza is a worldly person and makes the best informant in the entire area. Without him I'm finished.

I thanked Gomeza profusely and said, "Let's go to the store and buy some tobacco, and some grass (*bangui*) across the street." We were back on the best of terms.

I think all in all it was good it happened. It put me in line and has stopped me from committing a possibly worse crime. Maybe something I would have tried to do during the elephant hunt.

16

I LOST several days because of the incident. All my papers had to be dried out and all my clothes washed. It was the first time I ever washed my clothes in the woods. It was hard work because they were so dirty, and in general, it's harder in the woods than in town. I beat my lathered up clothes down on a log while I sat on an overturned termite mound that had *mongongo* leaves placed on it.

This new camp is probably one of the most, if not *the* most beautiful I've ever seen, and what is more is that I am living in it.

Monday my hut was nearly finished. I've decided to live in a hut the same size as everyone else's and not cause any of the women a lot of extra work. This time, *I* cleared the ground and cut the *mongongo* leaves and saplings. The women built the hut. Yesterday I built a bed and table, and cleaned the weeds from the front of my home for a hearth to cook on and sit around at night. I have been eating lots of antelope and getting along very, very well with everyone, especially the children.

I'm completely over the culture shock sitting five kilometers out in the forest in a beautiful camp eating antelope, fetching water, visiting nearby camps, playing with too many children, and writing a little. I could very easily come back one day. I would know a lot more before I did, however. It's a bit ironic. The day I feel I could easily stay on,

I know I must return. And I'm not just saying that as though I had no say and wasn't responsible for my returning. I'm very much at home. I can sit for hours on end doing nothing, like these people do, and it doesn't bother me one bit. I sit and think and look at the forest. There are always plenty of kids to amuse myself with.

While living at Camp Andilifo, I realized that my mind had already left the Ituri. This camp has made all the difference in the world and it's good that I was able to see that camps differ in moods as well as surroundings. It's nice getting water from the river without wallowing through the mud this time.

Odds and ends: When I feel depressed, the village especially, looks poverty-ridden. When I'm fine, I don't notice the poverty. Poverty means something different to me now. Pygmies never look like they're poverty-stricken.

I have become attached to this band and especially to Zatu; my cook, general helper, and close friend. That goes for Gomeza also, of course. How do you like that? I've got the pygmy chief cooking my meals!

I have finally learned to "cup" my elbow and make the loud clapping sound the pygmies make, just as well as the adults, and better and louder than most children.

I don't think I'd ever live in the village again now that I've taken a good look at the forest world. I could come back here anytime I'd like to. I'd get a business visa. Keep a little shop in the village with someone to run it while I did research in the woods.

Gomeza's father is said to have killed one hundred elephants. They express one hundred as, one zaire, meaning one hundred makutas. "Zaire moja," they say.

I've got a couple more holes in my teeth due to rice that was poorly cleaned. I now only give my cook rice to prepare in the daylight, not at night by a lamp. Teeth don't pain me yet though. Only when I chew hard sometimes.

Gomeza's young son made an animal trap near camp. Apparently it could have hurt someone. I never saw a kid punished as severely in all my trip so far. His bottom was beaten with a stick while he rolled in the mud. His head was whacked with the stick. He went running from his father to his uncle and his uncle threw him down on the ground, having caught hold of his arm. Then his mother yanked him by his arm back to their fire.

This same kid, about a week earlier, ate his father's leftovers that his mother had put aside for Gomeza to eat when he returned from the village. His bottom had some cuts on it by the time Sakina (Gomeza's wife) was finished with her son.

Because of the "sleep-in-the-forest-alone" incident, the chances have been lessened that I'll do something dangerous again. Things are only safer now because of what happened. The forest is a safe place generally. I feel safer here than at home where I drive a truck on busy roads.

The animators that dance at official occasions are actually abused, used. Mobutu has created legalized prostitution. They select attractive girls and guys. Then the officials use the girls sexually. They can not refuse or they will suffer the consequences if they do. (No women hold governmental positions that I know of.) The guy who leads the animators of Nduye has profited at least twelve girls. (*Profiter* is what they say in French.) He said none can refuse him due to his position.

The Brother gave me a small plastic envelope with cognac in it. Tasted fine. They give them to sentinels in Italy at night so if they get the urge to go drinking while on duty, they just drink a few and it supposedly satisfies their thirst.

Several nights ago, when I was back at the old camp, a forest scorpion fell on me from the ceiling of my hut. Pascal brushed it off and it spiked him. Not seriously though. He impaled it with a splinter of wood, telling me that had he placed it in the fire it would only bring others.

I made a whistle out of an antelope bone I had eaten the meat from. They took the whistle away from me and threw it in the fire, telling me I'd scare the game away. There are lots of small superstitions as these.

Zatu's never heard an elephant trumpet and I have, and I don't even live among elephants. Contemplative isn't it?

I could easily live in "my shack" in the woods at home now. I've picked up some good camping tricks—use of fire, ways of cooking meat and vegetables.

Saturday May 14th
Next day

There have been moments before this very one when I've said to myself, "Ah . . . I would have worked ten years for this," but I would have to say that this one is exceptional for more reasons than one. I guess the first one is that I feel at home among these people like I've never felt before. The culture shock is gone. They like me. *How* we should get along so much better if I spoke more of their language.

It is nighttime. I see glowing campfires from the doorway of my hut. This camp is particularly musical. I hear two finger pianos being played. I don't think I'd ever want to live in the hot, sunny, village again.

First of all, it is lonelier in the village than when I'm here among this big family which is loaded with kids. When I step out of the forest into Nduye I have to look down at the ground because the sunlight immediately hurts my eyes. That is when I understand Turnbull say-ing the village is hot, dusty, and its water sources polluted.

Gomeza is the "Kenge" [Turnbull's key informant in Epulu] of Nduye if ever there were one, and I'm certain that if Turnbull arrived here he would make the same choice for his key informant. He is the head of all the Bambuti in the collectivity of Nduye.

This afternoon the lively children chopped down a huge tree. I stepped over my desk and stuck my head out of my hut just in time to see it crash the last half of the way down. I asked them if they were just playing but they said, "No," they were getting a section of log out of the tree to make a wooden drum from.

They were euphoric when the tree hit the ground, whooping, "Uo! Uo! Uo! Uo!" I chimed in and they kept mimicking me. All I could think of was these children living on another planet or in another world.

What fun these children are. I carry them piggyback around camp (sometimes four at a time) and chase them, acting like a ferocious monster.

I see it as either plunging in all the way or going home. And I'm not ready to dive in yet, though I think it's very likely I will one day.

This morning they spotted a crocodile down at the small river. We swim and bathe there! But they know all dangers in the forest and how to avoid them.

Sunday May 15th
Next day

Something that is slightly exceptional is that Gomeza has three brothers all about the same age as he. Two live in this camp and one is in another camp less than ten minutes away. I'm hanging out with the Four Fearless Bambuti Brothers! To hear them talk about elephant hunting! There is Gomeza, Sililo, Pascal, and the fourth ones name I don't know. They are all friendly as hell. The fourth one I'll call "Smiley," for practicality's sake. I went over to his camp yesterday with Gomeza. The camp had just arrived that morning. I said, "Hello," and shook everyone's hand. It's always a little surprising when a white man, or even a villager, arrives at a camp in the middle of the woods. Many of them knew me and greeted me by name. I noticed many hunting nets around, which I thought peculiar, for this area is hunted with bow and arrow, lance and dogs.

I remarked about them and then I was shown their spears, which I recognized as the type used in Epulu. That's when I realized that the strangers had come from far off. From Banana they told me, which is before Epulu traveling toward Mambasa. Directly from here to Banana, they said, is ninety kilometers, and their sense of distance is excellent. (From here to town, Gomeza always marks off the kilometers by the halves as we arrive at certain trees along the way.) They said they came this far because Apuobo had called them to catch antelope for him. How he contacted them I can't imagine. I found the story a bit hard to swallow. They said when their work was done they'd return home.

Monday May 16th
Next day

Here I sit on a coiled up hunting net near the central campfire watching and listening to the men, and one very old woman, sing in praise of the day's hunt. Over the fire stands a smoking rack with five antelope on it. I trade a bar of laundry and dish soap for the upper half of one of them with one of the hunters.

They sing so very seriously—about as seriously as they hunt. It is a very important part of life here. The woman is clapping her cupped hands together, creating a loud, high-pitched rhythm, and singing about me, *muzungu* (white man). The best male singer is keeping time with a stick that has had its one end splintered, "*O-u-o-o-a-o-e-i-e-i.*" "*Um . . . um . . . um . . . ,*" they chorus. Then one breaks into a solo backed by the others. I start to add softly to the chorus, as I've done

before, but this time I am politely asked to refrain. It appears very
serious. I guess they are thankful for the good hunting they've found here.

They pay no attention to my presence until I am tired and rest
my head on my hands. I learn that only women sit this way, never men.
Men hold their head up without their hands and sit with their arms
rested across their thighs or on their knees. They want me to act like
one of them. They all like me and I talk to them with my small
vocabulary of Kingwana and hand gestures.

Two hours later, the singers pause. The old woman has just finished
a wonderfully hypnotic, trance-like dance, oblivious to her surroundings. It doesn't matter the least bit that I, a stranger, am present.
Actually, after ten months of living in the area, I'm no longer so much
of a stranger.

The men and children from our camp signal it's time to return.
They light their large, bright-burning "match sticks" to follow the forest
path by. I help them see with my "flashlight" (just kidding). I believe
in authenticity but have decided to keep the few things I possess, including my flashlight. It sure makes getting up in the middle of the
night to answer nature a lot easier. I try to keep all my things to myself
as much as possible so as not to change this camp in any way.

That was last night. Today, the plentiful children are playing in
the nearby woods catching crabs, minnows, and then eating them in
their tiny play domes. They are playing house in immitation of their
parents and this is how they learn to become adults.

We arrive back at camp howling and singing. A nice ending to
a productive day. I sure did know I was in deepest, darkest, Africa listening to those pygmies from Banana sing and dance.

Tuesday May 17th
Next day

All in all, this week has been the most enjoyable I've ever spent
among the Bambuti. I've seen that one camp can vary tremendously
from another. This one is rolling and plenty of sunlight gets in where
I sit. The towels I hang on the roof of my hut are always dry, which
is a nice change. In the old camp, they were always moldy-smelling.
At Andilifo, I waited three days for my wash to dry out, and finally
resorted to taking it along with me to town to dry it out.

The second day we arrived here, Sililo shot an antelope with one of my arrows, so he was obligated to give me the entire back half of the animal. Guess he won't make that mistake again. I gave him a cluster of plantains and two handfuls of salt so he didn't lose out on the deal.

If I stretch my arms out, my fingertips touch the walls of my dome. I can't stand erect inside. It doesn't matter, because all I do in my leafed cave is sit and write or eat and sleep. I put my stick bed and table in last Tuesday.

Wednesday May 18th
Next day

Today I didn't do a shred of writing or studying. I sat back—almost —with what I guess is malaria again. (I woke up four mornings ago to see mosquitos living in my water bucket.) The thing I hate about it is not its physical discomfort so much, it's what it does to me mentally. It makes me want to leave the forest and Nduye practically instantly.

At one point I was sitting on my bed at my desk looking out through the opening to my hut at several children, and because my consciousness was altered it was as though I was watching some film about primitive people. I may have some other sickness too. I've had a head cold for the past week. I've got an extremely sore throat and slight pains shoot through my stomach occasionally. The latter causes me to believe I may have dysentery.

I stopped writing, finding it difficult because I was still sick. I've been taking Nivaquine and am just about cured. I feel fine at the moment but I still need to complete the treatment.

Earlier I said, "I sat back—almost— . . . " during the entire day. I said "almost," because I washed so many dirty pots and dishes—about three hour's worth.

Saturday night was the first time I had seen them singing and dancing in camp. I have always seen it take place in the village, except for Sunday night at the Banana camp. I have heard them sing enough that I can imitate them perfectly. The songs usually don't make any sense. They are composed of vowel sounds placed back to back, so I never needed to memorize any words.

I sat down and sang with them, which they encouraged me to do. Gomeza would stand up next to the fire now and then and dance in place, sometimes holding his right arm outstretched as though he were looking over something. He'd move it from left to right in a sweeping motion. One time he got up and told me to join him, so I did, dancing and singing in place. Sometimes I'd break into a lead, "*E-e-ma-i-e-e-o-u-o-o-i-e-a-o-u-i,*" and they would chorus, "*Uhm-m-m-m-m-m-m.*" I did chuckle at myself at first. No one else did though, except maybe Gomeza. It was hard to tell if he was just plain happy. They'd all been smoking marijuana, as they are accustomed to doing all day long.

Many boys begin shortly after ten years of age. Zatu smokes it unmixed with tobacco. The tobacco is strong and makes one unaccustomed to it dizzy, if not sick, if too much is smoked. Turnbull writes that the Epulu pygmies on very cold nights smoke tobacco so heavily that they sometimes pass out and fall in the fire.

I was going into town the next day to market so I donated some leftovers I had of rice, beans, oil, and salt to the campfire, which all were happy about. By the time it all had been cleaned and cooked, three more hours of dancing and singing had gone by, which was longer than it usually would have lasted, I feel. I thought about home and what I'd be doing on a Saturday night, and recognized that not much had changed.

Gomeza got very mad at me yesterday morning, forbidding me to give anything to anyone in camp. "No food, salt, oil, tobacco, nothing. You can give things to me or to Sakina, but to no one else, or I'm moving back to the old camp near the village."

Maybe he thought I was changing the camp's atmosphere in a bad way. I only give something when I'm asked for it, and even then, not always. Or if someone works for me, I give them some food or salt usually.

I don't know what set his temper off but I have an idea. It's interesting he threatened to move back to the old camp rather than kick me out of this one. Maybe he thought it was getting too much like the village here and people were getting lazy and asking me for stuff they'd have earned from the villagers before I arrived. When I used to visit them in the old camp in the abandoned plantation I would give them salt and tobacco, and very occasionally, some food.

Gomeza had been elephant hunting the day before yesterday, claiming they walked one hundred and twenty kilometers round trip. I find it hard to believe, considering they left about eight-thirty, nine o'clock, although they didn't return until after dark.

Yesterday he was tired, obviously, and wanted to stay in camp. I had to go into town because I had an affair to be settled before the chief. Gomeza asked Sufelo, one of the bachelors, to walk me in but Sufelo refused. This is what I think ticked Gomeza off. Maybe he thought it was pathetic that Sufelo had refused to do me a favor, considering all I contribute to camp, as well as what I've given Sufelo.

Gomeza changed into his Western villager's clothes and we went into town together. We arrived at Apuobo's office but he became too busy to see me. A woman arrived with a long, deep, gash on the back of her head and a large bloody scab on her upper back the size of my outstretched hand. Some of the blood had dried, what was still fresh was trickling downward. She had a skimpy piece of cloth tucked around her groin like a diaper, and wore a dress that hung below her waist by several inches, looking more like a smock.

The story was, as I had assumed, her husband had beaten her. And as is usual, she probably had been adulterous, as the Walese are known to be. John says, more so than many other people. I'd say it's true.

I told Gaduma (the assistant chief) I'd return later. I went to the mission, ate oranges on the hill with Gomeza until Father Louis woke up and I was able to get my money from the mission's safe, and bought eight bottles of palm oil in town.

I learned that Father Louis is leaving for Italy Sunday for a three to four month vacation. He hasn't been home in four years. Comparatively speaking, it doesn't seem like a very long vacation.

I remarked to John, after Gomeza and I had left the mission and I saw him at his girlfriend Harriet's house, that a study of Father Louis' life—or for that matter, another missionary's—would make a more curious study (though probably not as interesting) than that of the pygmies'. Consider he gets up about five. Goes to church at six, and leaves at six-thirty to walk back up to the mission for breakfast. Then he sits out on the porch, or at his desk in his room, reading until ten-thirty. Then he takes a siesta until lunch is ready at twelve-thirty, one o'clock. After lunch, he sits on the porch looking down into the village smoking a cigarette (boredom caused) until one-thirty. By one-thirty it's time for his afternoon siesta, which lasts until nearly three. Then it's more sitting and reading of the Bible until dinner time. Early to bed at about eight o'clock, having talked on the porch until that time with the other missionaries. There is now a strange twist to the pattern. He gets up at two in the morning and reads, I assume, until four and sometimes five.

When I spent my first two weeks in Nduye at the mission, I'd get up to piss and have to go outside. (I can't begin to imagine what it would be like to find a Third World mission with a toilet in every bedroom!) My room was next to his, and when I'd go outside I'd see a glow coming from his translucent window. I'd done this enough times that I knew that he didn't sleep with a light on (a lamp burning). I was eventually able to determine which hours the light stayed on. I was surprised he didn't sleep when everyone else does. Although, who sleeps before *and* after lunch? The only variation in his life is when he drives the Sisters on a safari or goes to Bunia on business.

He spent fifteen religious years in Italy before he came to Nduye. He has now spent twenty-five here because he believes in God. And I imagine if I asked him why he lived here for so long he'd tell me, just like all the other missionaries do, that his place was God-chosen and he has sacrificed his life for God. *Sacrifice* is the perfect word, to him. To me, the prime word is *waste*. John agreed. But one of the most important things I've learned since I left home is that there is no "right" life style and that "there must be room for all and all respected," to quote my other friend at home named John. I realize I've just criticized Father Louis' lifestyle but that doesn't mean I can't respect it at the same time.

The Provincial Father of the Upper-Zaire region once asked me what I thought of missionaries and I told him truthfully what I thought. I told him, in general, I didn't agree with what they're doing. "Every culture has their own god. How can you say yours is absolute?" I asked. "Man created God, not the converse." He just pointed out that change is inevitable. We agreed. He said that was his main interest in Africa.

There was a missionary in Kisangani who told me God had chosen Kisangani for her, and because of that, she loves Kisangani and would rather be there than any other place in the world. (Some people need a definite reason for living, others are content to believe in God and, or, life's little pleasures.)

I thought I might find what was left of the "right" life among the last of the purest of hunter-gatherers. When man became a cultivator was he kissed by death? Are we nearing the end? Research shows it was inevitable: The transition from hunter-gatherer to cultivator was due to increased population.

I was called to Apuobo's office at two. When I arrived, I found two of my former workers. One of them (Musafil) accused me of not paying him for two and a half weeks of work.

I had needed a cooking shelter built (Kingwana; *baraza*), so I asked the chief if he could give me two prisoners because I always have so much trouble finding workers. He gave me one, Musafil. Musafil dragged a one week job out to two and half at the rate of forty makutas per seven hour workday. After the third day, I found another guy who worked for a week. When he (Mungeli) left, the job was nearly finished. Musafil finished the job.

I was in town one day, not too long ago, when I saw Musifil and told him I wanted to pay him. I had paid Mungeli already. A discrepancy came up. I said I'd pay him for his work, and not more. He told me he worked seven hours a day for two and half weeks and that I owed him six zaires. So we had to see the chief.

The chief was fighting for Musafil because Musafil had committed a crime, was therefore a prisoner, and owed the collectivity money in the form of a fine that would go directly into Apuobo's pocket. The fine was five zaires.

The chief went through the penal code book and told me I was subject to a fine of ten zaires for refusing to pay my employee. Or, he'd send us both to a higher court in Bunia. (Like I've got time for that!)

I admitted it was truly my fault for letting a poor, lazy, workman continue to work for me, and ended up paying Musafil four zaires and thirty makutas.

I hate them because they all lie for each other because they're all relatives of each other. The whole thing was a farce and they laughed all the way through it.

I gave the chief the money and did not act my polite self by walking out, only shaking the chief's hand. (Chalk up my third case lost to a Zairean. I've yet to win *one*!)

Thursday May 19th
Next day

Two days ago I had the best hike through the forest to date. Sililo, Gomeza, Dominica and her girlfriend, and I, left the village for camp. It was getting dark so we were moving along at a snappy pace. I set the pace. I walked as fast as possible about three different ways without running, while they tried to keep up with me. I may not be able to run through the forest as fast as a pygmy but I can walk faster than one. Although . . . I did trip over a root along the way and fell flat on my face, unhurt.

We came to a special patch of leaves to the side of the trail. They stuck them in their hair, as they are accustomed to doing. My straight hair wouldn't hold the stems so they stuck them between my cap and my head. I found a black hawk's feather and stuck that in too. Then we continued, I chanting, "*D'authenticité!*" This is a very popular nationalistic word in Zaire which everyone knows.

Before we arrived in camp I signaled our arrival by clapping my bent elbow held against my side. Everyone had a good laugh when we entered camp.

17

I MOVED out of the forest back to my village home on Thursday the 19th. April 19th was the day I moved into the forest, making a stay of exactly one month.

The thing I was finding about being out there was that without the tools to go about the work, one doesn't progress. The work doesn't get more interesting, as it would if one thing led to another and then left me with only more that would need to be figured out. Without Kingwana, I was at a standstill. I didn't even have to think about it. I knew it was over.

I told the children and people sitting and standing outside my home around my hearth. Then Gomeza came back from bathing in the river and he heard the news. He was sick in the stomach so he'd find someone else to carry my things into town. It didn't take long to pack my things; about twenty minutes. Then when I was ready, they started hitting me for *cadeaux* (gifts, in French). "Give me this. Give me that," they asked. I gave them all the salt I had left, soap, and white beans. I gave Gomeza my file; Zatu, some palm nuts.

The children and I had gone down to the stream earlier to draw water so I could wash the dishes. On the way down they pretended to be crying because they were sorry I was leaving. When we got to the river Biasa (I called it a stream above. It's small) they shaped leaves into cones, dipped them in the water, and poured the water on their eyes while continuing to moan, looking like they were really crying. I was touched. I knew I would miss them.

Monday May 23rd
Next day

We hiked into the village. Two bachelors carried my two baskets, and several children, a few odds and ends. I was happy to leave the forest. There probably isn't another place on earth where life moves more slowly. Imagine living in such close, constant contact with nearly always the same people for your entire life! You'd know everyone nearly as well as you knew your spouse. I was happy to get out of the forest even though the month had gone by fast and without any trouble.

On the way into town they begged me endlessly like I'd never been begged before. I guess it was because it was their last chance. I ignored them and thought about other things until I'd just finally get mad and tell them to, "close their teeth."

We rested at the camp in the plantation. I'd just told them to shut up at the top of my bloody lungs so they would know I was serious, when Zatu asked me to buy everyone raffia wine when we arrived. I was sitting in my reclining chair at that moment. I grabbed him and threw him over my knees and began whacking his buttocks until he fell on the ground pouting. I hadn't hurt him, but when I unexpectedly tossed him on the ground, it got him angry, as I hoped it would. He threatened to not carry my plastic jug of oil any further, and Dominica said she'd tell Apuobo what I'd done and then he'd lock me up in prison. I knew they weren't serious and we'd be on our way shortly.

We reached town about one o'clock—just in time for some *mabondo* (raffia wine). There were so many people, as usual, that we only got one calabashfull. Which was good, however, because it didn't end up costing me much that way.

I bought some rice cakes for my helpers to eat and gave Dominica and her friend ten makutas each. We walked to my hut and deposited my belongings, gave them some salt, a little money for some tobacco, thanked them, told them to say hello to all back at camp, and then they were off.

Friday the 20th I was working in my hut when I heard some kind of commotion going on down the road that morning. Out of the glass window in my study, I could see my neighbors flock to the road's edge. Of course I had to join them. It was a rare but familiar sight. The Bambuti from Andili had arrived to dance, only this time it was an extra special occasion because two village girls had "seen their blood" for the first time. Menstruation had begun.

These two enormous amazons were being carried on a chair sitting on a litter supported by the walking men. Each woman required her own group. At the head of the mob was an old villager woman dancing, singing, and leading the whole thing. She had a hat on made from the skins of a small leopard-like animal that lives around here, and feathers. The tails of the two animals hung down her back like a coonskin cap.

All the semi-sweet chocolate bodies were glistening in the sun having been rubbed down with palm oil. They looked gorgeous, to say the very least. They all wore leg bands just below the knee and resting on the upper part of the calf. Painted bark loincloths were tied around their waists with different-colored beads. The two girls to be initiated into womanhood wore grass streamers from their upper arms. Some wore a string over one shoulder that made a loop around the other side of their ribs, which had small wooden pieces that looked like spools of thread strung on it. Each piece was decorated with burn marks. They wore small baskets as caps that had a large cluster of brilliant crimson feathers attached on top. Their bodies were carefully painted with black dye. Their faces were exquisitely done. Some wore earrings. Some made me think I'd never seen more beautiful girls. There were no women over fifteen perhaps among the pygmy females and the two amazons. They carried specially carved and painted logs that they used as walking canes—obviously phallic symbols.

And here I was without my camera! It was a sight never to be seen in a book about Africa that had photos in it. And if a photo of what I saw were to be shown at home, it wouldn't be able to be placed. It was atypical somehow, and extremely outstanding in all it's authenticity.

They would stop in front of each hut and wait for a gift for the two initiated girls. Then after receiving it, there was a special chant ending with a long, high, drawn out, "Whoooooo!" And then they'd march on to the next hut swaying forward and backward as they continued. The initiated girls shook their heads in a certain way. They reached me, and I reached into my pocket to see what I could find for the lead woman. I handed her a half-full pocket of coins. They all were content and ended with that melodious, "Whoooooo!" again before they carried on to the land bordering Apuobo's house to dance where they always do, under the border of tall, shady trees.

The men began beating the tam-tams and the circle of dancers began rotating, a mixture of pygmies and villagers. The oiled bodies always stayed together behind one another while everyone else moved where they liked when they wanted to. We continued around into a circle, or several circles, revolving together. Then the drum beat changes and everyone takes a twirl and a spin inside the circle. Every so many seconds the drummers would hit the drums extra hard and that's when everyone thrusts their genitals forward toward someone of the opposite sex. Just as your body has reached the peak of its arc and thrust, the drums sound, "Whap!" or a double or triple "Whap!" which requires two or three more thrusts crotch to crotch.

Not everyone gets involved. There are more men running up to women than the converse. Many women scream or whoop and run away laughing out of the men's reach. Some get annoyed as though they're saying, "Don't get fresh with *me*." Even some youngsters are to be found participating.

The dance is more than suggestive, yet there are some that take it farther, always being men. Sometimes two men (usually villagers) will come up and attack a woman from both sides. Several moved toward one and she backed away from them into me accidently and I "whapped" her. Everyone was holding their sides in laughter. It is a most appropriate dance for such adulterous people. It also gives people a chance to know whom they can profit. Undoubtedly, some slip off for the real thing eventually.

I don't know if it was because it was particularly amusing or what, but I had quite a few women come up to me, more than the other men had, even several pygmy belles. Even ancient ladies. The pygmies were usually scared of me. I guess everyone knows about the facts of life shortly after they are able to talk. Children run around naked until they are nearly eight sometimes.

There was one extremely beautiful pubescent villager. She wore a purple, white, and blue cloth wrapped around her head with the crimson-feathered hat on top, dangling gold earrings and a myriad of waist beads. It made me lament the entire time not having a camera. I'd never see such a sight again. Even if I came back ten years later she would have grown older. The young will grow older but beauties will always be born again. This is something I've been thinking about a lot lately. So much that I see will never be the same. Usually the children get me thinking about this, but no matter how unique they all seem, there will always be others. They will have their own children.

Tereza, the woman next-door, has been caught in the bushes behind her house with other men by her husband several times. Her husband Mima let Mamadu (my neighbor to the other side of my house) use his house one afternoon to profit a woman when all had gone to drink wine. Somehow the secret got out and there was a big stink. Two days later Mamadu profited Mima's wife Terezal I sat in the middle of the feuding Mima and Mamadu denying it.

The fight was rather humorous. Mamadu began cursing out Mima in French, which Mima doesn't speak or understand. Mamadu therefore told Mima how ignorant he was. They were each yelling at each other from their property calling the other one over to his for a fight. No one finally arrived at the other's place so Mamadu went to the road and called Mima there. We all knew the fight would never take place—as they never do—because Mamadu is twenty years younger than old Mima and would kill him.

They finally talked themselves out. Mamadu kept going back to his house and then Mima would say something that would aggravate him so he'd come over and yell at Mima from my property. Of course, I couldn't get any writing done so I sat down and listened to it for an hour.

Friday night we went out the road toward Mai Tatu to see the Bambuti dance where they'd spend the night. John found a girl to profit. As he was slipping off from the dance area, he tumbled into an enormous ditch, dirtying his pants at the knees. He was going to take her into the bushes but she insisted on her house. He tried to refuse but finally followed her. She said no one was there. She opened the door and he said he had to step over the bodies sleeping on the floor to get to her room.

He gave her a cigarette after they were finished, bragging to me once again how he has become as good, if not better, than a Mulese at exploiting people to the fullest, using their own tactics.

Saturday night I had quite a time dancing and singing with a band of pygmies in town. They were from the left side behind the mission. The moon was full white and bright enough to read by.

In the beginning some villagers danced, but as it got later, the pygmies took over the dance. We got to the good ol' pelvic-thrusting part and many of the women kept coming out into the middle of the circle to meet me. I guess they find extra enjoyment in whapping a strange white man mostly because they can't believe one is really dancing and singing with them. Some of them nearly fell down dead with laughter.

I returned to the circle's edge feeling that things were getting out of hand and I was disrupting the dance. I also didn't want to make any of the males jealous of me. As I stood there, a youth stretched his arm in front of me and said softly, *"Pole pole,"* which means slowly. I got the message to slow down.

I began beating the *banja* sticks for a change. A *banja* stick is a foot-long stick that is split about eight times at one end. Two of these beaten together make a nice-sounding rhythm. Then a youth tied ankle bells to each of my feet and I began dancing like mad, throwing in my own innovations now and then or copying the others. Innovations are perfectly acceptable. We would take spinning hops over the fire. Somehow I managed to never break the rhythm. I was not the least bit inhibited. Dance is a serious art form to them and if I had laughed at myself a lot they might not have appreciated it, thinking I was disrespectful. We got on tremendously. Again I wished I knew the language. How it would be nice to speak the language with subtlety. I hardly had a chance to speak to those nice young girls.

It got hot so I took off my shirt, and in doing so I realized I was the only one who'd been wearing one. I gave out tobacco twice during the night. At about one o'clock I went home to sleep. They danced until sunrise, caught a quick nap, and continued Sunday.

I stayed with them as late as I could since it would be my last night with them before my departure, but at one o'clock I'd had enough. I'd been drinking late into the night the day earlier.

I made the mistake again of telling people too soon that I was leaving. I had done this once before when I thought I was leaving in December. Everyone flocked here asking for souvenirs and gifts. What a pain in the ass they are. Saturday night was the limit.

Mima burst into my house drunk and asked where his *cadeau* was, furiously. I told him to get the hell out of my house. The man doesn't make a shred of sense when he's drunk. The chief's wives arrived to buy a saucer but Mima's wife grabbed it and bought it, laying her money down on the dirt floor. During the confusion, Mima insulted Machozi, the chief's first wife. The wives left and shortly after we heard a knock on the door. It was Apuobo's messenger calling Mima. I put on my shirt, knowing I'd be included eventually, and walked to the chief's house with them. Suddenly Mima lost his boisterousness before the chief. He was like a little child. The chief heard the matter and told Mima to stay at home when he's drunk, and sent him to prison. Mima was enraged as he walked away. He had gone ten yards when he threw his lamp to the ground and made a run for it into the blackness. The two guards caught him. He was running aimlessly anyway. Where would he run? He was running in anger.

Just about all my things have been sold or given away so I'm not bothered as much. My house, and some other things I need, will be sold when I leave here for good.

Now I'll try to finally get rid of the notes I've made that have built up: Zatu cut down a tree out of boredom, showing the pygmies do kill without reason always.

A man here (Andilifo) has two wives, which is rare. He has a hut for each one, just as the Walese (or all villagers) have a separate room for each wife. They take turns sleeping with each wife. It's normally two days in a row with each one. I assume this man moves back and forth from dome to dome. I found him to always stay with his older wife. Once, the younger one cursed him out for two hours, probably because she wasn't getting any of his attention.

John and Harriet's relationship was discovered by the chief finally after one year. Apuobo noticed some stranger's clothes drying on his clothesline and thought one of his wives had washed her paramour's clothes, as is the custom. Upon asking who's clothes they were, Harriet told him they were John's. Harriet lived at the chief's compound at that time. No one up til then had known about their relationship.

I heard an airplane overhead this morning (May). Everyone tried to spot it through the clearing in the trees. They know I drive a truck and asked me if I knew how to fly a plane. Planes evoke wonder and fear in them. I told them what it was like to sit in a plane and look down at all the small things. I told them about the World Trade Center and its elevator, and the view from its top.

The pygmies and I laughed together saying how the god of the mission doesn't exist and that it is just a big tale and how the only real god is the god of the forest, Tore.

Falling asleep at night in the forest made me think I could have been anywhere in time, either thousands of years in the past or the future, because the forest and its sounds are unchanging.

I gave Pascal some palm kernels to roast in his fire while he was roasting his. He set mine to one side on the coals, and his on the other, and began turning them all with a stick to evenly brown them. Mine were chock-full of palm fat. The best I ever ate. While he was pushing them around I noticed that one of my nuts had slid over into his pile and I pointed it out to him. We had a big laugh as we rocked backward.

18

I JUST this minute witnessed a classic nuptial dispute between our good friend Mima and his wife Tereza. His house sits next to mine with my glass window staring at his property. He was in front of his house getting mad again. Then I realized someone had shut the door, which stopped him from walking in and out of the house screaming at the top of his lungs, as he had been doing.

I saw his other wife, Emelia, and stepdaughter Christina, behind the house at the *baraza*, so I assumed Tereza was inside and had shut the door. He kept running up and throwing his body against the door trying to smash it down, but it was useless. He went to the *baraza*, picked up his favorite chair and placed it about ten yards in front of his house. Just as he was about to sit down, he took another lunge at the door. I could see the anger mounting. He just couldn't wait to get in and beat his wife silly. She finally opened the door and he walked in and began beating her until he dragged her out in front of the house.

By this time a small crowd had gathered, and all the people who'd just returned from the raffia trees had arrived in front of the house on the passing road as well. Everyone was enjoying watching the fight. Tereza grabbed his testes and began pulling and squeezing them off. She eventually got on top of him and, with her free hand, began slugging him into the ground. Mima had tried to swing at her but kept missing and then yelled, "You've got me by my testes. Let me go!"

Two men stepped from the crowd to pull Tereza off her husband before she killed the puny, toothless, man. They were both held but wanted so much to continue the fight. Tereza walked off into the nearby forest and Mima went into his house to begin destroying his wife's possessions by throwing them against the walls and the floor, making a big racket. Probably feeling he had been publicly shamed by his spouse, he began throwing all of her things, along with everyone elses, out the front door (the only one there is) to show everyone how enraged he was.

Thursday, May 26th
Next day

While he was doing this he threatened to kill her. Christina (daughter of Emelia and stepdaughter of Mima) went into the house and brought all the knives, a machete, and a bow and arrows out of his reach.

He had once picked up his bow and arrows, noticing Tereza wasn't around, and went to look for her in the woods behind their hut. He knows her hiding places and surprised her fornicating. When he reached the place where she'd been lying, he found one of her wraps spread out as a blanket and brought it as evidence to show the nearby palm wine drinkers how unfaithful his wife is.

She appeared out of the brush eventually, and had her back facing Mima at one point. He picked up a large wooden pestle and went running toward her. Just as he was about to bring it down on her head, the palm wine drinkers shouted warning and she turned around just in time to see the mad man coming after her and took off. He might have killed her.

Mima continued heaving suitcases of papers out the door to everyone's amusement. He picked up one of the metal trunks and continually threw it against a tree stump, bashing it in.

He walked out to the road and John tried to calm him down by talking to him, but Mima just accused him of being one of the men fornicating his wife. Then he walked back toward the house and Angapalaembi (his stepson of two years) was in his path so he knocked the kid down, who in turn began to cry. At this point he was furious at the whole world. He picked up the child by the wrist, looking as though he were going to stand him up, but instead hurled the infant into a patch of weeds fifteen feet away.

That was it, no one could tolerate this mad man any longer. John dashed forward and got hold of him, just as Mima was about to hurl a tin trunk at Angapalaembi. I never saw John so enraged in my life. He yanked one of Mima's arms up behind his back and told him he was going to prison, while Christina got hold of the other arm.

Emelia ran forward cursing him out at the top of her lungs. It was the first time I'd ever seen her have a quarrel with her husband and I had noted earlier how it was always Tereza who fought with Mima. After she finished every sentence she'd exclaim, "Nabode!" (I die) two or three times. She was crying without showing any tears as they marched him away.

I sat here beginning to write this down when he returned to his house from the woods, obviously having escaped from prison. He told his wife *he* was not staying in jail but that *she* was. (Tereza had returned by now in her wraparound that had been ripped while they were fighting.) He threw some more things, including glass, out of the house and then paced around until he demanded where his black shoes were. He never did find them, but instead, opened one of the trunks that lay ten feet in front of my window and pulled out a black shoe polish tin. He pushed the lip of a glass into it to scoop some up and then he smeared it around the inside of the glass with his fingers. I thought perhaps he was going to stain his wife's clothes.

He went down the road toward the filthy stream (in which I've seen excrement floating), and came back with the glass full of water and announced to me that he was going to drink the concoction and die. (By this point I had opened my window so I could hear everything clearly, instead of standing outside where I would have appeared nosey.) I responded with, "Kwa heri," (good-bye) and told him that what he was about to drink was not poisonous.

He sat on the ground in front of his house while the rest of the family sat under the *baraza* not paying any attention to him. I thought he was just threatening. He began eating something off of a piece of paper and then finally pushed the paper into his mouth. I didn't know what was in shoe polish but I decided he'd better not drink it. Although, I wasn't quite sure what to do. "Should I interfere?" I asked myself, "or should I let the incident run its course?" Here I sat with possibly less than five seconds to make a decision.

At first I was going to observe the thing as it was, feeling, I am studying them and should not be responsible for altering the circumstances even if someone were going to die. I'm supposed to look at things objectively. It reminded me of Jane Goodall feeding her chimps and therefore influencing the data she collects. Then I decided to stop the man, feeling I had a chance to prevent a possible death, and that it was my duty as a fellow human to do such even though I doubted the quantity he might swallow could kill him. I thought it would make him sick, especially because of the polluted water that no one drinks, but bathes in.

Then I was certain I would try to stop him. I remembered it was I who'd given him the shoe polish as a present, at his request, because I was leaving (the opposite of how we give presents, but they'll think of any occasion from which they may profit). I could just see it then. I'd be responsible for his death by supplying the poison.

The crowd had long gone and I was surprised the officials hadn't come to look for their escapee. I was going to run and tell Apuobo but remembered he was in Mambasa, and as Mima's family wasn't showing any concern, I ran to my other neighbors, but neither man was home. So I told the two wives what was about to take place and they slowly walked up behind Mima to ask him what he was doing. He told them to get away and they told him what a fool he was.

Then he got up and walked around to the side of his house in front of my window and drank it in one shot. I thought how ghastly it must have tasted. He smeared the polish around the inside of the glass again and headed down the road for the water. "He did not receive a gift from me to abuse," I thought, "and I will not let him." I somehow needed to justify my getting involved. Here he was, trying to kill himself with my present to him.

I walked behind him. He asked me where I was going but I didn't answer. I came up alongside of him and took the glass out of his hands without any struggle; leading me to believe that's just what he was hoping someone would do so he wouldn't have to go through the ordeal again. But he did manage to scrape a finger's worth of polish out of the glass before I got it away from him, and thrust it into his mouth.

I began walking back to his house to get the tin also. (Earlier, I had asked Christina for the tin to see if it's contents had been written on it, but they hadn't, as I suspected.) I met Gaduma (Apuobo's next youngest brother, and assistant chief), and told him the man was trying to kill himself by drinking shoe polish mixed with water. (I doubted he consumed very much because it doesn't mix with water and most of it remained stuck to the inside of the glass.) The military man who accompanied him got hold of Mima and began slapping his face as he was questioned by Gaduma. Then Tereza came over and began shaking her finger and yelling at him as they hauled him away.

The first question Gaduma asked was where the shoe polish came from. He tried to tell me how I was responsible because I'd given it to him. I told him I could have given the man a bucket of water and if he decided to stick his head in the bucket and drown himself it was his fault, not mine. Gaduma didn't say much after that. He sat down in one of the chairs and talked to the family. Tereza got up eventually and sat in front of the house. She'd had too much. She broke down and began sobbing. Maybe she really does love her husband. They've been together for a long time.

By this time it was dusk. I walked into town to the store and to the tailor, and after my business was through I walked to John's hoping we'd walk down to Harriet's together for supper. He then related how the dispute had arisen between Mima and his wife.

Mima went to drink wine that afternoon. Sometime after they had been seated under the tree, Tereza arrived. Mima gave her a hard look and asked her where she'd been drinking that day since her eyes were so red. She didn't answer and continued looking down at the ground as she does when she's drunk. He asked who'd bought her wine but still she said nothing. The other drinkers tried to calm him down, telling him that if fighting goes on under the tree it will dry up and give no more wine to anyone, as they believe. John told me he thought they had been drinking together earlier, and couldn't understand why Mima asked her where she'd been drinking.

A villager John and I call Hitler (because he wears a Hitler mustache), handed Mima a calabash of wine which Mima in turn poured half of out on the ground and gave back to Hitler, demanding it back only seconds later. He was more drunk than his wife and John and I suspect he smokes marijuana. We don't know how alcohol would possibly make someone so mentally disturbed. I also feel the villagers get intoxicated as easily as they do because of such a lacking diet. I eat a lot of meat compared to them. I've been eating meat three times a day for the past six weeks.

As the wine was nearing depletion Tereza slipped off ahead of the crowd that was about to leave, hoping to get free of Mima. While walking the path to the Mai Tatu road from the raffia tree, he said over and over, "Tereza has got to leave *today*. She's getting out of my house!" And then when he returned, that is when the fighting began, he first trying to break down the door to get at her.

Today the wives are still next door, but Christina has left. I don't know where she has gone, but I doubt it's far away because her boy Tabo is with the wives and still needs to be breast-fed.

Yesterday was quite a day. After John and I had taken dinner at Harriet's, we went across the river to see his old woman Maria, to whom he supposedly has given a baby boy. She told him she'd be distilling manioc alcohol that night in the forest and would like him to arrive to help and keep her company. Of course we didn't tell Harriet where we were going.

Several hundred yards after the bridge we met Maria coming toward us, along with a woman who has just arrived from Isiro (her husband kicked her out, is one story; the other, is that she left him), a woman teacher who is known for being an absolute fool when she drinks, Maria's mother and sister, and her new child and daughter, along with some children. They were on their way to our side of the river, but feeling we had money, they decided to return to Maria's house with us and see what they could get out of us to drink. They had had enough already it was quite evident.

We strolled to Maria's and seated ourselves in her house, whereupon she served John and I a cup of *kaikbo*. Then when I decided it was strong enough and worth buying, I laid one zaire down on the ground. But there was no more left she told us, to our surprise. She had distilled some but it was gone (We knew where it had gone too because of such a carousal going on), and said she'd make a lot more the following day and that that was when we should return.

John stayed in the room while I went outside to sit by the fire. The nonsense was too loud and absolutely empty. Fifteen minutes later the noise grew louder and I saw John exit the hut by moonlight with drunken women clawing him. He began to walk away with them all around him and told me we were going. I began shaking everyone's hand to say good-bye when I turned around because of a sudden great commotion. The women were hanging on him trying to pull him down playfully I thought, until I heard John yell, "Let's get out of here!" Then I realized a fight was going on. He handed me his radio and I began pulling some of the women off of him with my free arm but it was difficult. One of them had hold of his belt. When they were crouched down low enough, I stumbled forward and ended up sitting on three of them. Maria tried to grab his testes but he gave her a good kick which stopped her cold. They had hold of his shirt so he unbuttoned it in order to slip out of it and away. Meanwhile, there were children around and several young boys delivered blows with their fists to his head. Just as he was nearly out of his shirt I heard, "R-i-i-i-i-i-p!" They had his shredded shirt but not him, and I dashed off behind him noticing Maria coming from behind me trying to catch John. I made a quick decision, thinking, "We are trying to run away from trouble and here she comes asking for more. I don't know who's in the wrong but I know this woman is looking for more trouble, and *that* is wrong." So when she came right up next to me I tucked my bent arms close to my sides and gave her a football block that sent her sprawling. I utterly surprised her and she said, "Josef. It's me," as though I had mistaken her for someone else. By the time she got up we had sprinted way ahead of her and the enraged mob down the road. I was cringing as I ran, believing stones might have been thrown at us.

After we were well out of their reach we ducked into the brush to watch them pass. Now I could see how burning angry John was now that he was standing still. It reminded me exactly of the time earlier that day when he took Mima off to prison.

We walked back out to the road and just as we neared Harriet's house we met them again. Maria began talking loudly to John until he finally lost his temper. He demanded why she had followed us and then answered for her. "You've come to get the beating you deserve!" In his fury he said to me, "I am going to beat this woman!" He searched frantically for a stick while Maria stood quietly, still, in the road (thinking he was joking, John told me later).

While he was searching for his switch I wanted to prevent any more fighting and asked if what he was about to do was according to custom. All he answered was, "I shall give this woman a beating." (A certain amount of wife-beating is also considered in line among the pygmies.)

He looked on the ground, at the trees for a limb to break off, but finally went as far as the chief's compound to his bamboo dish-drying rack and yanked a strip of the bamboo from it, crashing it down to the ground. He bent it in the middle to shorten and strengthen it and stepped up to her to deliver his first blow smack across her buttocks, "Whop!" He gave her a second quick one and she reached out to get hold of him. The third swing cut her index finger, which made her lunge at him, bringing John down on the roadbank. The group moved closer.

John quickly reversed the positions so that he was on top of her and gave her a few hefty slaps. Her daughters began wailing and others began whimpering. Then her daughters moaned, "Mama! Mama!" in terrible fear. The eldest daughter moved forward to interfere but I stepped in front of her. By that time John had tried to disengage himself so he could run free, but Maria grabbed on to one of his legs and he dragged her on the road several yards until she let go.

I continued to my house to heat my bath water. They came by looking for him, saying they would wait until the morning for him to show up, but finally went back to their side of the river. He had been watching them all the time from the chief's back porch. It was lucky Apuobo was in Mambasa. It was also a lucky thing Harriet was not at home at that moment or she would have come out and probably beat up Maria.

John appeared and related what started the incident. Maria is jealous of Harriet because she is receiving all of John's attention. She rightly accused him of not devoting any of his time to their child. (Although, there is another man claiming the child is his.) Maria and two other women kept criticizing him while he turned a deaf ear, trying to avoid an argument. Maria got up out of her seat and slapped him across the face. "We have been together two years now and this is the first time you've ever done that. Now what is wrong with you?" he demanded. He got up to leave and that's when the drunkards began climbing on him.

My work has been going along very slowly because I've been letting myself get distracted by those good ol' village distractions. I may leave Monday after having ended the week here. I've been eating meat every meal and consuming lots of *mabondo* and a little *kaikbo*. I've also got good ol' diarrhea again. I heard the loudest clap of thunder yesterday while I was sitting here.

June 3rd
One week later

I am leaving Monday. I want to wrap up the weekend here, eat a chicken on Sunday, and begin answering some of the many letters I've received from home.

Wednesday night I heard two whites with Land Rovers had arrived from the north going toward Mambasa. The general impression was that they weren't tourists, so I assumed they were possibly plantation owners. I didn't go to see them.

Yesterday morning I heard they were still here, so assuming their
cars weren't broken down, I figured they must have had a reason for
staying over. Being whites, it was highly unlikely they were visiting
relatives. I was walking up from the river about to turn down the Mai
Tatu road to my hut when my curiousity got the better of me and I
went to investigate. I asked Omari the shopkeeper if the whites were
still here and he pointed the direction to the hotel. (Not a hotel in our
terms. They are rooms to sleep in.) I wandered in to see some blacks
and greeted them. I could see from their city dress that they were part
of the Land Rovers, and stepped into the central lobby to see through
an open door a white and a black man sitting on a bed. The white man
introduced himself, "Henault, Kinshasa." I awkwardly answered, "Jay
Bone, American."

We shook hands, the three of us. Henault sat with books and papers
on his lap. We got to talking and then I said, "Your first name is Charlie
isn't it?" He replied, "Yes." Then I explained how I knew his friend in
Kisangani, Mr. Harvent, a pharmacist. Harvent had urged me to go
to the large art museum in Kinshasa and look up his friend Charlie.
Harvent had told me about Charles and how he lived with the pygmies.
Charles' last voyage through the Ituri was in order to collect *mulumbas*
(painted bark loincloths) for the museum. I saw the ones Charles had
given Harvent.

We had a nice talk. He's forty-nine, a Belgian like Harvent, and
has been working for the museum for the last seven years. Every year
he says he's going to quit. He used to be a professional drummer in
Kinshasa (formerly, Leopoldville), beginning before independence. He
had a month's break so he hitched through the Ituri. He got back to
Kinshasa too late for his job and someone else had taken his place, so
he then landed a job with the museum. When he's not in Kinshasa he's
out in the bush collecting artifacts, information, and photos for the
museum. He told me how handicapped he is because he never had any
formal anthropological training. I had asked him about his background
and told him how I was going home to complete my education first.
He agreed it was the best idea.

He accepted my invitation down to my place to see my small
collection of mulumbas. As we were walking out the door we were
admiring a young villager girl who looked familiar to me. They had
picked her up in Epulu and she'd been traveling with them for the past
two weeks. I guess I'd seen her in Epulu. Commenting on her beauty

gave him the excuse to tell me a story. He replied (He also spoke broken English), "She's nice but I prefer pygmy women."

He told me how he spent two months in the forest around Epulu living in a hut with a married pygmy woman who's husband had gone on a safari somewhere. "Did you live in the same hut in front of all the other pygmies?" I asked. "Yes," he replied.

One day they were walking through the village hand in hand when the woman saw a truck coming down the road and exclaimed, "That's my husband!" But she refused to let go of Charlie's hand. The husband got down off the truck and walloped her across the face. The whole affair was finally settled by Charlie giving the sore husband five zaires and several bottles of beer which they drank together.

John told me the pygmy women often refuse to sleep with villager men, complaining their penises are too long. This, I know is not true. He also keeps telling me how much he wishes he had a car so he could take pygmy women on dates. He thinks that if he had a car he could lure them away from Nduye, and then it would be a lot easier to distract the women into being seduced by him.

Duabo, the head of the girls school, was caught with teachers' mail in the bottom of his w.c. (outhouse). Apparently, there are teachers who've requested positions elsewhere and their answers have ended up in his w.c. because he doesn't want them to leave Nduye. He collects all the mail in Bunia, and often the teachers' mail is addressed care of Duabo. So he opens it up and does what he likes with it. John suspects his answer about getting into U.N.A.Z.A. in Kisangani has ended up in Duabo's w.c. because he can't figure out what's taking them so long. Duabo is very peculiar indeed.

An old man here named Primus is a confirmed miser. He planted so many raffia trees eight years ago that now that they are mature he's raking in the money. He had money stashed away to begin with. He is stingy as can be. He delights in taking an afternoon walk to the store to buy his daily tin of sardines (sixty makutas a piece). Then, if anyone asks him about his taste for sardines he tells them how he's bought them for his hungry son. (Primus also refers to me as his son.)

Apuobo got back from Mambasa yesterday evening and I saw him this morning. He was hung up in Mambasa because the zone needed eighty zaires from his collectivity. So he had to send a foot messenger the sixty kilometers from Mambasa to Nduye to let Gaduma know he was to squeeze the money out of the population by collecting taxes early;

about six months early, as a matter of fact. They went around at night to collect the money when they could be sure everyone was at home. It caused some pretty big fights. I heard something to the effect that one of the tax collectors got into a big physical fight with a girl John and I have named "The Sex Machine." Her real name is Louise. She's aborted so many times she's under constant menstruation. She can no longer conceive.

The fight went on and on until she arrived with the tax collector on this side of the river. Outside Apuobo's house, she stripped down to her bathing trunks (used as underwear) and beat up the forty-year-old guy. She was about to finish him off when he grabbed a rock and brought it down on her hand that lay on the ground.

These Walese women can put up a good fight by God! Which reminds me: Mima is keeping a hawk's eye on his wife Tereza. He's still in prison, but when hard labor is over or it's time for lunch, he comes home.

Other nicknames John and I have are, "Hitler," for the man who wears the Hitler mustache, "Madame Bonshoir," for a woman who says bonshoir when she's drunk, instead of *bonsoir*. I usually reply, "S(h)alamu," (greetings). We hate her. She's an absolute wretch. A real case study.

Then there's a girl pygmy we call, "The Tank." She nearly made our eyes pop out when we first saw her. She's short, squat, muscular, and she's got two of the most unsensual breasts hanging on her chest like Christmas tree ornaments.

In general, all the Walese are known as Iks to John and I. We decided it was the perfect name for such incomprehensible, self-centered people. John and I refer to each other by "Iky" or "Ik Man," being that we live here and have been unable to fight off being swallowed up by the Ik culture until we've actually become one of them ourselves. John keeps seriously worrying he's going to be a bad person by the time he leaves Nduye.

19

NOW that I've left the forest people and will be spending more of my time in more civilized places it will be nice for a change to dance without smoke in my eyes.

Before I left, and even still true now, is that I was beginning to feel close to the people. They are so pathetically open compared to how we are to each other. I could talk to an old woman as easily as I could converse with a twelve-year-old. I love the casualness and unpretentiousness of these people. I despise and outright loathe the majority of missionaries I meet. They're cold as ice. Consequently, they build and live in worlds of solitude. And what have I discovered? These people come down with ulcers. Probably because of their artificial surroundings. They might eat five meals in one year with a female at the table, or the converse for Sisters. One Sister from Nduye is back in Italy taking it easy because she's got an ulcer. And now Mrs. Lenhartzen might have one. She was here for ten days being tested and they still couldn't find what was wrong with her. She's still miserable and eats nothing but papayas. That can't help much. But all else she vomits up. If she's not better in a week she'll come back to have some more tests done, and if they still don't find what's wrong, she'll return to the States.

Part Four

Part Four

20

EVERYONE was surprised, all well as happy, to see me. The night I arrived I was swamped with handshakes from the pygmies who were dancing in town. Many thought I had left for good, while others swore I'd return, despite my telling them I'd be gone not much more than three months. [I was in East Africa and the Kalahari Desert of Botswana with the Bushmen.]

At first I didn't recognize my helper in the woods, Zatu. I had forgotten how small the pygmies are. In the dark, they all looked like kids among all the ones that really were kids. Most surprising of all though, was being hugged by certain villagers, mostly my neighbors, and I felt they did so more out of desire than obligation. Rarely do the Africans publicly show affection, and I, being a white man, was impressed all the more. Most of them desired to hug me more than I desired to hug them, and therefore, it generally looked a bit awkward.

Mima, the toothless chap who got his testicles pulled by his wife, was his usual drunken self and even hugged Day (the American photographer I've returned from Kenya with). Harriet came charging toward me from her rice patch and nearly tackled me, she embraced me so hard around the waist. John acted strange, as though I were a spirit risen from the dead, and appeared to not recognize me with my longer hair. When I approached him he lurched back at first, as though I were going to attack him. He had gone around one side of a building, while I had gone around another in order to sneak up behind him and surprise him, and since he caught me half way, that may have added to his surprise.

Sunday we moved into my home and my pygmy friend Emile swept out all the cobwebs with a large palm frond. Likambo patched the roof with *mongongo* leaves and I cut down some of the overgrown grass in front. Day chopped a path to my outhouse and John cut a border around my hut. I got some things sewn by Isiaka the tailor, and we sold various things to the mission because we arrived here makutaless. I am forced to sell my home afterall. If Likambo is unhappy living in the chief's compound he can build his own home somewhere else, just like every other man.

Apuobo was invited to Kinshasa by the government for a reunion they hold there every five years. Two weeks are up, so we are expecting him any day now, and shortly after he is at home and working I will ask him for permission to take photos of the pygmies.

We expect to spend a week in the woods and then head for home. I'm overjoyed that they are camped now where I left them six months ago. Gomeza's wife told me they will remain next to the Biasa River for the next two and a half weeks. The camp's composition has changed and gotten larger too, I believe.

Wednesday December 7th
Six days later
Camp Biasa

Here I am again out at Camp Biasa, five kilometers from the village. I haven't had even a second to write since Apuobo returned from Kinshasa a week ago. I've been occupied taking care of all the last things I wish to take care of before we head for Khartoum, Sudan. We are very close to being ready. By Sunday we'll be back in town, and hopefully by Wednesday, on the road.

I began answering letters when it came time to go on a short safari to Andili. Day, John, and I left Nduye about four o'clock Saturday after-noon. With us we had soap, salt, leaf tobacco and cigarettes to barter for *mulumbas* (painted bark cloths). I carried the seven kilo's of salt because Day thought I was a fool to not have bought mostly tobacco, which is lighter. At his suggestion, I inquired in the village as to what was in greatest demand along the path to Andili, and it was salt, as I suspected. It didn't matter though because Day was determined to carry a light pack. I will say now that my companion is a pain in the ass, mainly for two reasons: He's too self-centered and incredibly argumentative. If I say white, he'll surely say black, even if I'm so much as voicing an opinion. So, I never initiate conversations that concern little more than trivia. It doesn't matter what I say, he will try to find some way to show me that what I've just said is not absolute. I haven't let him have it yet with what I think about this problem he has but I blew up once already, telling him to get off my back regarding how I wish to live my life, and since then he's left me alone. It's my business how many times I take a shower in a week, or if I want to even up my shoe laces before I tie them, or if I wish to brush my teeth at night, or how much I wish to write to answer each letter. Unfortunately, I am dependent on him for these photos, as well as funds that are supporting me now and since somewhere in Tanzania. We are getting along fine because I'm controlling all my reactions to what Day says or does, and it ain't killing me.

The photo situation with Apuobo turned out like this: Because we don't have a photo permit from Kinshasa, he can not authorize us to take photos within his collectivity. So he said we can take as many as we like away from town in the bush and he'll pretend he knows nothing about it, yet we can tell the subjects beforehand that Apuobo gave us the OK.

Thursday December 8th
Next day

It began raining just after we entered the forest. About a kilometer in, the path takes a turn around a termite mound and I realized at that moment that it was also the point marking my being in the forest nearly eighteen months after my arrival, as had been anticipated. Something about that point on the path always made me ask myself how many more months were left. All those months weren't spent in the forest, but it still was a gratifying feeling to walk past that spot in the forest seventeen months later.

The forest world is different from that of the village. I can see how Turnbull saw such a sharp contrast between the two because he spent long stretches in the forest, consequently enhancing the contrast for him. Many who read his work find his contrasts too severe and clear-cut. Their criticism is partially valid.

All the smells of the forest environment brought back a full flood of memories and images upon reentering it. Needless to say, some of them were fearful ones that such a foreign environment produced and continues to produce now and again.

Two days from now it will be nice to be back in the village because I know that the episode is finished and new things are awaiting me, things very different from what this experience has been in many ways.

We've been out in the forest since Tuesday afternoon and we're still working on getting Gomeza's OK. This morning Gomeza tried to tell me that tomorrow we can take photos, and not today, but after a short discussion we settled for two o'clock this afternoon while the sun will be out, hopefully.

Now he's demanded ten arrow tips for his brother Pascal, plus copies of the photos, and a pair of shorts with a shirt from the States for each of them. "OK. As long as we get the photos," I responded. Just now, a guy making a bark cloth refused to have his photo taken unless we gave him a zaire. Here we are now, getting down to dealing with the individuals.

I decided I didn't have enough time to build my own hut, so Day and I are living together in the one Gomeza and his family were living in until we arrived. Tuesday night we slept inside it while Gomeza and his family slept outside around the fire. Contrary to what he expected, it rained, and they crowded into a friend's hut for the rest of the night.

Because we are together in the same hut, I have had to construct a portable table made from the usual sticks and vines. As I sit outside now by the daylight through clouds, last night's rain falls irregularly from the leaves it collected on overhead. A foot away I keep my hand-kerchief ready. Luckily my Bic is indelible.

Day took a few photos of me this morning while I was building a table dressed in my very own *mulumba* and feline skin cap. The appearance of the camera sent many children running to their huts.

Sunday December 11th
Three days later
Nduye

It's really very nice to be back in the village. Colin Turnbull how did you ever stay six months on end out there?!!!

Tonight is really the first time I've had a chance to make an entry.

Let me see . . . At about two-thirty p.m. on Thursday, Sitala (Gomeza's sister) said that we had better get our photos while there is plenty of sun. Now that I've just realized what I've said, it sounds humorous. I guess she must have overheard me mentioning something about the conditions concerning light.

Day brought out his camera, and between that afternoon and Friday evening we "shot them full of holes," as I put it several times. By the time we left the forest Saturday, Day had shot roughly one hundred and eighty people dead.

It was the palm oil that got us our photos. I rarely saw oil in a pygmy camp compared to the amount I've seen in villages. It's liquid gold. The only thing we have at home that comes to my mind at the moment that is comparable is caviar, or pure malt whiskey, perhaps. Actually, maybe champagne is the best synonym.

Monday December 12th
Next day

I have to go right this minute nearly. It's late at night. We're just about all set to shove on. Wednesday we are hoping to get a ride with a Father from the mission toward, or even to, Isiro on his way to a reunion in Wamba.

Very early this morning I went down to the high river to do my last wash here and didn't finish until about midday. That was all that was left that I had regretted doing because it can be a task. I did the works; sleeping bag, coat, bags, and so on.

Whew! I just wish I had the time to really convey on paper what it is like and means to leave here. I'M SO HAPPY! but it surely ain't like I'm leaving hell, or heaven either, for that matter. It's just time. Day is referring to home as "the other end of the rainbow." He's really ready to push on.

The reason I don't have the time to write more about all this is because the *mundane's* got hold of me again. I wanted to go out into the forest from the camp before I left and say good-bye to it properly and offer my thanks, but I ended up drinking some palm wine. Sililo arrived from the forest singing, with a bottle of palm wine in his hands and some bright green leaves stuck in his hair. And then while intoxicated, I said to myself, "Your last day. Stop working. You've got your photos and that was the main objective of coming out here. Sit back and relax in the amber sunlight filtering lazily in through the trees." I knew it would be dark before I could blink an eye, and sure enough it was. I had acted like a pygmy during those last hours and sat idly, totally idly.

Earlier, I had wanted to walk out of the camp into the forest alone and do something closer to meditating for an hour. What I really had in mind was recording what the flora is really like, which I never did, and what the forest's smells make me think, and what it's like to say good-bye to the pygmies and their home. It doesn't matter though that much. Don't try to fight the *mundane*. The *mundane* has prepared me for Wednesday's road. If I still get a chance, I'll go into the forest (though not virgin, most likely) and have a sit.

I had no party in the village afterall. I had wanted to have a goat with rice—too broke and sick of being exploited. Friendship around here is so very different than what I define it at home as. I've got less than five friends here, according to that definition. One could question my saying I have pygmy friends, or even call me an outright liar! I begin now to remember stories I heard while in Epulu about Turnbull's "friends" and the way even Kenge treated him . . . .

Day has been sick. Sweating at night. He may have malaria, so I'm treating him. This may be affecting how he acts toward people, so what I said about him earlier may be unjustified. I won't know until I get to know him better after he gets well, hopefully. He's been like this for a long time.

I feel like I'm just a hop, skip, and a jump from home now. Amazing what the mind can come up with, envision, no? Still got some time on the road ahead of me, some good European food, and a few civilized surprises I imagine, and hope for.

21

"WE'RE in like Flint," as Day says, from the 007-esque movie, *Our Man Flint*. It means everything is just peachy. We use the expression a lot when we're being served a good meal or have caught a good ride.

Right now I am very comfortably set up at a woman's house at a table sipping tea. The truck we arrived on last night is having its brakes worked on, so I'm trying to get some writing out of the way meanwhile. Yesterday was eventful. We are at this moment fifty kilometers below Watsa, which is below Faradje, and not too far from Aba or the Sudanese border. Our truck is overloaded. Consequently, we are making only fifteen kilometers an hour over the bumps and holes.

We left Mungbere yesterday morning. Thirty kilometers or so out of town we came across some officials with a prisoner. His torso was thoroughly tied up. They loosened the man's hands so he could climb up on top of the truck and he was made to hold his captor's hat, the type cops at home wear; plastic visor, plastic lined-interior. His hat and uniform were something left behind by the Belgians. This whole Belgian influence thing is extremely interesting and really worth commenting on.

So much of Zaire's terrain is spooky because of all that still stands that was abandoned in 1960. I'm constantly finding it difficult to imagine life here with the Belgians in the past. Everywhere I look I feel I am living and witnessing things at a time that archeologists of the future would envy me for. I should compare it to my walking the alleys of Etruria [roughly corresponding to modern Tuscany] in order to render the feeling (an idea of the feeling) I often get.

The clash of two cultures. The results. The dying culture. And also finally grasping what it was like before the Belgians arrived. I have begun to have a very real image of that life long ago. By piecing all the old remains together in my imagination, I have an ever-increasing picture.

This leads me to some of my most recent thoughts concerning the amount of comprehension I had of what life meant in Nduye, and in turn, to many Africans. It was enough of an understanding, and a feeling of comfortableness combined, that I often thought how easy it would have been to have made a life of it perhaps. You take a wife, keep a garden, have kids, and I would have a small enterprise of some kind on the side, such as making palm oil. Or I would grow some cash crops. With the money after the sale, I would have enough for necessities such as medicine and so forth. It's a very easy life in many ways, with so much leisure time. I am talking about life as a Mulese, and not a Mbuti. The latter would be more difficult for me, at least at first. I would learn a lot.

Will life at home now be much of a challenge? What a relaxed life it is here. I would have to forget about being ambitious and wanting to accomplish things. It is for this reason that I am going home now, in addition to other ones. I'll take a breather on the way home and have a second look through different eyes now. Can my attitudes toward various things be considered apathetic now? What really does matter in life? Are the Africans really apathetic, as I had thought previously, or is it just that they value less the things that we consider important? What more do they need? What more do *we* need? It's very, very bizarre how my thinking has changed. What's the value of a life? That's a common question that I am always asking myself. But why should I try to valuate it. My feeling is, or my conclusion is, that life wouldn't be life if no mysteries, uncertainties, inexactnesses, inequalities, and imperfections didn't exist. It's perfect and imperfect simultaneously.

I like to think of life and nature as synonomous. But there would be a slight difference between the two perhaps, if I were to think of nature as water and everything that we do with it as adulteration, and those adulterations as beverages.

I was content, satisfied, to see "even" a pygmy in the same human boat we're in. We are brothers and it doesn't matter that I'm living thousands of miles away from them very differently. Change must always occur, and the pygmies aren't going to get down on me for being one of the world's number one consumers of its resources. And it's not because they are totally ignorant of what it all means. Do people at home criticize one another's lifestyle? No one is ever in a position to do so. Criticism would only reveal the critic's ignorance.

There was something I held myself back from writing about six months or more ago because I wanted to think about it more. Suppose life for each African is more similar to every other African's than would be true of each American, or European, for example. For the Africans, less variation is to be found, and consequently, each personality is not as different as each American's? Would this explain why the choice of one's spouse is seemingly so casual to my eyes? The pygmies, for example, only swap sisters. All one would want in a spouse is good basic qualities. And this is exactly how I looked at many of the women who were roughly my age.

When I first arrived in Nduye, I remarked that love to Africans is different than our conception of it. But at home with all the openings for variations, decisions, and choices I never had a girlfriend. It had something to do with my scrutiny, no doubt.

I write too slowly when I think and daydream so I shall stop for the moment and continue briefly with the prisoner.

No sooner had the prisoner gotten on, when he received a hard slap or two across his back for not holding the hat properly. We were at that point well into the Lingala-speaking area and all I had to hear was the French word *buvette*, to figure that the captive had robbed one. A *buvette* is a small bar. I assumed the warden and his men were headed for a certain prison. An hour or so later we arrived at a small village mainly to pick up a drum of gas. We also had to wait for some guy who kept inventory of what the truck was transporting, because he wanted to continue with us after he had taken inventory, I assumed.

It was at this village that the warden got down still clutching his two and a half foot whip that was made from a forest vine and knotted at one end to be gripped by. The prisoner (whom, I later learned, was originally from Wamba. I assumed from his small stature and certain physical attributes that he had some pygmy blood in him from somewhere along the way) immediately got slapped around a bit, which is par for the treatment of prisoners, particularly thieves. (I won't even attempt to put down the extreme brutality thieves receive in Africa. It's a wonder there are so many.) I can't remember exactly how the transaction took place, but the warden received one hundred zaires tied with a piece of light-blue cloth.

We were smack in front of a tiny shop with the typical tailors going about their business. The air was broken by the prisoner's arrival, and apparently they had brought the prisoner back to the town of the crime.

At one instant, one of the two tailors couldn't control his anger any longer and he attempted to maul the prisoner, who was clothed in a bathing suit (which is typical. They are stripped of their clothing immediately after capture).

The worst was yet to come, and as the minutes ticked by in the broiling sun I could see the crime had been considerable. All that were around abused him either verbally or with a hefty slap or more on the face. The prisoner was somewhere between twenty and thirty and looking like he was about to cry, but throughout the whole, short ordeal there was never a tear shed by him.

The warden finally folded the one hundred zaires in half and slipped the wad into his back pocket. He handed his whip to one of the two tailors and let go of the cord he held the prisoner by. He was whipped so hard I imagined he would pass out because of shock, just like the guys in the old days who were flogged on ships. The whip, or switch, had its end reversed so he was beaten with the knot until a piece of the knot had broken off and stuck out of the upper part of his back. The welts even showed up immediately through the black skin, unless I imagined them having to have resulted from such a flogging. All the helpless man could do with his arms and hands bound was yelp like a dog and hop from one foot to the other.

Finally, the prisoner's scab (of considerable size over one of his eyes, which he had probably received soon after having been captured) was ripped open by the whip's knot and hung there just barely attached, dripping blood on the ground.

I think the prisoner was grateful for that moment because it signaled enough, as he held his head back like someone with a bloody nose, or at least I thought so.

Since there was only one whip (which fell apart eventually. It looked like the same vine the pygmies make their bowstrings from), the other tailor resorted to kicking the guy in the stomach and punching his head with all the might he could muster.

The warden made the tailors (just country tailors!) back off (and I think this is actually when he took the money off the table, creased it, and put it into his back pocket). Just after he had taken several steps to carry the prisoner away, he returned in front of the few onlookers. He dropped the cord by his feet and stepped on it while reaching into his back pocket to pull out a large pocketknife, just long enough for me to admire its beautiful wooden handle and wonder why the villagers in Nduye never made them.

"Was he going to stab the prisoner?" I asked myself, looking on in disbelief. And even if he was going to kill him, I knew from all I'd seen and learned previously in Africa that I wouldn't intervene, and would sit there helplessly.

He walked up to the prisoner as though he were going to commit a public execution, and with the edge of the blade, not the point, he pressed it repeatedly against the victim's face and pulled it downward as though he were trying to shave his facial hairs with a dull blade by force. The prisoner stood and beared as much as possible without backing away. The warden was not getting the results he wanted, obviously, so he changed his grip slightly on the four inch blade's handle. With a downstroke, he repeatedly scarred the man's face with the tip of the knife, digging harder and harder until he finally got the bloody gashes he was looking for and knew would mark the thief for life. It was gory and pitiful but I have been tempered, and my interest was great enough that I never blinked an eye, let alone wince. Finally the prisoner was carted away.

My sense of compassion has been dulled. I really had begun looking at that prisoner as though he were a piece of meat. He just no longer resembled a human the way he was being treated and never retaliated. I could have watched them beat him to death, perhaps without ever turning my head away or trying to stop it. I began believing he deserved it for whatever he had done. And I couldn't believe what I heard myself saying to Day afterwards. I told him I wished all thieves got the same treatment, except for the scarring. Next to murderers they are the worst scum of the earth. Maybe even worse than murderers, allowing lives can be stolen.

The thought of my dying arrived. I became overwhelmed by a sense of well-being, of some kind of neutral euphoria. My mind faded from a stagnant, timeless realm into a hypnotic stupor, numb to the simple sounds around me. The world of the Africans that I had come to know was abruptly transformed into a cyclical blur. Before me were people and their huts built of human frailty. All else was taken up by the voracious forest. It became difficult to tell one from the other. We all seemed to have appeared from nowhere, as though vegetation and minerals combined on yet another jaunt through the wellspring of consciousness. The only way I could tell I was alive was by looking into the sun. And I knew then that being dead was . . . the same . . . , and I was completely content and ready. But some sort of effort would be required, so I gave up on the thought, and in so doing, felt life's insistent nudging from where I sat.

Jay Jasper Bone was educated at the State University of New York at Empire State College and at Stony Brook before receiving his B.A. in anthropology from Stanford University in 1983. He has done fieldwork for Seton Hall University, Virginia Commonwealth University, the University of Bordeaux and Harvard University.